RODALE'S CHRISTMAS

Needlecraft
Collection

RODALE'S CHRISTMAS · Needlecraft Collection

Over 100 Easy Projects for Gifts, Decorations and Bazaar Best-Sellers

Cross Stitch · Plastic Canvas Crochet · Knitting · Sewing

Jean Leinhauser, Rita Weiss and the Editors of the American School of Needlework®

Rodale Press, Emmaus, Pennsylvania

American School of Needlework® Editorial and Design Staff:
President: Jean Leinhauser
Executive Vice President: Rita Weiss
Vice President: Bobbie Matela
Art Director: Carol Wilson Mansfield
Project Director: Mary Ann Frits
Creative Director: Jane Cannon Meyers
Cross Stitch Editor: Ann Harnden
Plastic Canvas Editor: Carly Poggemeyer
Quilting Editor: Linda Causee
Knitting and Crochet Editors: Kelly Robinson,
   Sandy Scoville, Kathy Wesley
Associate Editors: Meredith Montross, Pam Nichols
Production Assistants: Pat Hawes, Mary Hernandez,
   Terea Mitchell, Brent Rathburn
Administrative Assistant: Candy Matthews

Rodale Press Editorial and Design Staff
Editor: Jane Townswick
Copy Editor: Gayle Putman
Cover Designer: Linda Bossard
Cover Photographer: John Hamel

Rodale Press Home and Garden Books
Editor-in-Chief: William Gottlieb
Executive Editor: Margaret Lydic Balitas
Senior Editor: Cheryl Winters Tetreau
Copy Manager: Dolores Plikaitis
Art Director: Michael Mandarano

Book Design
Joyce Lerner, Fred Huetter
Graphic Solutions, Inc-Chicago

If you have any questions or comments concerning this book, please write to:
Rodale Press, Inc.
Book Readers' Service
33 East Minor Street
Emmaus, PA 18098

Library of Congress Cataloging-in-Publication Data
Leinhauser, Jean
   Rodale's Christmas needlecraft collection : over 100 easy projects for gifts, decorations and bazaar best-sellers : cross stitch, plastic canvas, crochet, knit, sewing / Jean Leinhauser, Rita Weiss and the editors of the American School of Needlework.
      p. cm.
   ISBN 0-87596-678-0   hardcover
   1. Christmas decorations. 2. Needlework. 3. Fancy work. 4. Sewing. I. Weiss, Rita. II. American School of Needlework. III. Rodale Press. IV. Title. V. Title: Christmas needlecraft collection.
TT900.C4L43   1994
746.4—dc20   94-19736
                                        CIP

Distributed in the book trade by St. Martin's Press

2 4 6 8 10 9 7 5 3 1 hardcover

Contents

Contents

Introduction

The very word "Christmas" symbolizes joy, excitement and enchantment for young, old and in-betweens. And Christmas is extra special to those of us who are needleworkers.

We love to crochet, knit, embroider and sew Christmas gifts, decorations and wearables. A handcrafted gift makes a statement of caring that no purchased item can convey.

Hand-stitched decorations become family heirlooms, cherished by many generations.

We at the American School of Needlework®, create books of designs all year long — but our favorites are the Christmas projects that we share with you in this book.

Even if you've never stitched before, you can use this book. We've included basic instructions for cross stitch and plastic canvas embroidery, knitting and crocheting.

Cross stitchers will find Santas, angels, snowmen and reindeer frolicking through their section.

Crocheters can create a blizzard of snowflakes, lacy angels, a little village, a warm afghan and a colorful stocking.

Knitters can make an afghan and pillow, stockings to hang and to wear and even Mary Janes for baby.

Plastic canvas lends itself to wonderful tree and package ornaments, doorstops and table decorations.

Sewers will delight in our easy fabric tree skirt and patchwork ornaments — perfect for the beginner. A Christmas Teddy Bear and Merrie Rag Doll are great for filling stockings for youngsters of all ages.

Whatever time of year you sit down with this book, you're sure to hear sleigh bells in the background and a faint Ho! Ho! Ho!

Jean Leinhauser   Rita Weiss

Cross Stitch

Cross Stitch How-To

Cross stitch, in recent years, has bloomed as the most popular type of embroidery. There is a wide array of designs being published each year, with projects ranging from framed samplers to kitchen mugs.

It's wonderful to start with blank fabric and some embroidery floss, follow the chart and watch a colorful design appear. Cross stitch is easy to do, it's not messy and the results are handsome. Even the smallest cross stitch ornament makes a very special gift.

The following pages give you all the information you will need to become adept at cross stitch. If you're already addicted to this needle art, you will find the information inspiring and useful to your continued interest in cross stitch. We've included counted bead embroidery on perforated paper that is done in much the same way as counted cross stitch.

Materials

The materials required for counted cross stitch are few and inexpensive: a piece of evenweave fabric, a tapestry needle, some 6-strand cotton floss, and a charted design. An embroidery hoop is optional. All of these are readily available at most needlework and craft shops.

EVENWEAVE SURFACES

These are designed especially for embroidery, and are woven with the same number of vertical and horizontal threads per inch. Cross stitches are made over the intersections of the horizontal and vertical threads, and because the number of threads in each direction is equal, each stitch will be the same size and perfectly square.

AIDA CLOTH

The most commonly used fabric for cross stitch is cotton Aida cloth. It is a basketweave fabric in which horizontal and vertical threads are interwoven, making the intersections for stitches very easy to see. Aida is woven with the intersections (or squares of the fabric) spaced in several sizes, including 11-count (11 stitches to the inch), 14-count (14 stitches to the inch), 16-count (16 stitches to the inch), and 18-count (18 stitches to the inch).

The number of stitches per inch of any evenweave fabric determines the size of a design after it is worked. The photos in **Fig 1** show the same heart design worked on all four sizes of Aida. The more stitches to the inch, the smaller the design will be. Thus a design stitched on 18-count fabric will be considerably smaller than one stitched on 11-count fabric.

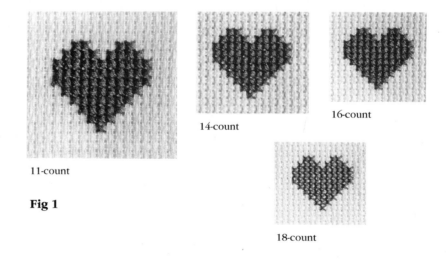

11-count

14-count

16-count

Fig 1

18-count

There is also vinyl Aida-looking material sold under the name Vinyl-Weave™. Its washability makes it ideal for placemats, and it is often sold as the insert material for mugs and other gift items.

AFGHAN FABRICS

Afghan fabrics are evenweaves that come in a variety of sizes and patterns. They are purchased as full size afghans, and the dimensions differ between manufacturers. Each fabric has a specific thread count and a woven layout that creates specific areas for stitching. They may be cotton, synthetic, or a fiber blend. An afghan fabric is usually coarsely made with a simple over-and-under weave, so stitches are made over two horizontal and two vertical threads. The design on page 8 is worked on an afghan fabric.

DECORATIVE FABRICS

Decorative fabrics will give your projects added interest. For the holidays there are Christmas fabrics which may be pre-finished. The designs on page 68 are worked on a plaid napkin and place mat. The plaid fabric contains gold threads as part of the woven pattern.

PERFORATED PAPER

This unique product is a pressed paper with evenly spaced holes, traditionally used for counted cross stitch embroidery. The paper is stiff and resists tearing, but should be handled with care. It is purchased in sheet form, usually 9" x 12" pieces. The beaded ornaments which begin on page 13 are worked on perforated paper.

PERFORATED PLASTIC

Perforated Plastic looks like perforated paper, but it is really a 14-count plastic canvas. It comes in several colors and you can stitch just as you do on perforated paper. When a more durable surface than paper is desired, the plastic will work very nicely. The design on page 78 is worked on this surface.

When you want to work on a non-evenweave surface, a product called "waste canvas" can be used. Directions for working on waste canvas are on page 25.

PRE-FINISHED PRODUCTS

Do you want to make a cross-stitched fingertip towel, pillow or perhaps a Christmas stocking, but you don't like to sew? Then you will love the many pre-finished accessories available with the evenweave fabric made part of the construction. You'll find so many lovely pre-sewn items; in addition to those we've mentioned, there are more table linens, kitchen accessories, bookmarks, and many baby and bath accessories.

HOOPS

Counted cross stitch can be worked on fabric with or without a hoop. If you choose to stretch the fabric in a hoop, use one made of plastic or wood with a screw-type tension adjuster. You may use a hoop large enough to accommodate the whole design or choose a small hoop, whichever you prefer. Placing the small hoop over existing stitches will slightly distort them but a gentle raking with the needle will restore their square shape. Be sure to remove the fabric from the hoop when you have finished stitching for the day.

Center the hoop on the fabric with the tension screw at 10 o'clock if you are right-handed or at 2 o'clock if you are left-handed. Pull fabric taut and tighten screw.

Paper, plastic, and vinyl surfaces are quite firm and do not require a hoop.

NEEDLES

Cross stitch is worked with a blunt tapestry needle. The needle slips between the threads, not through them. **Fig 2** will tell you which size needle is appropriate for each count of fabric or surface.

FLOSS

Any six-strand cotton embroidery floss can be used for cross stitch. The six-strand floss can be divided to work with one, two or more strands as required by the fabric. **Fig 2** tells how many floss strands to use with the various fabrics.

For our charts the brands of embroidery floss colors are specified by number. Each brand has its own color range, so these suggestions are not perfect color matches, but are appropriate substitutions. Cut floss into comfortable working lengths–we suggest about 18".

Generic color names are given for each floss color in a design; for example, if there is only one green, it will be so named, but if there are three greens, they will be labeled lt (light), med (medium), and dk (dark).

Thread Count or Mesh Size	Number of Strands for Cross Stitch	Number of Strands for Backstitch	Tapestry Needle Size
14-count (when worked over 2 threads)	6	3	20
8.5-mesh	6	3	20-22
10-mesh	4	2	22
11-count	3	1 or 2	22
14-count	2	1	24 or 26
16-count	2	1	26
18-count	1	1	26

Fig 2

A "blended" color is one that is created by using one strand of each of two floss colors and is so noted in the Color Key.

Blending filament can be added to provide sparkle to your work. It is listed by color number. Use two strands of filament along with the usual number of strands of floss when stitching.

Metallic gold thread also can be used to add a festive touch. Choose a brand that is comfortable to work with. The number of strands required will depend on the thickness of the brand you choose; experiment with a few stitches to achieve the effect you like.

SCISSORS
A pair of small, sharp-pointed scissors is necessary, especially for snipping misplaced stitches. You may want to hang your scissors on a chain or ribbon around your neck–you'll need them often.

CHARTS
Counted cross stitch designs are worked from charts. Each square on a chart represents the space for one cross stitch. The symbol in a square specifies the floss color to be used. Straight lines over or between symbols indicate backstitches. Each chart is accompanied by a Color Key, which gives the number of the suggested color by brand. If a color name appears without a preceding symbol and equal sign, the color is only used for one of the following decorative stitches. Backstitches and straight stitches are indicated by straight lines and should be worked the length and direction shown. French knots are designated by a dot or starburst symbol, lazy daisies and eyelets by their shape. Each chart also gives you the number of stitches in width and height of the design area.

Charts can be foolers: the size of the charted design is not necessarily the size that your finished work will be. The worked size is determined by the number of threads per inch of the fabric you select and the size of the design. For example, if you work a motif that is 44 stitches wide and 55 stitches high on 11-count Aida, the worked design will be 4" wide and 5" high. Worked on 18-count Aida, the same design will be 2 1/2" wide and 3" high. **Fig 3** shows how much stitching area is required for designs up to 50 stitches in either direction.

Getting Started

Unless otherwise directed, work your design centered on the fabric or background surface. Follow arrows to find center of charted design; count threads or fold fabric to find its center. Count up and over to the left on chart and fabric to begin cross stitching.

To begin, bring threaded needle to front of fabric. Hold an inch of the end against back, then anchor it with your first few stitches. To end threads and begin new ones next to existing stitches, weave through the backs of several stitches. Trim thread ends close to back of work.

THE STITCHES
Note: Unless otherwise noted in the Color Key, use two strands of floss for all cross stitches, straight stitches, French knots, lazy daisies, and eyelets, and one strand for backstitches.

CROSS STITCH
A single cross stitch is formed in two motions. Follow the numbering in **Fig 4** and bring threaded needle up at 1, down at 2, up at 3, down at 4, completing the stitch. When working on Aida cloth, as in **Fig 1** on page 2, your stitch will cover one "block" of fabric.

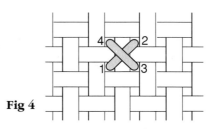

Fig 4

Thread Count or Mesh Size	Number of Stitches				
	10	20	30	40	50
14-count (when worked over 2 threads)	1 1/2"	2 3/4"	4 1/4"	5 3/4"	7 1/4"
8.5-mesh	1 1/4"	2 1/4"	3 1/2"	4 3/4"	6"
10-mesh	1"	2"	3"	4"	5"
11-count	1"	1 3/4"	2 1/2"	3 1/4"	4 1/2"
14-count	3/4"	1 1/2"	2 1/4"	2 3/4"	3 1/2"
16-count	3/4"	1 1/4"	2"	2 1/2"	3 1/4"
18-count	1/2"	1"	1 1/2"	2 1/4"	2 3/4"

Fig 3

(measurements are given to the nearest 1/4")

Work horizontal rows of stitches, **Fig 5**, whenever possible. Bring thread up at 1 and down at 2; repeat to end of row, forming first half of each stitch. Complete the stitches (3-4) on the return journey from right to left. When a vertical row of stitches is appropriate, complete each stitch then proceed to the next, **Fig 6**. No matter how you work the stitches, make sure that all crosses slant in the same direction. Work second and subsequent rows below first row.

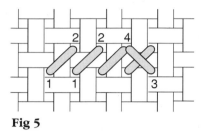

Fig 5

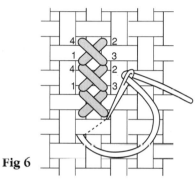

Fig 6

When working on perforated paper or plastic, each cross stitch is made over a square space that is surrounded by four holes, **Fig 7**. Make horizontal rows, **Fig 8**, whenever possible, working on the perforated surface as if it were fabric. Be very careful not to carry threads more than the distance of two or three stitches on the back because the threads will be visible on the front.

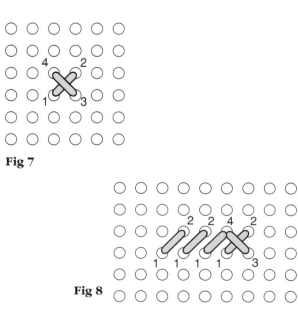

Fig 7

Fig 8

BACKSTITCH

Backstitches are usually worked after cross stitches have been completed. They may slope in any direction and are occasionally worked over more than one fabric block or thread. **Fig 9** shows the progression of several stitches; bring thread up at odd numbers, down at even numbers.

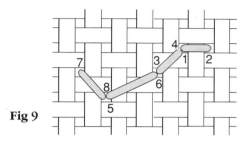

Fig 9

STRAIGHT STITCH

A straight stitch, **Fig 10**, is made like a long backstitch. Come up at one end of the stitch and down at the other. When making several straight stitches close together, occasionally weave through some stitches on the back to secure the thread.

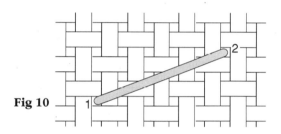

Fig 10

FRENCH KNOT

Bring thread up where indicated on chart (this may be the middle of a block or between blocks). Wrap floss once around needle, **Fig 11**, and reinsert needle close to where thread first came up. Hold wrapping thread tightly, close to surface of fabric. Pull needle through, letting thread go just as knot is formed. For a larger knot, use more strands of floss, but wrap only once.

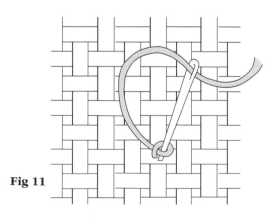

Fig 11

5

When working on vinyl or a perforated surface, French knots are made a bit differently than on fabric. Weave your beginning thread through some stitches on the back as usual, then make a small knot before bringing floss up where indicated on chart. Wrap floss once around needle, **Fig 12**, and reinsert needle next to where floss first came up. Hold wrapping floss tightly and pull needle through, letting thread go just as knot is formed, but do not pull through to the back of the vinyl. For a larger knot, use more strands of floss, but wrap only once.

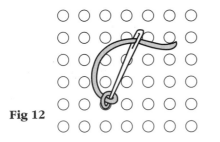

Fig 12

LAZY DAISY STITCH

This stitch creates pointed oval shapes that resemble flower petals. Bring thread up at center hole (1), **Fig 13**. Loop floss, insert needle in same hole, and bring it out two squares from center (2) or as indicated on chart, with loop beneath point of needle. Pull needle through, adjusting size and shape of loop. Stitch down over loop, one thread farther from center, to secure it. Repeat for each oval shape. Anchor ending thread especially well on the wrong side.

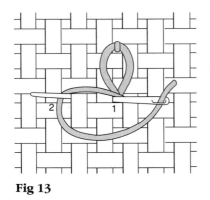

Fig 13

EYELETS

Eyelets are isolated stitch patterns formed by straight stitches that radiate outward from the center, **Fig 14**. They are made over a specific number of fabric blocks as shown on the individual chart. Bring threaded needle up through fabric at any location on the outside of the shape, then stitch down at the center. Continue in this manner around the shape to complete the eyelet.

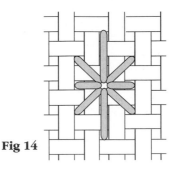

Fig 14

DOUBLE CROSS STITCH

This version is created with a cross stitch covered by two straight stitches. To begin, follow the numbering in **Fig 15** to make a single cross stitch (1, 2, 3, 4). Then come up at 5 and down at 6, to make a vertical stitch and finish (up at 7 and down at 8) with a long horizontal stitch.

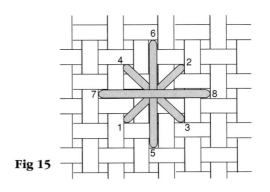

Fig 15

Planning a Project

The designs in this book are shown as finished projects. You may wish to apply some of these cross stitch designs to other uses. Whichever project you work, begin by selecting your chart and type of fabric. Next, determine the finished dimensions of the stitched area. Divide the number of stitches in width by the number of stitches per inch of fabric. This tells you how many inches wide the fabric must be. Repeat for the height of the design. Use the chart on page 4 for quick reference.

Add enough additional fabric for unworked area around the design plus an additional 2" or 3" on each side for use in finishing and mounting. If your design is a small one, be sure to allow enough fabric to fit over your smallest hoop. The excess fabric can be cut off after stitching.

Cut your fabric exactly true, right along the holes of the fabric. Some raveling will occur as you handle the fabric; however, an overcast stitch, machine zigzag stitch, or masking tape around the raw edges will minimize raveling.

It is best to start stitching at the top of the design (or the top of a color area) and work downward whenever possible. This way your needle comes up in an empty hole and goes down in an occupied hole. This makes your work look neater because completed stitches are not disturbed.

To begin stitching, count up from the center of the fabric to the top left group of stitches on the chart.

Most cross stitch may be carefully washed. When you have finished stitching, dampen embroidery (or wash in lukewarm mild soap suds if soiled and rinse well); roll it briefly in a clean towel to remove excess moisture. Place embroidery face down on a dry, clean terry towel and iron carefully until dry and smooth. Make sure all thread ends are well anchored and clipped closely. Then proceed with desired finishing.

INITIAL AND DATE YOUR WORK

It may not seem important to you now, but a piece of embroidery that has a signature and date will be much more valuable as time passes. Choose a thread color that has been used in the piece and position your initials and date unobtrusively at or near the bottom.

Below are the alphabet and numerals to use to personalize your projects.

Christmas Tree Afghan

designed by Carol Wilson Mansfield

Get ready to enjoy a crackling fire and the scent of pine while the north wind howls! This warm and snugly afghan is a perfect "pick up and put down" project, as it uses only one floss color (lots of it!) and each section can be completed in a relatively short period of time. It's an extremely effective country accent.

Stitching Notes

AFGHAN FABRIC

This design was created to fit 14-count Hearthside afghan fabric. All stitches are worked over two threads to produce seven cross stitches per inch. We used beige Hearthside with green cross threads. The fabric contains 30 large squares (five wide x six high) plus partial squares for fringing. Each square has 97 x 97 threads and measures approximately 7" x 7". Each design portion fits a fabric section, so if you want to substitute one design for another or work with a different fabric, make sure you have the right number of threads to do so.

Additional Supplies

Cotton embroidery floss is used for all stitching. Use six strands in your needle; separate them and realign before threading the needle.

You will also want a pair of sharp embroidery scissors and size 20 or 22 tapestry needles. The use of a thimble and/or a hoop is optional. You should also have a yardstick or tape measure, straight pins, and basting thread.

WORKING OVER TWO THREADS

Each cross stitch is made over two vertical (top to bottom) threads and two horizontal threads of fabric. These afghan fabrics are all constructed with areas having a simple weave which creates intersections that have alternating vertical or horizontal threads on top.

To make a cross stitch, begin below and to the left of an intersection with a vertical topmost thread. Bring thread up at 1, down at 2, up at 3, down at 4, to make one complete stitch (**Fig 1**). Make horizontal rows of stitches wherever possible, working the first half of each stitch (1-2) left to right and the second half (3-4) on the return (**Fig 2**). On vertical rows, work each stitch individually.

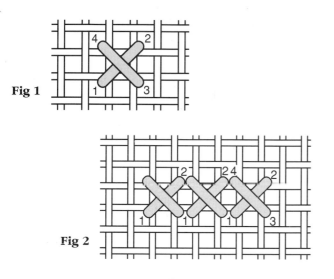

Fig 1

Fig 2

Pay special attention to the threads on the back of your afghan. With only seven stitches per inch, you'll need to bury fairly long ends to secure the floss, especially backstitches, from normal wear and tear. You may even want to run floss ends through in two directions by including a "U-turn." Occasionally, stitching will be visible on the back, so if it's tidy, it will just look like any other wrong side.

Design Placement

Make sure the fabric cut is the size and layout required for the design. Mark the top of the fabric and keep it at the top while stitching the entire design so that all stitches cross in the same direction. If a portion of the design changes direction, turn the chart(s), but not the fabric.

It is sometimes difficult to tell one side from the other on afghan fabric. One way is to check the selvages. If thread ends are visible where they turn back on themselves, that will be the wrong side. Also, look at the decorative section bars or bands—one side may appear more "finished" than the other and should be chosen as the right side. Finally, if you absolutely cannot tell the difference, then it really doesn't matter!

Place fabric on a flat surface. Refer to Layout Guide below and make sure all sections needed for afghan design are complete.

Use the floss listed in the Color Key to stitch each design in its appropriate section according to the Layout Guide.

Center the 43w x 43h designs within each square. Center the 43w x 22h designs (Reindeer and Inside Border Trees) between sides, but stitch the lower edges even with those of the adjacent designs.

Finishing

Fringe makes an attractive and easy edging for an afghan. First, cut off the selvage ends. Along each side to be fringed, use matching thread to machine zigzag over two threads, right next to the woven pattern at the base of where you wish the fringe to be. Trim fabric to desired fringe width. Carefully remove the cross threads, leaving the fringe intact.

			Fringe			
	Outside Border Corner	Outside Border Trees	Cabin	Outside Border Trees	Outside Border Corner	
	Cabin	Inside Border Corner	Reindeer	Inside Border Corner	Cabin	
Fringe	Outside Border Trees	Inside Border Trees		Reindeer	Outside Border Trees	
	Outside Border Trees	Reindeer		Inside Border Trees	Outside Border Trees	Fringe
	Cabin	Inside Border Corner	Reindeer	Inside Border Corner	Cabin	
	Outside Border Corner	Outside Border Trees	Cabin	Outside Border Trees	Outside Border Corner	
			Fringe			

Layout Guide

9

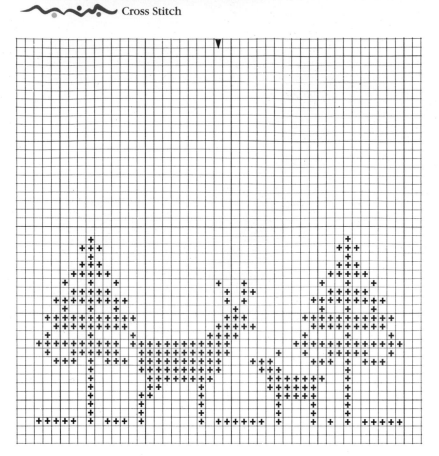

Reindeer design area: 43 wide x 22 high

COLOR KEY

	DMC	Anchor
+ = green (50 skeins)	367	216

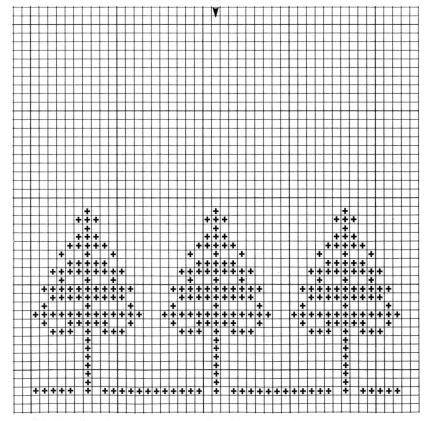

Inside Border Trees design area: 43 wide x 22 high

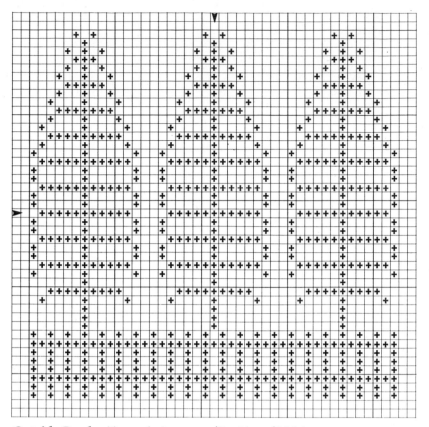

Outside Border Trees design area: 43 wide x 43 high

COLOR KEY

	DMC	Anchor
+ = green (50 skeins)	367	216

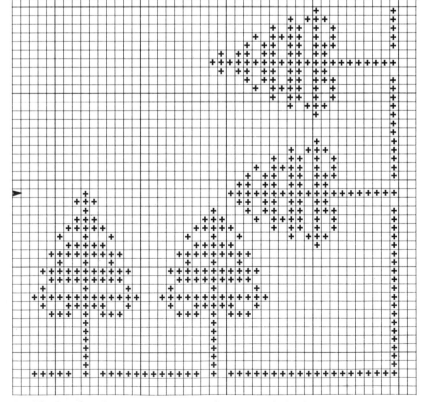

Inside Border Corner design area: 43 wide x 43 high

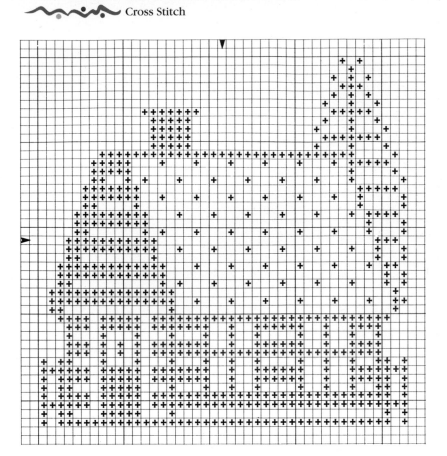

Cabin design area: 43 wide x 43 wide

COLOR KEY

	DMC	Anchor
+ = green (50 skeins)	367	216

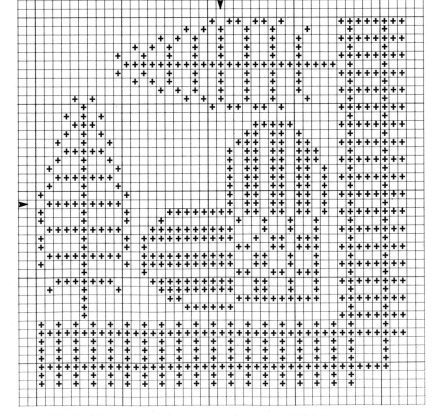

Outside Border Corner design area: 43 wide x 43 high

Beaded Ornaments

designed by Sam Hawkins

What a sparkling holiday you'll have with these charming ornaments! Decorate the tree, tie them onto gifts, hang them from hooks, or even add a magnet. They're created on a perforated background using seed beads instead of cross stitches.

Stitching Notes

PERFORATED PAPER

The right side of the paper is the smoother side. There are 14 perforations per inch, a size similar to a 14-count cross stitch fabric. However, rather than using cross stitch, we are going to use only beads to produce these ornaments.

Neutral paper shades were favored during Victorian times, but the recent popularity of this product has inspired manufacturers to produce perforated paper in several colors as well as white, black, gold, and silver. We have used white, cream, gold and brown for these ornaments.

BEADS

These designs use glass seed beads that come in a marvelous array of colors. They are basically the same size, although irregularities in size—and occasionally color—will occur. When a design requires many closely packed beads, try to use beads that are about the same size. If you find some unusually large ones, save them to use singly. If a bead has too narrow an opening for your needle, it's best to discard it. Mill Hill seed beads were used and are identified by name and number in each Color Key.

EMBROIDERY FLOSS

Since these designs are composed entirely of beads, with no cross stitching or backstitching in the design, the floss used for beading will match the background paper. Unless otherwise directed, use one strand of floss. We have not listed floss colors, only bead colors. Choose a shade of your favorite brand of floss that is close to the paper color—it probably will not show. So, without having to change thread colors, you can concentrate on picking up the right color bead!

NEEDLES

Although a long, thin beading needle is often used, we suggest a #8 quilting needle for counted bead embroidery. This needle has a large enough eye through which to thread a single strand of floss, yet a small enough eye to pass easily through the center of a seed bead. Purchase an assortment of needles and find which one works best for you; needle choice can be very personal, depending upon the length of your fingers or use of a thimble.

SCISSORS

You will need small sharp embroidery scissors for cutting floss. You will also want a pair that can be used to cut the paper—3" or 4" is a handy size. Stitch-removing scissors or slant scissors are very helpful when cutting tiny areas.

MISCELLANEOUS SUPPLIES

Select a thin metal or plastic ruler for measuring. Use a fine graphite pencil to lightly mark along rows of holes before cutting the paper. A kneaded eraser should remove any unwanted pencil marks—be sure to test erasability on a scrap of perforated paper.

CHARTED DESIGNS

Each square on a charted design represents the space where a bead can be attached. On perforated paper, this space is a small square of paper surrounded by four holes. Each symbol on the chart shows you that a bead is to be attached in that square and the bead color to use. For accurate counting on perforated paper, count the squares where stitches can be made instead of counting holes.

The stitch width and height accompany each chart and centers are shown by arrows. The finished design size as well as the cut size are noted so you can plan placement on your stitching paper. The cutting line for each shape is shown as a heavy outline around the design. Most of these designs can be stitched on a 4" square of paper; larger ones require a 5" square.

GETTING STARTED

Make sure your hands are clean—skin oils or lotion residue can permanently stain perforated paper. Cut the paper an inch or so larger on all sides than the cut design size and be sure it is large enough to hold comfortably. If the paper is too small, your hand may feel cramped. Trim (or tape) edges so they are smooth to the touch; this will help prevent floss from snagging as you stitch.

All these designs have cutting outlines. Stitch the design before cutting out the finished shape. Unless otherwise directed, plan to work your design centered on the paper. Measure to find center of paper; follow arrows to find center of charted design. Count up and over to the left on chart and paper to begin stitching.

Cut floss into a comfortable working length—we suggest about 24". To begin, bring threaded needle to front of fabric and hold at least an inch of the tail end against the back of the paper. If desired, make a half cross stitch to anchor this beginning thread. Anchor the tail of thread as you attach the first few beads. Or, instead of holding the beginning thread with your finger, use a tiny piece of repositionable tape on the wrong side of the paper, then remove it after the beginning thread is secure.

Pull floss completely through each time the needle goes through the paper. Try not to carry threads across unstitched areas on the back of the paper, as they may show through to the front. To end threads and begin new ones next to existing stitches, weave through the backs of several stitches. For added security, weave the thread in two directions.

Attaching Beads

Half cross stitches are used to attach the beads, and you will work in horizontal rows just as you do for counted cross stitch. Thread needle with floss color to match paper.

Begin at the left side of the row to be beaded. Bring needle up at 1 and slip the appropriate color bead on the needle (**Fig 1**). Insert needle at 2 to complete the half cross stitch (**Fig 2**). Continue across the row from left to right adding the appropriate color beads (**Fig 3**) as directed in the Color Key.

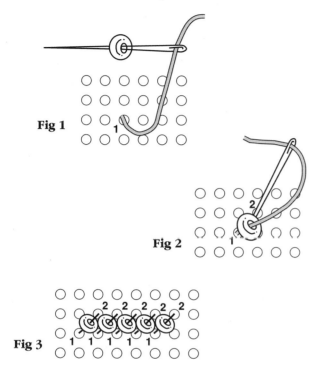

Fig 1

Fig 2

Fig 3

Now, bring floss up at A, the hole below the hole you just entered, then insert the needle from right to left through the centers of the entire row of beads (**Fig 4**). Pull needle through and stitch down at B, (the same hole as 1). Repeat for each row of beads, returning to the left side ready to begin the next row. This stitch realigns the beads into a straight row and reinforces the attachment.

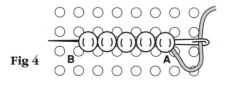

Fig 4

If a design requires an isolated bead, attach it with a half cross stitch, then work a second half cross stitch through the bead for added security. To attach beads that form a vertical row, begin at the top and progress downward on the paper (**Fig 5**).

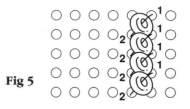

Fig 5

Stitching Tips

The following suggestions will be helpful when working on perforated paper:

• Hold light-colored paper over a dark surface (or dark paper over a light surface) to make the holes more visible.

• When possible, begin stitching in an area of the design that has several closely spaced stitches so your beginning floss will be well secured.

• When you are ready to add a bead, pierce it with your needle, use a scooping motion to slip the bead onto the thread, then insert the needle into the appropriate paper hole.

• Pull floss through the holes in a smooth, even motion; do not tug or pull on it.

• As you work, make sure beginning and ending threads are carefully hidden on the back side and trim ends closely.

• A small tear in the paper can be easily repaired. Apply a small piece of transparent tape to the wrong side of the paper, covering the tear and adjacent holes; then proceed to stitch as if the tape were not there, piercing it when stitching through the hole it covers.

Finishing Ideas

One of the most exciting aspects of this neat paper is its ease of finishing. Perforated paper can be easily cut horizontally, vertically, or diagonally.

Follow the cutting lines shown on the chart after beaded design has been completed. The cutting lines will be at least one square away from any stitching but may be several squares away, especially if the background paper is part of the design. It may be helpful to lightly pencil this cutting line along the holes first to avoid cutting in the wrong place.

When you cut along a row of holes a scalloped edge is created. If desired, you can carefully trim this a bit more to create a smooth edge, but take care not to weaken the edge of the paper.

Note: When tidying up the edges, you may find it helpful to turn the paper over and trim from the wrong side, as irregularities are a bit more visible from the back. To make a neat inside corner, cut into it from both sides in two motions rather than trying to cut around it in one motion.

For a simple ornament, glue the ends of a decorative thread loop to the top back of the stitched shape. If you wish, you can cover the wrong side of your stitching before cutting out the shape. Attach a piece of fabric print with fusible web. Or, glue on felt, ribbon,

construction paper, or a fancy decorative paper. You can also add a self-backing of plain perforated paper in a matching or contrasting color.

There are other uses for these little ornament designs:

• Glue a magnet to the back.

• Attach a pin back to make jewelry.

• Use them as package tie-ons.

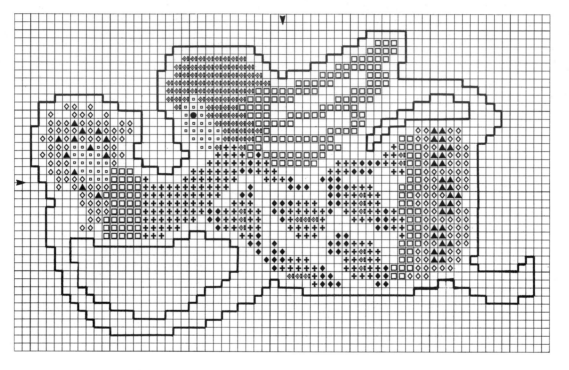

Angelique

Design size: 54 wide x 31 high
Cut size: 63 wide x 38 high
Paper color: cream

		Mill Hill
□	= White	479
▲	= Royal Plum	2012
▫	= Peach Cream	2003
⧆	= Yellow Cream	2002
◇	= Ice Green	561
◆	= Christmas Green	167
+	= Sapphire	168
●	= Royal Blue	20

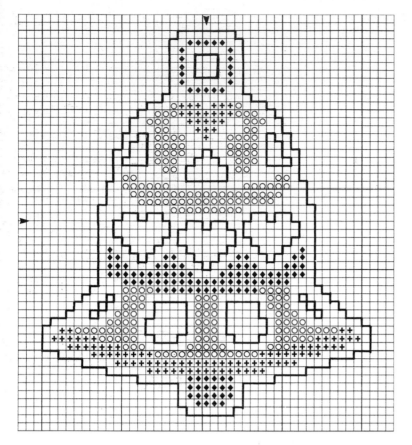

Christmas Chimes

Design size: 39 wide x 46 high
Cut size: 41 wide x 48 high
Paper color: brown

		Mill Hill
+	= Old Rose	553
O	= Victorian Gold	2011
♦	= Christmas Green	167

Della Robbia

Design size: 39 wide x 31 high
Cut size: 44 wide x 45 high
Paper color: gold

		Mill Hill
–	= Dusty Rose	2005
☆	= Red	968
★	= Garnet	367
O	= Tangerine	423
▫	= Yellow Cream	2002
©	= Gold	557
◇	= Ice Green	561
♦	= Emerald	332
+	= Royal Plum	2012
✖	= Iris	252

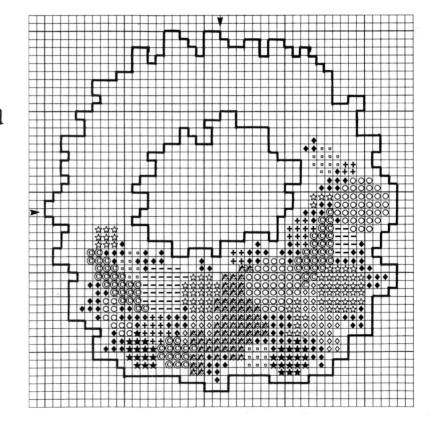

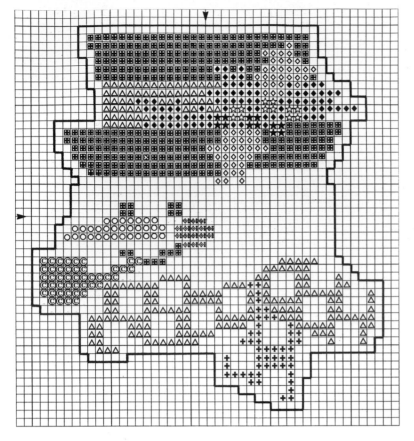

Frosty Man

Design size: 42 wide x 46 high
Cut size: 44 wide x 48 high
Paper color: white

		Mill Hill
◈	= Dusty Rose	2005
☆	= Red	968
★	= Garnet	367
○	= Tangerine	423
◇	= Ice Green	561
◆	= Emerald	332
△	= Sapphire	168
+	= Cobalt Blue	358
©	= Antique Copper	3006
⊞	= Black	2014

Holiday Rocker

Design size: 41 wide x 44 high
Cut size: 43 wide x 46 high
Paper color: cream

		Mill Hill
+	= Dusty Rose	2005
©	= Red	968
−	= Tangerine	423
◇	= Ice Green	561
◆	= Emerald	332
●	= Jet	81

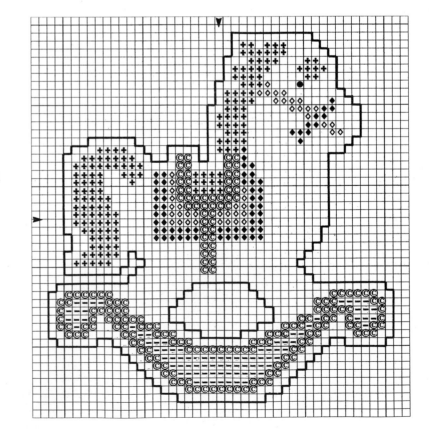

18

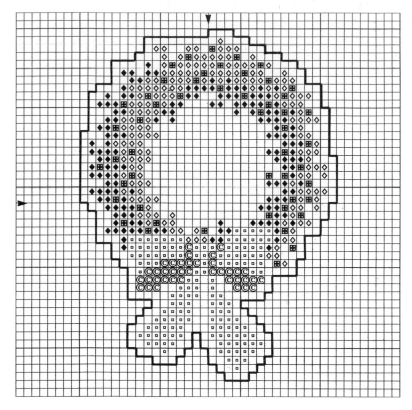

Holly Berry Wreath

Design size: 30 wide x 42 high
Cut size: 32 wide x 44 high
Paper color: white

		Mill Hill
□	= Dusty Rose	2005
©	= Red	968
⊞	= Red Red	2013
◇	= Christmas Green	167
◆	= Emerald	332

Jolly Old St. Nick

Design size: 38 wide x 36 high
Cut size: 49 wide x 55 high
Paper color: white

		Mill Hill
◈	= Tea Rose	2004
+	= Dusty Rose	2005
⊞	= Red Red	2013
▫	= Coral	275
◇	= Robin Egg Blue	143
✖	= Jet	81

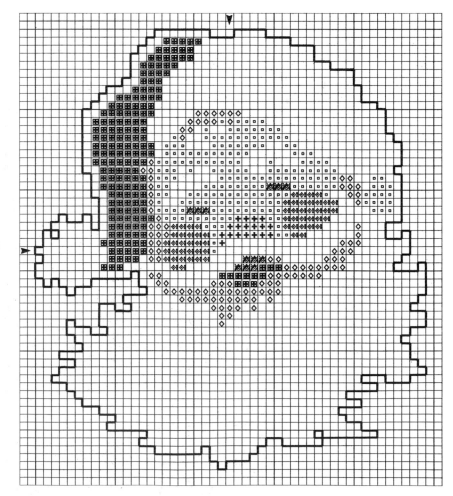

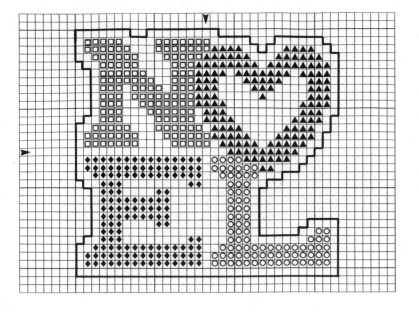

Noel

Design size: 31 wide x 29 high

Cut size: 33 wide x 31 high

Paper color: white

	Mill Hill	
▲ = Red Red	2013	
O = Yellow Cream	2002	
♦ = Christmas Green	167	
☐ = Royal Blue	20	

Old-Fashioned Christmas Tree

Design size: 31 wide x 31 high

Cut size: 40 wide x 40 high

Paper color: white

Note: This ornament should hang diagonally; center hanger above top of stitched tree.

	Mill Hill
− = Pink	145
+ = Red Red	2013
▫ = Yellow Cream	2002
◇ = Light Green	525
♦ = Christmas Green	167
⬦ = Royal Blue	20
☆ = Iris	252

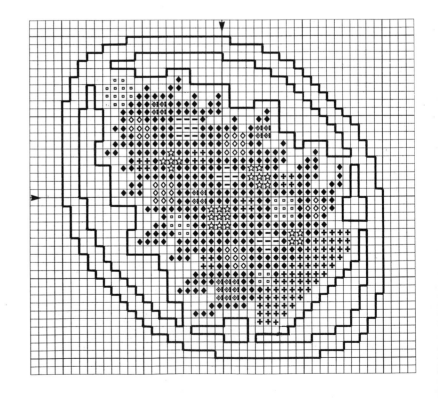

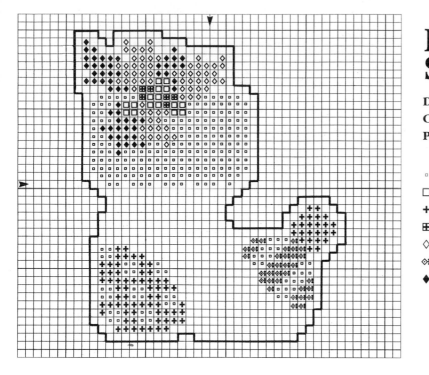

Patchwork Stocking

Design size: 32 wide x 37 high
Cut size: 34 wide x 39 high
Paper color: brown

			Mill Hill
▫	=	White	479
▢	=	Dusty Rose	2005
+	=	Red	968
⊞	=	Red Red	2013
◇	=	Christmas Green	167
◈	=	Ice Green	561
◆	=	Emerald	332

Poinsettia

Design size: 37 wide x 39 high
Cut size: 39 wide x 41 high
Paper color: white

			Mill Hill
△	=	Dusty Rose	2005
▲	=	Red Red	2013
⊞	=	Royal Plum	2012
◈	=	Victorian Gold	2011
+	=	Ice Green	561

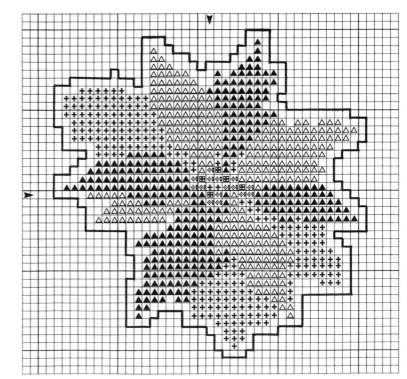

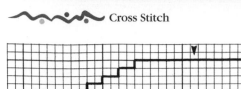
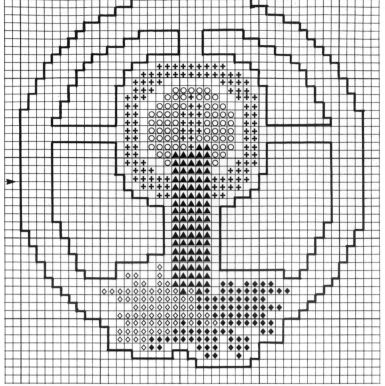

Shimmering Light

Design size: 24 wide x 37 high
Cut size: 43 wide x 46 high
Paper color: gold

		Mill Hill
▲	= Red	968
○	= Tangerine	423
+	= Victorian Gold	2011
◇	= Christmas Green	167
◆	= Emerald Green	332

Sleigh Full of Goodies

Design size: 46 wide x 43 high
Cut size: 48 wide x 45 high
Paper color: brown

		Mill Hill
△	= Dusty Rose	2005
▲	= Red Red	2013
©	= Gold	557
⊞	= Bronze	221
◇	= Light Green	525
◆	= Emerald Green	332
+	= Sapphire	168

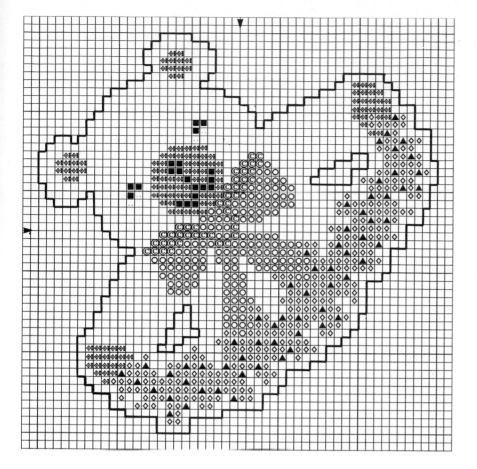

Teddy Christmas

Design size: 47 wide x 47 high
Cut size: 50 wide x 50 high
Paper color: brown
Note: This ornament should hang diagonally; center hanger at top of head.

		Mill Hill
▲ = Royal Plum	2012	
◇ = Christmas Green	167	
O = Robin Egg Blue	143	
© = Satin Blue	2007	
✧ = Pale Peach	148	
■ = Copper	330	

Candy Cane

Design size: 37 wide x 41 high
Cut size: 39 wide x 43 high
Paper color: white

		Mill Hill
▫ = White	479	
△ = Dusty Rose	2005	
▲ = Old Rose	553	
+ = Red Red	2013	
◇ = Christmas Green	167	
◆ = Emerald	332	
O = Sapphire	168	
★ = Royal Blue	20	

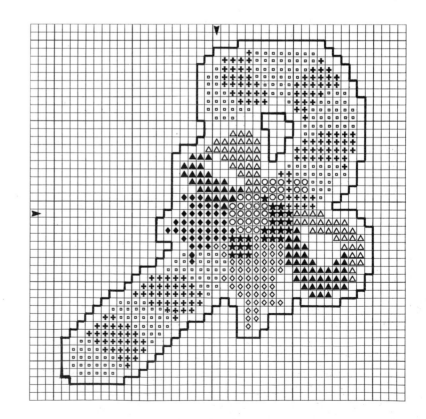

23

Joyful Wearables

designed by Sam Hawkins

Here's a wonderful way to show off your stitching talents this holiday season—cross stitching with waste canvas on a sweatshirt! You'll love watching these designs come to life as you work over the waste canvas threads basted to the garment. To soften stitching, remove the canvas threads and voilà–the design comes into full view.

Special Notes for Waste Canvas

DESCRIPTION OF WASTE CANVAS

This unique canvas, also called tear-away waste fabric or blue-line canvas, is a disposable counted cross stitch surface. It is actually an inexpensive double-thread canvas that provides a temporary, countable surface on a non-evenweave fabric. The design size and sweatshirt color are given with each chart.

Waste canvas comes in several mesh sizes, ranging from 8 1/2 to 16 threads (actually pairs of threads) per inch. Every 5th pair of threads on the canvas has a dark blue thread as a counting aid and also to distinguish the piece from regular needlepoint canvas. These designs are worked on 8 1/2-mesh and 10-mesh waste canvas. The chart on page 4 shows the approximate finished sizes of designs worked on different mesh or count backgrounds.

The canvas is basted on the front of the garment or fabric. Then the design is stitched with embroidery floss, the surface dampened, and the canvas threads are removed, leaving the wonderful stitched design.

SUPPLIES

Unless otherwise noted, we used 6 strands of embroidery floss for cross stitches and 3 strands for backstitches on the 8 1/2-mesh waste canvas; on 10-mesh, we used 4 strands for cross stitches and 2 strands for backstitches.

Note: When working on a dark sweatshirt, light floss colors may require more strands for proper coverage.

Because finished work may be dampened when canvas threads are removed, it is wise to test dark floss colors for colorfastness especially the reds. Just stitch an inch or two of floss through some white fabric, dampen it, and let dry. If there is any hint of dye on the fabric, do not use the floss unless you pre-wash it to remove excess color.

Use a tapestry needle large enough to carry the number of strands with which you are stitching. A size 22 or even the smaller 24 can be used for 6 strands or less of floss.

You will need some extra supplies in addition to the usual embroidery scissors and thimble, if you use one. Have on hand some shears (not good ones) for cutting canvas, a sewing needle and thread, and a few safety pins. You will also need a spray bottle with water and tweezers to use after the design has been stitched.

PREPARATION OF CANVAS AND FABRIC

Note: You may want to pre-wash your sweatshirt to remove any excess dye and to allow for possible shrinkage.

Determine the finished size of the design on your chosen mesh (number of stitches divided by mesh size equals number of inches in width or height), then cut canvas two or more inches larger on all sides. If canvas piece is quite large or feels coarse, tape sides so threads and fabric do not snag on rough edges.

Baste a vertical center line down front of garment as a guide for positioning the design. Align blue canvas threads (horizontally or vertically) with weave of fabric and/or seams of garment. Pin canvas over center of area where design is to be stitched; if canvas curls, turn it so edges curve downward. Baste canvas in place, **Fig 1**. On a large design you can also baste across the centers so canvas doesn't shift; or, use randomly placed safety pins to hold canvas until area has been stitched.

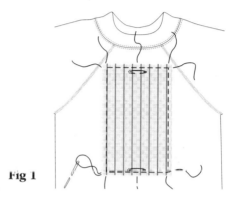

Fig 1

GETTING STARTED

Count canvas threads, treating each pair as a single thread, and stitch design as you would on any evenweave fabric. Specific stitch instructions follow. Make sure to work design centered (or in desired position) on garment. Start stitching at the top of the design and work downward. This way the needle comes up through fabric at a hole that is empty and goes down through fabric at a hole already occupied by a stitch so you avoid disturbing the stitch.

STITCHING TIPS

• Some canvas brands have a lot of sizing and are stiff to work on; others are quite soft and will conform to the surface of your fabric. If needed, add more safety pins to keep the canvas and garment together while you are stitching. A piece of cardboard or foam core board placed between the front and back of the sweatshirt keeps a good separation between the layers and provides a convenient work surface as you pin and baste.

• Because garments are laundered frequently, you may wish to begin and end threads with a small knot for added security. Here's a neat way to make knots and keep the back tidy so thread ends do not catch when item is worn. When beginning a thread, weave through some stitches on the back, then make a knot on the back and proceed to stitch. When ending threads, make your last stitch and end with a knot on

the back, but do not cut the thread. Weave the thread end after the knot under some stitches on the back then clip the end. All the little tails will be secured.

• Use the stab stitch method of pulling thread completely through the fabric each time the needle goes in or out. It is hard to make accurate stitches with the sewing method (in and out in one motion) when working on a thick fabric plus waste canvas. Try working with one hand above the fabric—stitching downward—and the other hand beneath the fabric to catch the needle and send it back toward the top.

• The neckbands on some sweatshirts tend to pill from a lot of handling. If you baste or pin a fabric scrap over this area, it will be protected while you are stitching.

THE STITCHES

The construction of cross stitches and backstitches on waste canvas is the same as for regular counted cross stitch.

CROSS STITCH

The woven canvas intersections are treated as if they were squares on evenweave fabric. The needle goes into and out of the centers of the larger canvas holes. To make a single cross stitch, bring needle up at 1, down at 2, up at 3, and down at 4, **Fig 2**. Follow this sequence for single stitches and all vertical rows of one color. For horizontal rows, work half of each stitch (1-2) from left to right across the row and complete each stitch on the return journey (3-4), **Fig 2**.

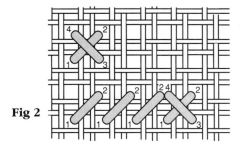

Fig 2

Stitches that are next to each other must share the same fabric holes to keep their shape. This placement involves a bit of guesswork because of the size of the canvas holes, but you'll get the feel of it rather quickly.

BACKSTITCH

Work backstitches after cross stitches have been completed. Backstitches can slope in any direction and are occasionally worked over more than one square. Follow the numerical sequence in **Fig 3**.

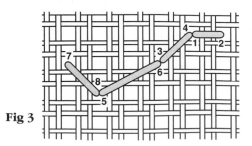

Fig 3

REMOVING WASTE CANVAS

Now comes a special fun part! Make sure your stitching is completed. Cut away the extra canvas, leaving about 1/2" all around the design. There are two ways to remove the canvas threads; choose the one you prefer and that gives the best results with your brand of waste canvas.

MOIST METHOD

Dampen the right side with a spray or two of water and let it rest for a few minutes until the sizing softens. Use your tweezers to pull out each of the canvas threads. Pull them one at a time—resist the temptation to do more. Add moisture if needed and remove all canvas. Like magic...the finished design!

DRY METHOD

For fabrics which are dry cleanable only, soften canvas threads by rubbing (or scrunching) them together. It is then possible to remove threads one by one without using water.

TRIMMING

Some designs have been embellished with ribbons or other trimming; they are listed in the Color Key—add them if desired. *Note: Do not use beads or other small decorations for young children's garments.*

Ribbons can be tacked on with strong sewing thread. Bells and other non-washable trimmings can be attached with small safety pins or Velcro® patches and removed for cleaning.

To attach sequins, use small seed beads, **Fig 4**. Use doubled thread and begin with a knot on the wrong side. Stitch up through the center hole of the sequin, slip on the bead, and stitch back down through the same hole; knot thread on back and clip end.

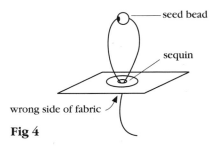

Fig 4

To make a ruffled edging on the neckband or sleeveband, such as on the "Naughty or Nice" or "Joyful Santa" designs, use thread to match sweatshirt and set your sewing machine on a wide zigzag with a short stitch length. Stretch the folded edge of the band and zigzag completely around it; as the tension is released, the ruffled edging appears.

As with any special article of clothing, hand washing is safer, especially if it has been embellished. If you prefer to machine wash, turn garment inside out and use a gentle cycle. Dry flat.

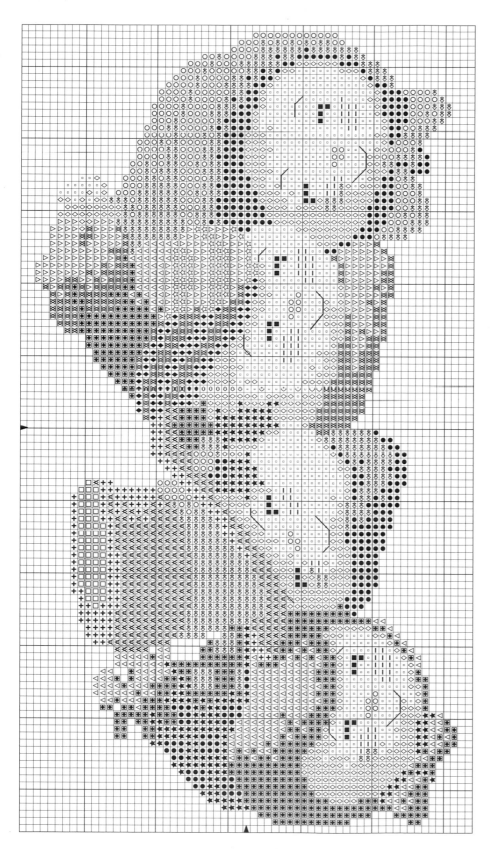

Here We Come A-Wassailing!

Design area: 110 wide x 59 high
Model: stitched with 10-mesh canvas on red sweatshirt

	DMC	Anchor	Coats
∘ = white	blanc	2	1001
− = very lt pink	776	24	3125
O = lt pink	957	50	3152
◈ = med pink	956	40	3153
● = dk pink	309	42	3000
☆ = lt orange	3340	329	2329
◆ = dk orange	947	330	2330
▽ = yellow	725	306	2307
⬚ = gold	782	308	2308
△ = lt green	704	256	6238
◉ = med green	702	239	6226
★ = dk green	700	229	6227
☐ = lt brown	842	376	5388
+ = med brown	840	379	5379
✻ = dk brown	839	380	5360
◇ = gray	318	399	8511
■ = black	310	403	8403
ǀ = Backstitch: black			

Note that yellow and lt green symbols are similar.

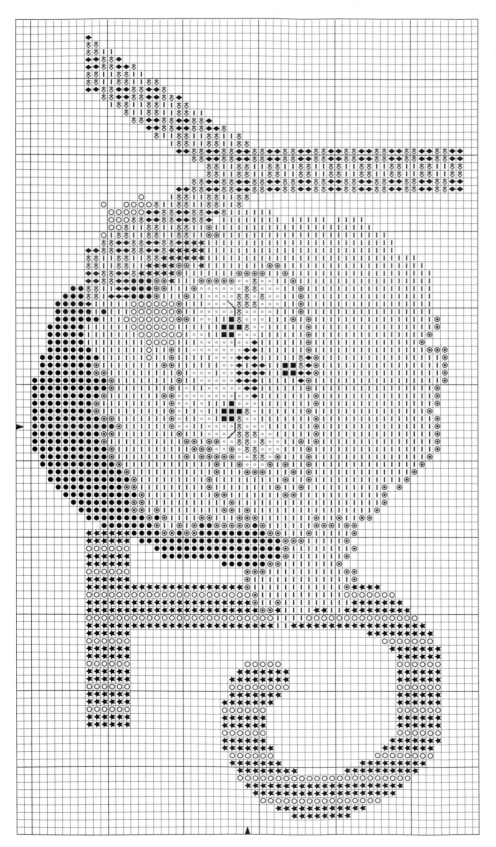

Joyful Santa

Design area: 103 wide x 57 high
Model: stitched with 8 1/2-mesh canvas on lt blue sweatshirt

		DMC	Anchor	Coats
−	= white	blanc	2	1001
○	= peach	818	48	3067
✿	= pink	3708	26	3126
◆	= lt red	3705	35	3012
●	= red	666	46	3046
○	= lt green	702	239	6226
★	= dk green	910	228	6031
⊙	= gray	318	399	8511
■	= black	310	403	8403
|	= Backstitch: black			

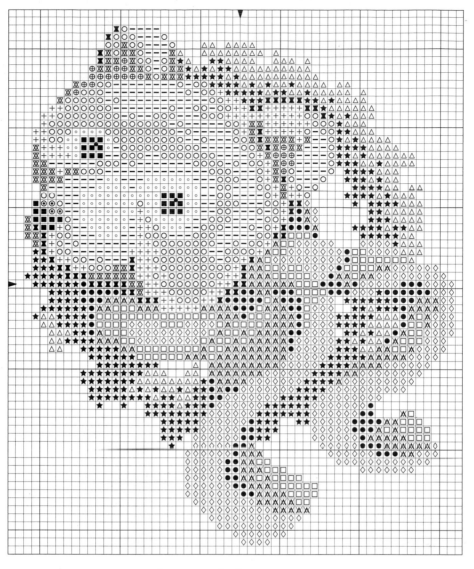

My Friend Teddy

Design area: 54 wide x 65 high

Model: stitched with 8 1/2-mesh canvas on yellow sweatshirt

		DMC	Anchor	Coats
∘	= ecru	ecru	926	5387
◇	= lt pink	3708	26	3126
□	= med pink	3706	28	3127
※	= med red	3705	35	3012
●	= dk red	304	47	3000
△	= med green	702	239	6226
★	= dk green	699	923	6228
—	= med tan	738	942	5372
O	= dk tan	436	363	5943
+	= lt brown	434	309	5365
⊠	= med brown	400	351	5349
▮	= dk brown	801	357	5475
⊕	= very dk brown	938	381	5477
⊙	= taupe	841	378	5376
■	= black	310	403	8403
•	= French Knots: ecru			

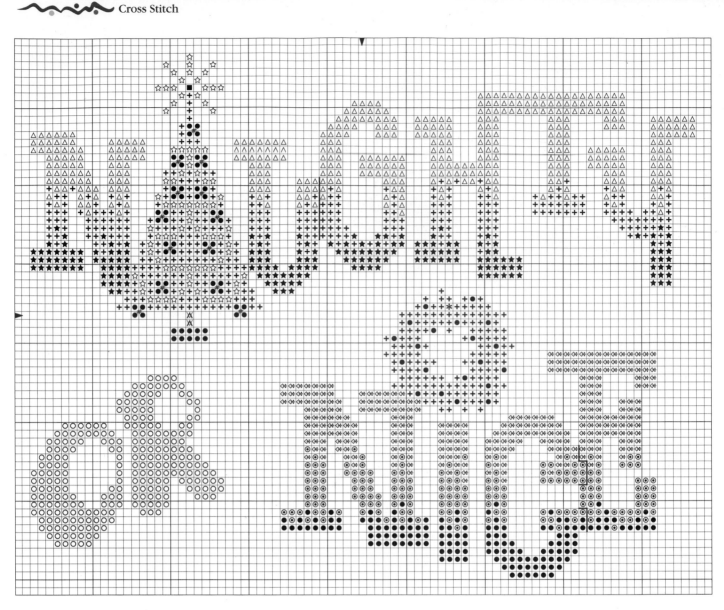

Naughty or Nice

Design area: 85 wide x 67 high

Model: stitched with 8 1/2-mesh canvas on black sweatshirt

Trimmings: one 1/2" scalloped gold sequin; fifteen 3mm gold beads; 1/8"-wide yellow ribbon

	DMC	Anchor	Coats
⬧ = lt red	776	24	3125
⊙ = med red	893	27	3127
● = dk red	321	47	3500
O = yellow	743	297	2296
☆ = gold	783	307	2308
△ = lt green	704	256	6238
+ = med green	702	239	6226
★ = dk green	700	229	6227
✖ = brown	839	380	5360
black	310	403	8403

| = Backstitch: black

■ = attach sequin & bead

= attach bead

✳ = attach bow & bead

Note: If no symbol is given, that color is used only for decorative stitches or backstitches.

Poinsettia Perfect

Design area: 87 wide x 75 high
Model: stitched with 8 1/2-mesh canvas on navy blue sweatshirt
Trimmings: 3/8" red/green/gold ribbon; six 3mm gold beads

		DMC	Anchor	Coats
∘	= lt pink	963	49	3150
◇	= med pink	899	27	3152
◎	= lt red	326	59	3019
⧆	= med red	321	47	3500
●	= dk red	498	20	3072
+	= gold	741	304	2314
△	= lt green	954	203	6020
◆	= med green	912	205	6226
▣	= dk green	910	228	6228
■	= attach bead			
✳	= attach bow			

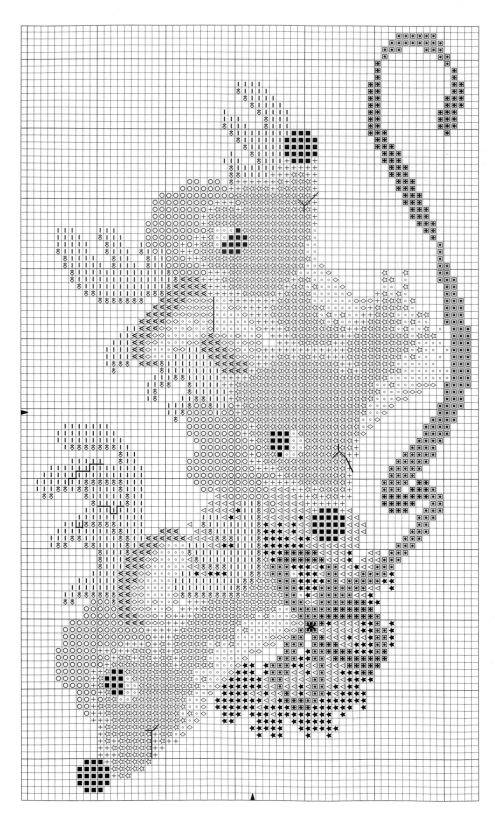

Reindeer Roundup!

Design area: 109 wide x 63 high
Model: stitched with 10-mesh canvas on red sweatshirt
Trimming: 1/8" blue ribbon; 18mm gold liberty bell

		DMC	Anchor	Coats
∘	= ecru	ecru	926	5387
△	= lt green	913	209	6020
★	= dk green	910	228	6031
▣	= lt blue	598	167	6185
▥	= dk blue	807	168	7168
−	= lt tan	437	362	5373
⬥	= dk tan	435	369	5365
O	= very lt brown	945	347	3335
☆	= lt brown	921	349	2326
+	= med brown	919	341	3340
✖	= dk brown	300	352	5471
■	= very dk brown	838	380	5360
◇	= gray	841	378	5376
│	= Backstitch: very dk brown (3 strands)			
✳	= attach bow & bell			

The Night Before Christmas

Design area: 83 wide x 85 high
Model: stitched with 8 1/2-mesh canvas on lt green sweatshirt
Trimmings: 3/8" red/green metallic ribbon; 1/2" white pom-pom; nine 1/2" gold sequins, assorted shapes; nine gold seed beads (for attaching sequins)

		DMC	Anchor	Coats
∘	= white	blanc	2	1001
⊗	= pink	350	11	3111
●	= red	817	19	3019
☆	= yellow	725	306	2307
◆	= gold	782	308	2308

		DMC	Anchor	Coats
△	= lt green	912	205	6031
★	= dk green	699	923	6228
+	= blue	825	162	7181
O	= tan	739	885	5387
◎	= lt brown	437	362	5373
✖	= med brown	434	309	5365
■	= dk brown	300	352	5471
|	= Backstitch: dk brown			
•	= attach bow			
✕	= attach pom-pom			
✳	= attach sequin			

33

Christmas Clippers

designed by Bette Ashley

These unique quick-to-stitch ornaments have wonderful wit and charm. Each one hangs from a jumbo 2"-long paper clip that is attached following our simple finishing instructions.

Stitching Notes

SUPPLIES

FABRIC AND THREAD

Our models are stitched on 16-count white Aida cloth, but they can be stitched on 14-count fabric (for a larger ornament) or 18-count (for a smaller ornament). The stitch width and height accompany each design.

On 16-count, the stitched designs vary from 2" to 3" in width and height, so cut a 5" fabric square and stitch the design centered on the fabric. You will also want a small piece of light-colored cotton fabric, either a Christmas print or a plain color.

Cotton embroidery floss is used for all the designs. If a design calls for metallic thread instead of floss, choose whatever brand you like and use two strands (or the amount that fits the fabric) for all stitching.

PAPER CLIPS

The clippers were made with giant (or jumbo) paper clips that are about 3/8" wide and 2" long. We used gold-tone metal clips plus vinyl-coated ones that are available in a variety of colors. Although color choice is optional, we have noted the clip color shown with each Color Key.

As a protective measure for the metallic clips, we suggest applying clear nail polish to the clip surface that goes between the layers of fabric. On vinyl-covered clips it's a good idea to use polish on the cut ends to prevent rust.

TOOLS

Size 26 blunt-pointed tapestry needles are suitable for 16-count fabrics. You will also need small scissors with very sharp tips to cut around the shape of the clip marks.

NEEDLEWORK FINISHER

This is a water-based stiffening solution that dries clear. Needlework finisher is sold under product names such as Liz Turner Diehl's Needlework Finisher, Aleene's Fabric Stiffener, and Stiffy® Fabric Stiffener. It is applied with a brush which should be cleaned with water before it dries.

TRIMMINGS

The addition of ribbon or other trimming, if used, is listed with each chart. These additions are optional and can certainly be changed if you wish. Use a clear drying craft glue to attach any embellishments after the ornament has been finished.

Finishing

MATERIALS (for each Christmas Clipper)

cross-stitched motif worked on a 5" x 5" piece of
   16-count (or desired size) white Aida cloth
cotton Christmas print or solid fabric for backing,
   slightly larger than stitched area
water-based needlework finisher
giant paper clip, 2" long, desired color
stiff, flat paintbrush, approximately 1/2" wide
sharp-pointed scissors
wax paper or aluminum foil
clear nail polish
desired trimming and glue
hair dryer (optional)

INSTRUCTIONS

Note: You may want to practice making a clipper ornament with fabric scraps before making one with your stitched piece.

Step 1. Apply clear nail polish to the cut ends of vinyl-covered clip and to the single-curve end of metallic clip. Set aside.

Step 2. Apply needlework finisher to right side of stitched piece with paintbrush, extending it slightly beyond stitched area. Coat the surface completely. Clean brush with water.

Place stitched piece right side up on wax paper and let dry. This can take from a half-hour to several hours, depending on temperature and humidity. You can use a hair dryer to speed up the process. When dry, the piece should be fairly stiff. If not, coat again and allow to dry.

Step 3. On the upper edge only, cut away the excess fabric, about 1/16" above the design. Be careful not to cut into the stitching.

Step 4. Coat wrong side of stitched piece with finisher. Cut a piece of backing fabric sufficient to cover the stitched area. Coat the wrong side of backing fabric with finisher.

Place the single-curve end of the paper clip centered on the trimmed edge. Cover with backing fabric so wrong sides are together with paper clip sandwiched between, **Fig 1**. Clip should be inserted about 1/2" between the layers, but make sure the cut end of the outside curve is visible so the clip can be opened or unbent (if desired). Press fabrics together with fingers and let dry on wax paper. The fabrics will adhere more readily after the finisher has become somewhat tacky. If needed, wait a bit and press together again to make sure clip is secure.

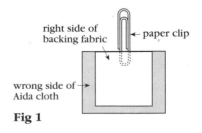

right side of backing fabric ← paper clip

wrong side of Aida cloth →

Fig 1

Step 5. When completely dry, cut away the excess fabric completely around the design. Be careful not to cut into the stitching. It is better to leave a little too much fabric around the edges than to cut away too much.

Step 6. Glue bows, streamers, or desired trim to Christmas Clipper. The trimmed ornament can be clipped (as you would clip papers together) to the side of a branch or a cluster of greens. You can also slip the clip over the end of a thin branch or it can be slightly unbent to create a hanger. If you prefer, you can suspend it by inserting a traditional ornament hook or fancy thread through the clip.

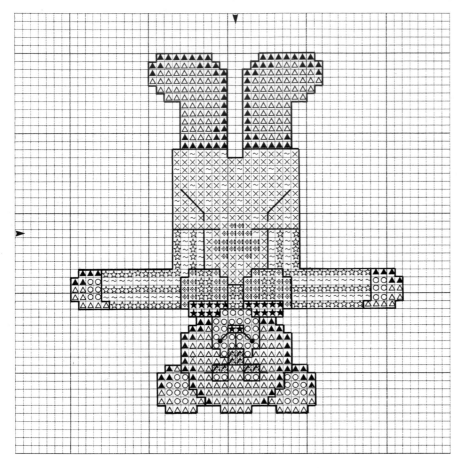

Bear on the Flying Trapeze

Design size: 42 wide x 45 high
Fabric: 16-count white Aida
Clip: blue, positioned horizontally
Trim: Glue feet between bars on one side of clip; secure with tiny fabric strips on back over the inner bar. Using 1/16" red ribbon, tie ends of an 8" piece to each side of clip; glue a tiny bow over each knot.

	Anchor	Coats	DMC
~ = white	2	1001	blanc
☆ = lt red	11	3011	351
⋇ = med red	35	3152	350
★ = dk red	20	3072	817
O = gold	362	5942	437
× = blue	137	7080	798
△ = med brown	369	5347	435
▲ = dk brown	371	5470	433
✖ = black	403	8403	310
• = French Knots: black			
| = Backstitch: black			

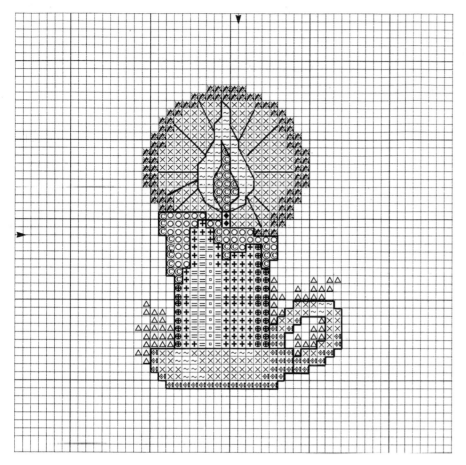

Holiday Candle

Design size: 26 wide x 38 high
Fabric: 16-count white Aida
Clip: gold

		Anchor	Coats	DMC
O	= white	2	1001	blanc
▫	= lt peach	8	3006	353
=	= med peach	11	3011	351
+	= dk peach	35	3152	350
⊕	= red	19	3500	817
✖	= orange	303	2303	742
~	= lt yellow	300	2350	745
✕	= med yellow	295	2295	726
◈	= dk yellow	306	2307	725
△	= green	227	6227	701
©	= blue	158	7053	828
◆	= brown	382	5382	3371
|	= Backstitch:			
	glow lines - orange			
	remaining outlines - brown			

Christmas Wizard

Design size: 30 wide x 47 high
Fabric: 16-count white Aida
Clip: purple
Trim: Glue a 6mm rhinestone to tip of wand

		Anchor	Coats	DMC
~	= white	1	1001	blanc
✕	= peach	868	3868	353
◇	= med purple	112	4092	552
◆	= dk purple	102	4101	550
▲	= fuchsia	94	4089	917
☐	= lt gray	397	8232	762
⊞	= dk gray	399	8511	318
✖	= brown-black	382	5382	3371
◈	= metallic gold			
✳	= Eyelet: metallic gold			
•	= French Knots: brown-black			
|	= Backstitch:			
	wand - metallic gold			
	remaining outlines - brown-black			

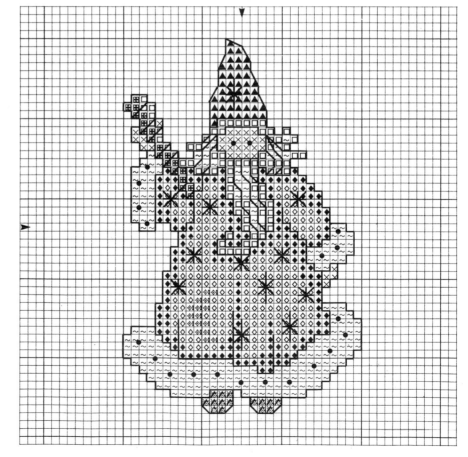

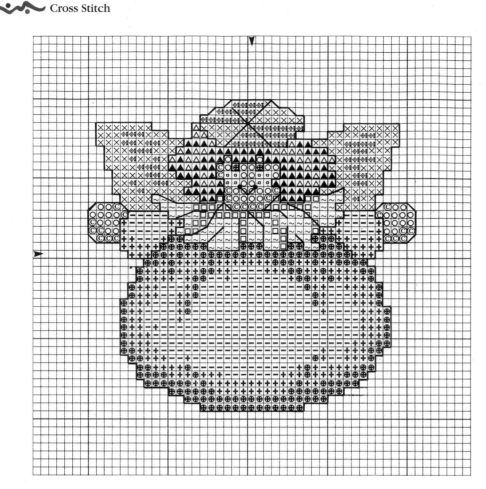

Fluffy Angel

Design size: 41 wide x 39 high
Fabric: 16-count white Aida
Clip: blue
Trim: Using 1/2 yard of 1/16" blue ribbon, tie a small bow and glue beneath chin. Tie center of remaining ribbon through end of clip, then knot ends and glue behind hands.

		Anchor	Coats	DMC
~	= white	1	1001	blanc
▫	= pink	36	3125	3326
O	= lt peach	868	3868	353
©	= med peach	882	3883	758
	dk peach	13	3013	347
✕	= lt yellow	293	2289	727
✥	= dk yellow	305	2295	743
—	= lt blue	130	7021	809
+	= med blue	131	7022	798
⊕	= dk blue	132	7080	797
△	= med brown	349	3336	3776
▲	= dk brown	351	3340	400
☐	= gray	397	8232	762
	brown-black	382	5382	3371
	metallic gold			

• = French Knots: dk peach

❘ = Backstitch:
   mouth - dk peach
   wing, halo - metallic gold
   remaining outlines - brown-black

Note: If no symbol is given, that color is used only for decorative stitches or backstitches.

Hanging Out

Design size: 37 wide x 40 high
Fabric: 16-count white Aida
Clip: red, positioned horizontally with shorter section bent upward

		Anchor	Coats	DMC
□	= white	2	1001	blanc
~	= lt red	47	3500	321
▲	= dk red	20	3072	498
✧	= yellow	305	2295	725
O	= med green	226	6227	702
♦	= dk green	229	6228	700
X	= lt brown	362	5942	437
◇	= med brown	369	5347	435
✕	= dk brown	357	5475	801
●	= black	403	8403	310
		= Backstitch:		

plaid pattern on vest - yellow
remaining outlines - black

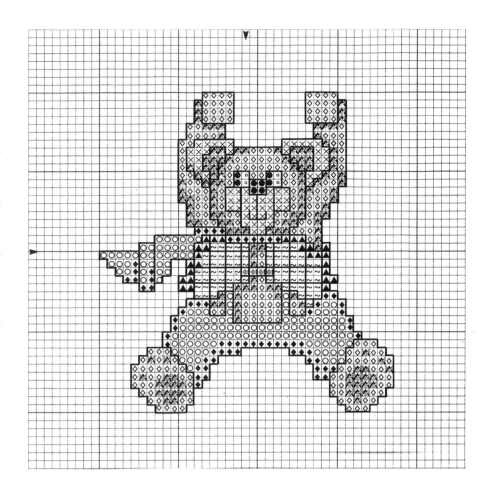

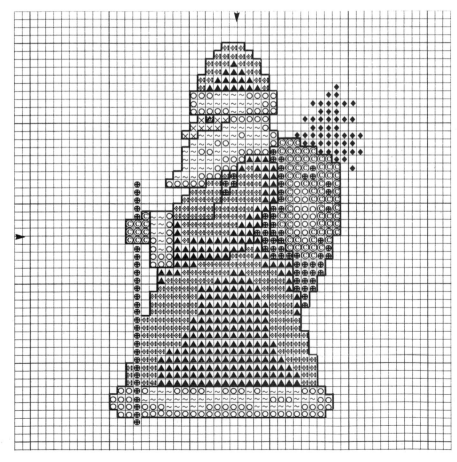

Folk Santa

Design size: 32 wide x 48 high
Fabric: 16-count white Aida
Clip: red

		Anchor	Coats	DMC
~	= white	2	1001	blanc
X	= lt red	778	3335	945
✧	= med red	35	3152	350
▲	= dk red	19	3500	817
♦	= green	227	6227	701
©	= lt brown	370	5349	434
⊕	= dk brown	357	5475	801
✕	= very dk brown	382	5382	3371
O	= gray	397	8397	3072
		= Backstitch: very dk brown		

Jingle Bell

Design size: 38 wide x 41 high
Fabric: 16-count white Aida
Clip: black

	Anchor	Coats	DMC
✕ = white	2	1001	blanc
☆ = lt red	35	3152	892
⊗ = med red	47	3500	321
★ = dk red	44	3073	815
○ = lt gold	305	2295	743
− = med gold	306	2307	725
+ = dk gold	308	5308	781
◇ = lt green	267	6267	3346
◆ = dk green	268	6269	469
✻ = black	403	8403	310
	= Backstitch: black			

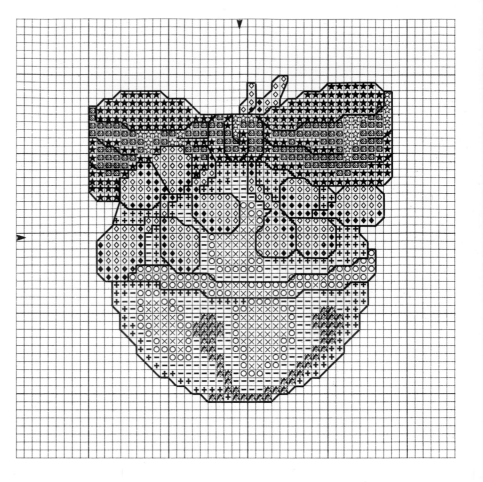

Li'l Sheriff

Design size: 34 wide x 46 high
Fabric: 16-count white Aida
Clip: red

	Anchor	Coats	DMC
▫ = white	1	1001	blanc
© = pink	36	3125	3326
☆ = med red	35	3152	892
★ = dk red	19	3500	321
~ = peach	868	3868	353
△ = lt gold	891	2874	676
▲ = dk gold	901	2876	680
◇ = green	227	6227	701
+ = med brown	936	5936	632
⊞ = dk brown	360	5476	898
□ = gray	231	8231	453
✻ = brown-black	382	5382	3371
⬦ = metallic gold			
✳ = Eyelet: metallic gold			

• = French Knots:
   bridle, buttons - dk red
   mouth, chaps trim - brown-black

| = Backstitch:
   reins, plaid shirt pattern - dk red
   remaining outlines - brown-black

40

Love

Design size: 30 wide x 46 high
Fabric: 16-count white Aida
Clip: gold
Trim: 1/16" dk red ribbon; tie bow and glue to lowest point of ornament.

	Anchor	Coats	DMC
~ = white	1	1001	blanc
▲ = red	47	3500	321
✕ = lt peach	6	3006	761
✥ = med peach	9	3008	352
+ = dk peach	10	3011	3712
O = lt gold	885	2386	739
✖ = med gold	886	2292	677
◇ = med green	245	6211	987
◆ = dk green	246	6246	986
black	403	8403	310
© = metallic gold			
| = Backstitch:			

    lettering - red
    banner, holly berries & leaves - black
    heart, vertical stripes below lettering - metallic gold

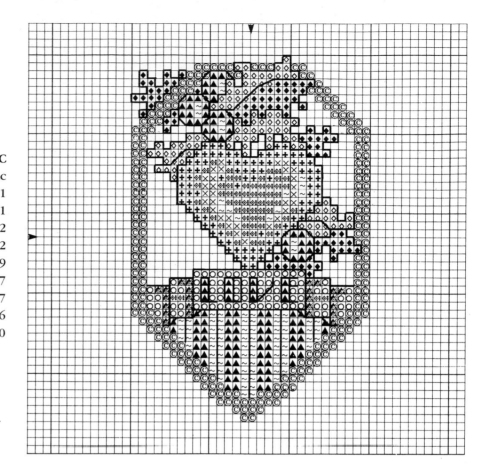

Note: If no symbol is given, that color is used only for decorative stitches or backstitches.

Noel

Design size: 44 wide x 37 high
Fabric: 16-count white Aida
Clip: gold

	Anchor	Coats	DMC
~ = white	1	1001	blanc
O = lt red	11	3011	351
© = med red	46	3046	666
⊕ = dk red	47	3500	321
✕ = med yellow	305	2295	743
▲ = dk yellow	306	2307	725
◇ = lt green	226	6227	702
◆ = dk green	229	6228	910
brown-black	382	5382	3371
• = French Knots: brown-black			
| = Backstitch:			

    "Noel" - med red
    remaining outlines - brown-black

Sleigh

Design size: 44 wide x 33 high
Fabric: 16-count white Aida
Clip: green

	Anchor	Coats	DMC
~ = white	2	1001	blanc
✕ = med red	47	3500	321
▲ = dk red	20	3072	498
⟡ = lt yellow	300	2350	745
⊠ = dk yellow	305	2295	743
◆ = green	227	6227	701
O = blue	137	7080	798
✳ = black	403	8403	310

• = French Knots: dk red

| = Backstitch:

    package ties, gold trim on sleigh,
      runner - dk red
    stems - green
    pattern on white package - blue
    remaining outlines - black

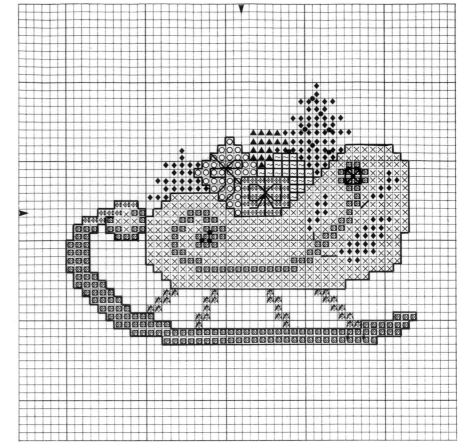

Note: If no symbol is given, that color is used only for decorative stitches or backstitches.

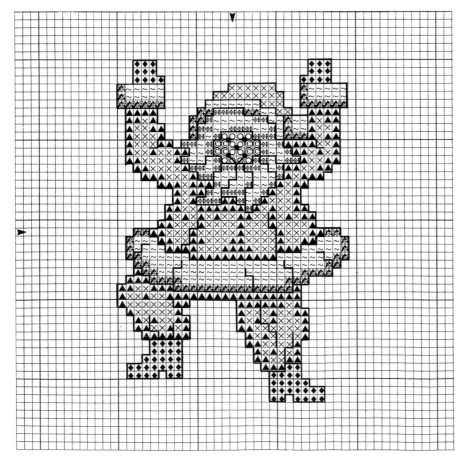

Swingin' Santa

Design size: 29 wide x 43 high
Fabric: 16-count white Aida
Clip: green, positioned horizontally with shorter section bent upward

	Anchor	Coats	DMC
~ = white	1	1001	blanc
© = pink	36	3125	3326
✕ = med red	47	3500	321
▲ = dk red	20	3072	498
O = peach	868	3868	353
◆ = green	229	6228	700
⟡ = blue	158	7053	747
✳ = gray	397	8232	762
brown-black	382	5382	3371

• = French Knots:
    nose - pink
    eyes, mouth - brown-black

| = Backstitch: brown-black

Test Ride

Design size: 39 wide x 50 high
Fabric: 16-count white Aida
Clip: red

	Anchor	Coats	DMC
~ = white	2	1001	blanc
△ = med red	47	3500	321
▲ = dk red	20	3072	498
− = peach	778	3335	945
✧ = yellow	306	2307	725
◇ = med green	226	6239	702
◆ = dk green	227	6227	700
○ = lt brown	370	5349	434
© = med brown	363	5943	436
● = dk brown	360	5476	898
✼ = black	403	8403	310

- • = French Knots:
  on hat, saddle - med red
  on rocker - med green
  eye, jingle bells - black
- | = Backstitch:
  ornament, bow - med red
  mouth - med red (2 strands)
  "SC" - black (2 strands)
  remaining outlines - black

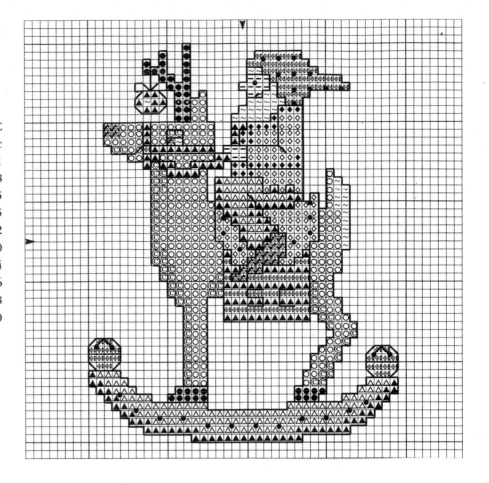

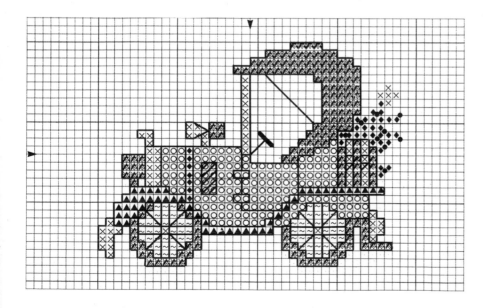

Tin Lizzie

Design size: 38 wide x 28 high
Fabric: 16-count white Aida
Clip: black

	Anchor	Coats	DMC
~ = white	1	1001	blanc
○ = lt red	35	3152	350
▲ = dk red	19	3500	817
✕ = yellow	295	2295	726
◆ = green	227	6227	701
✼ = black	403	8403	310

- • = French Knots:
  tree ornaments - lt red
  package trim - black
- ＼ = Straight Stitch: black (4 strands)
- | = Backstitch: black

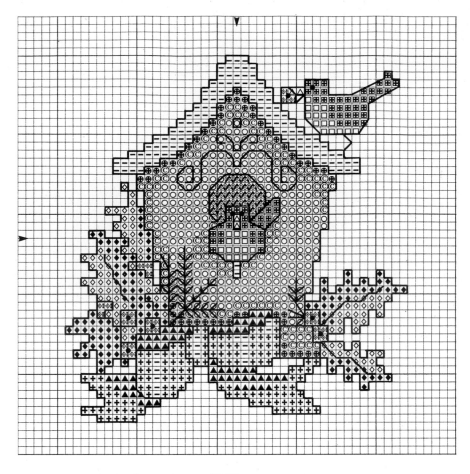

Home Tweet Home

Design size: 43 wide x 46 high
Fabric: 16-count white Aida
Clip: white

	Anchor	Coats	DMC
− = white	2	1001	blanc
⧆ = lt red	11	3011	351
✚ = med red	35	3152	350
▲ = dk red	20	3072	817
△ = yellow	295	2295	726
◇ = med green	227	6227	701
◆ = dk green	923	6228	699
O = lt blue	160	7159	3755
◎ = med blue	977	7977	334
⊕ = dk blue	979	7979	312
□ = lt brown	388	5831	3033
⊞ = med brown	903	5393	3032
⋇ = dk brown	381	5477	938
brown-black	382	5382	3371

• = French Knots: brown-black

| = Backstitch:
  pine branches, leaf veins - dk green
  remaining outlines - brown-black

Note: If no symbol is given, that color is used only for decorative stitches or backstitches.

Christmas Stocking Ornaments

They're sure to please all! These 4 3/4"-tall mini stockings are lovely for ornament exchanges, to fill with a small gift of jewelry, money or candy, or to adorn a special gift package.

Stitching Notes

SUPPLIES (for each ornament)

14-count Aida cloth, one 5" x 7" piece of desired color
cotton print fabric, one 5" x 7" piece, colors to match
   design
lightweight iron-on interfacing, one 5" x 7" piece
embroidery floss, appropriate colors for design
3/8" gold jump ring
additional trimming as desired

MISCELLANEOUS ITEMS:

tapestry needles
scissors
iron
pins
sewing needle and thread
tissue paper
sewing machine (optional)

ORNAMENT DIRECTIONS

Step 1. Stitch design centered on Aida cloth. Press embroidery on wrong side, making sure fabric threads are straight in both directions.

Step 2. Follow manufacturer's directions to fuse iron-on interfacing to wrong side of embroidery.

Step 3. Trace solid outline from the pattern on page 47 onto tissue or tracing paper and cut it out. Turn pattern over if stocking design faces opposite direction. Pin this pattern onto right side of embroidery, making sure edges are in same position as dots on the chart. If the pattern does not fit because your fabric count isn't exactly 14 blocks per inch, cut a slightly larger tissue pattern.

Step 4. Using thread to match Aida cloth, machine stitch just outside edge of tissue pattern along both sides and around foot; do not stitch across top. This stitching will eventually be turned under as part of the seam allowance. Remove pattern.

Step 5. Leaving a 1/2" seam allowance across the top edge and 1/4 " seam allowances around the rest of the shape, cut out stocking.

Step 6. Place print backing fabric and embroidery wrong sides together; pin pieces together at center. Cut backing fabric to match trimmed embroidery.

Step 7. On stitched front, turn under and finger press embroidery seam allowances, clipping as needed. At the top, turn under the side seam allowances first, then turn under the top edge. Repeat for backing fabric, making it slightly smaller than the front. Use pins to secure the folded edges together.

Step 8. Slipstitch the back to the front. Leave the top edge open.

Step 9. Sew or glue desired trimming to ornament. Tack jump ring (or a loop of trimming) to top back edge for hanging.

ATTACHING BEADS

The Beaded Medallions stocking design on page 49 uses seed beads in place of cross stitches. Use a half cross stitch to secure each bead over a block of fabric, **Fig 1**. Since beads must be attached securely, you can use a small knot to begin and end threads; use quilting thread, embroidery floss, or invisible sewing thread. Bring needle up at 1, pick up one bead with point of needle, then stitch down at 2; continue across row, adding beads as indicated on the chart.

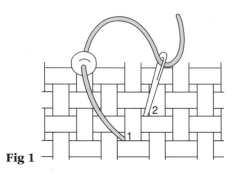

Fig 1

A straight line of beads can be attached with a straight stitch, **Fig 2**. Come up at one end of the line, add enough beads to cover the length desired, and stitch down at the end of the line. Be sure to secure thread well, and only use this method for a small number of beads.

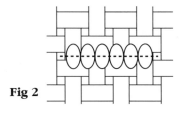

Fig 2

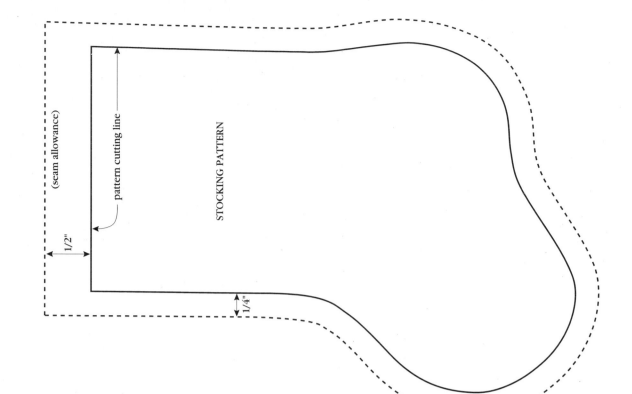

(seam allowance)

pattern cutting line

STOCKING PATTERN

1/2"

1/4"

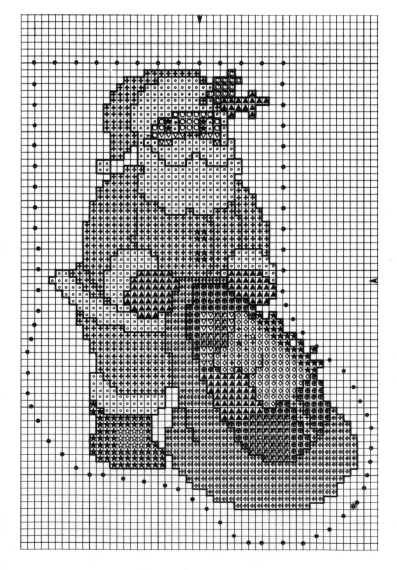

Santa's Pack
designed by Kathleen Hurley

Fabric: 14-count blue Aida
Trimming: one 5/8" gold jingle bell

	DMC	Anchor	Coats
∘ = white	blanc	2	1001
O = lt pink	963	49	3150
▽ = med pink	894	26	3126
+ = red	666	46	3046
☆ = yellow	743	297	2296
⬧ = gold	977	307	2306
© = lt green	912	205	6031
▲ = med green	909	229	6228
⚹ = blue	798	131	7080
⊕ = brown	975	355	5349
◇ = gray	452	399	8512
★ = black	310	403	8403
✳ = attach bell			
∣ = Backstitch: black			

A Purrfect Christmas
designed by Carole Rodgers

Fabric: 14-count pink Aida
Trimming: silver braid

		DMC	Anchor	Coats
◦	= white	blanc	2	1001
✧	= pink	962	76	3127
●	= red	326	59	3019
◇	= gold	726	295	2294
✻	= green	700	229	6227
△	= tan	435	369	5365
○	= lt gray	415	398	8397
☆	= med gray	414	400	8399
◆	= dk gray	413	401	5382
★	= black	310	403	8403
|	= Backstitch:			

    stems - green
    lettering - red (2 strands)
    cat - black

Note: If no symbol is given, that color is used only for decorative stitches or backstitches.

Bah, Humbug
designed by Anis Duncan

Fabric: 14-count cream Aida
Trimming: green metallic braid

		DMC	Anchor	Coats
+	= med red	321	47	3500
●	= dk red	815	43	3073
☆	= med green	702	239	6226
	dk green	909	229	6228
|	= Backstitch:			

    $, cook, clean, trim - dk green
    shop, wrap - dk red

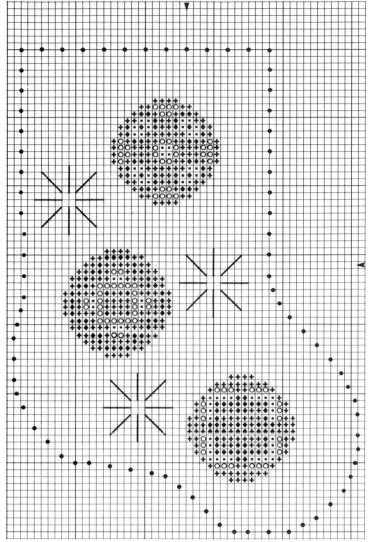

Beaded Medallions
designed by Carol Krob

Fabric: 14-count cream Aida
Note: See Attaching Beads, page 46, for attaching seed beads.

	DMC/Balger	Anchor/Balger	Coats/Balger
+ = blue	517/006	169/006	7162/006
O = white seed bead (medium)			
♦ = gold seed bead (medium)			
▪ = blue seed bead (small)			
	= string of blue beads (small)			

Beaded Wreath
designed by Carol Wilson Mansfield

Fabric: 14-count pink Aida
Trimming: pink lace; twenty pink glass seed beads

	DMC	Anchor	Coats
★ = pink	962	76	3127
O = gold	725	306	2307
− = med green	702	239	6226
♦ = dk green	991	189	6211
✳ = attach bead			

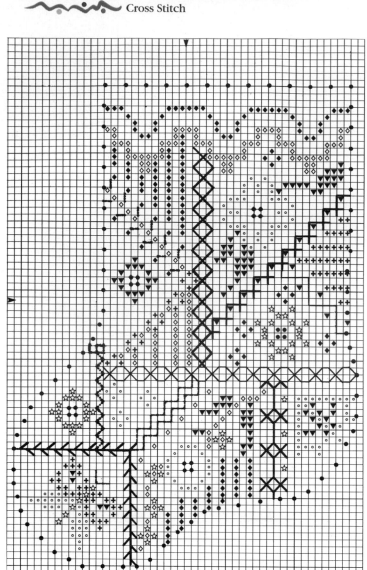

Button Patchwork
designed by Carol Wilson Mansfield

Fabric: 14-count cream Aida
Trimming: cluny lace; five assorted buttons

		DMC	Anchor	Coats
○	= pink	601	78	3063
◆	= red	498	20	3072
◇	= lt green	912	205	6031
▼	= dk green	909	229	6228
☆	= blue	825	162	7181
+	= purple	552	101	4101

| = red backstitch
| = dk green backstitch
⋮ = blue backstitch
| = purple backstitch
⁚⁚ = attach button

Note: If no symbol is given, that color is used only for decorative stitches or backstitches.

Cardinal Christmas
designed by Kathleen Hurley

Fabric: 14-count oatmeal Aida

		DMC	Anchor	Coats
	white	blanc	2	1001
◇	= red	321	47	3500
	dk red	816	44	3000
O	= gold	725	306	2307
	green	561	212	6211
+	= brown	632	936	5356
▲	= black	310	403	8403

• = French Knots: white
// = Straight Stitches: green
| = Backstitch: dk red

Country Church
designed by Kathleen Hurley

Fabric: 14-count cream Aida
Trimming: ecru lace

		DMC	Anchor	Coats
∘	= white	blanc	2	1001
☆	= lt red	899	27	3152
●	= dk red	326	59	3019
O	= yellow	743	297	2296
▽	= lt green	563	208	6210
+	= dk green	561	212	6211
−	= blue	813	160	7161
※	= lt gray	318	399	8511
	dk gray	317	400	8512
|	= Backstitch: dk gray			

Gander Greetings
designed by Kathleen Hurley

Fabric: 14-count cream Aida
Trimming: gold braid

		DMC	Anchor	Coats
∘	= white	blanc	2	1001
O	= lt red	3708	26	3126
◆	= dk red	3705	35	3012
©	= gold	977	307	2306
△	= lt green	704	256	6238
+	= dk green	992	187	6186
☆	= med blue	794	120	7021
▼	= dk blue	792	940	7022
◈	= brown	840	379	5379
※	= gray	414	400	8399
●	= black	310	403	8403
✳	= French Knot: white			
|	= Backstitch: black			

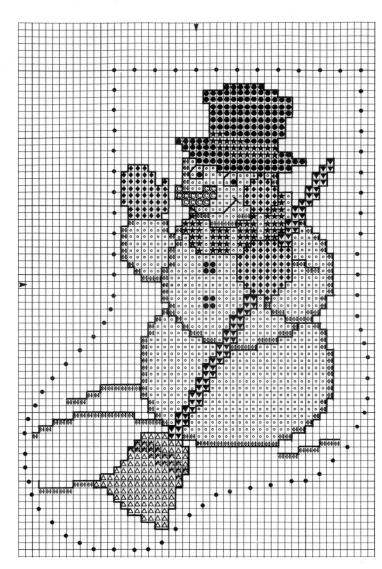

Howdy, Mr. Snowman
designed by Kathleen Hurley

Fabric: 14-count blue Aida

Trimming: green jumbo rickrack

		DMC	Anchor	Coats
∘	= white	blanc	2	1001
★	= red	321	47	3500
©	= orange	947	330	2330
△	= gold	402	347	3337
◆	= green	911	205	6205
✖	= blue	798	131	7080
▼	= brown	400	351	5349
◈	= med gray	414	400	8399
●	= dk gray	413	401	8999
	black	310	403	8403
|	= Backstitch: black			

Note: If no symbol is given, that color is used only for decorative stitches or backstitches.

Jingle Bell Tartan
designed by Carol Wilson Mansfield

Fabric: 14-count cream Aida

Trimming: three 3/8" gold jingle bells

		DMC	Anchor	Coats
★	= dk red	321	47	3500
◇	= med green	702	239	6226
+	= dk green	699	923	6228
◈	= blue	996	433	7010
◆	= purple	333	119	4101
✳	= attach bell			
|	= Backstitch: med green			

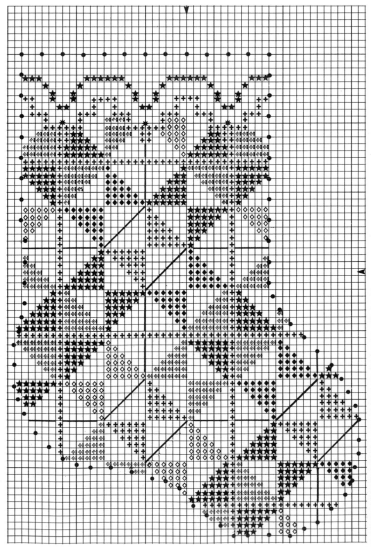

Time of
Laughter,
Joy and Fun
MERRY
CHRISTMAS,
Everyone!

Merry Christmas, Everyone
designed by Carole Rodgers

Fabric: 14-count cream Aida
Trimming: twelve red glass beads

		DMC	Anchor	Coats
+	= med red	321	47	3500
●	= dk red	498	20	3072
☆	= yellow	444	291	2298
O	= med green	700	229	6227
◈	= dk green	890	879	6021
✹	= attach bead			
•	= French Knots: med red			
|	= Backstitch: med red			

Merry Christmas
designed by Anis Duncan

Fabric: 14-count cream Aida
Trimming: gold braid

		DMC	Anchor	Coats
☆	= med red	666	46	3046
	dk red	321	47	3500
+	= green	699	923	6228
|	= Backstitch: dk red			

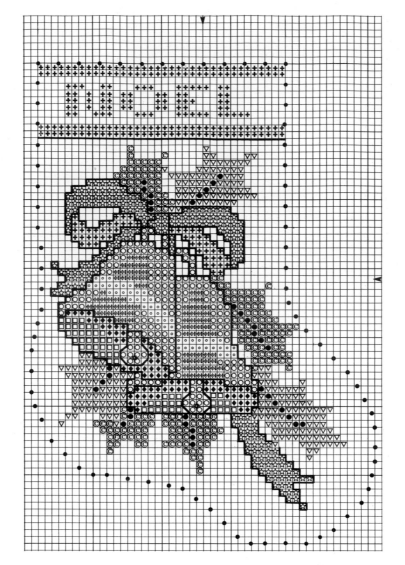

Noel Chimes
designed by Kathleen Hurley

Fabric: 14-count blue-green Aida
Trimming: two 4mm gold beads

	DMC	Anchor	Coats
○ = white	blanc	2	1001
☆ = lt red	891	35	3012
+ = red	321	47	3500
❈ = yellow	726	295	2294
O = gold	783	307	2308
▽ = lt green	704	256	6238
© = med green	562	210	6211
● = dk green	319	246	6246
□ = lt brown	301	349	2326
◆ = dk brown	898	360	5476
✳ = attach bead			
| = Backstitch: dk brown			

Christmas Borders

designed by Sam Hawkins

Christmas is a special time of year that inspires happy cross stitchers to take needle in hand and create wonderful decorations for their homes. These border designs by Sam Hawkins have been used on pre-finished Christmas stockings in various sizes as well as on a festive table runner for holiday entertaining.

Candleglow

Holly Bouquets

Parade of the Toy Soldiers

Dancing Angels

Rocking Horse Reunion

Bells, Bells, Bells

Ol' Santa Moon

Trumpeting Angels

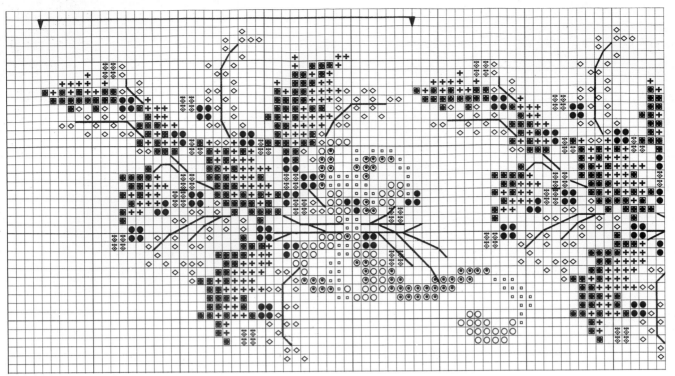

Holly Bouquets

Design area: 43 wide repeat x 39 high
Model: stitched on 14-count white Aida cuff of an 11" x 15"
quilted pre-finished print stocking

	DMC	Anchor	Coats
❋ = lt red	3705	35	3012
● = med red	321	47	3500
□ = lt yellow	744	301	2296
○ = med yellow	725	306	2307

Dancing Angels

Design area: 96 wide repeat x 34 high
Model: stitched on 14-count white Aida cuff of an 11" x 15"
quilted pre-finished red print stocking
Stitching Note: Tack three green bows below
stitched design.

	DMC/Balger	Anchor/Balger	Coats/Balger
ꝰ = white/pearl blending filament	blanc/032	2/032	1001/032
☆ = lt pink	3326	25	3126
❋ = med pink	894	26	3152
⊕ = dk pink	962	76	3127
◉ = red/filament	321/003	47/003	3500/003

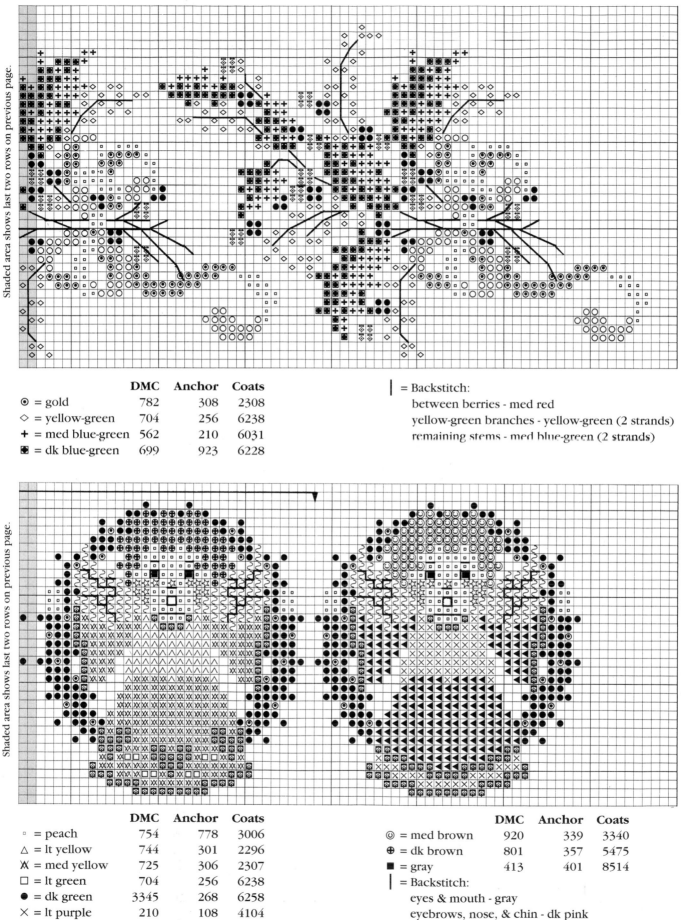

Shaded area shows last two rows on previous page.

	DMC	Anchor	Coats
⊙ = gold	782	308	2308
◇ = yellow-green	704	256	6238
+ = med blue-green	562	210	6031
▦ = dk blue-green	699	923	6228

| = Backstitch:
 between berries - med red
 yellow-green branches - yellow-green (2 strands)
 remaining stems - med blue-green (2 strands)

Shaded area shows last two rows on previous page.

	DMC	Anchor	Coats
▫ = peach	754	778	3006
△ = lt yellow	744	301	2296
⋇ = med yellow	725	306	2307
□ = lt green	704	256	6238
● = dk green	3345	268	6258
✕ = lt purple	210	108	4104
◀ = med purple	208	110	4101
∣ = tan	738	942	5372

	DMC	Anchor	Coats
◎ = med brown	920	339	3340
⊕ = dk brown	801	357	5475
■ = gray	413	401	8514

| = Backstitch:
 eyes & mouth - gray
 eyebrows, nose, & chin - dk pink
 wings - tan (2 strands)

57

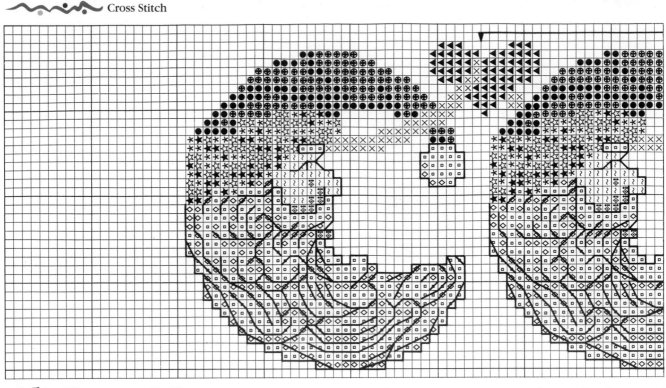

Ol' Santa Moon

Design area: 35 wide repeat x 38 high
Model: stitched on 14-count white Aida cuff of a
13" x 29" quilted pre-finished red table runner

	DMC/Balger	Anchor/Balger	Coats/Balger
▫ = white	blanc	2	1001
⸮ = peach	754	778	3006
✾ = lt pink	894	26	3126
◄ = dk pink/filament	962/007	76/007	3127/007
✕ = gold/filament	725/091	306/091	2307/091

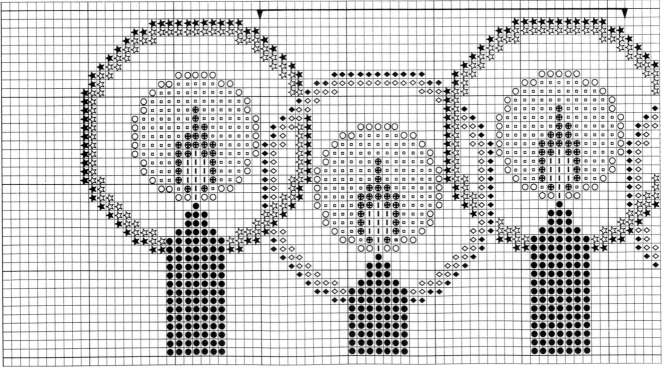

Candleglow

Design area: 42 wide repeat x 39 high
Model: stitched on 14-count ivory Aida cuff of an 11" x 15"
quilted pre-finished plaid stocking

	DMC	Anchor	Coats
I = white	blanc	2	1001
● = red	321	47	3500
▫ = lt yellow	744	301	2296

58

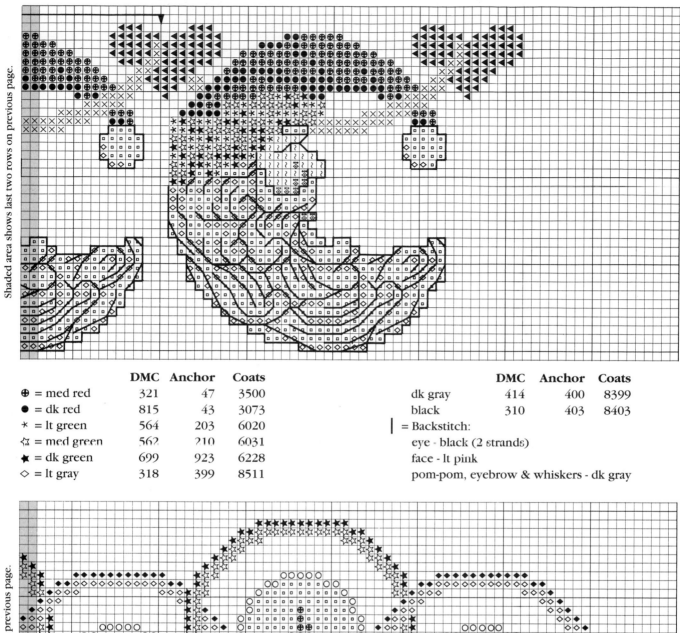

		DMC	Anchor	Coats
⊕	= med red	321	47	3500
●	= dk red	815	43	3073
✶	= lt green	564	203	6020
✿	= med green	562	210	6031
★	= dk green	699	923	6228
◇	= lt gray	318	399	8511

	DMC	Anchor	Coats
dk gray	414	400	8399
black	310	403	8403

| = Backstitch:
    eye - black (2 strands)
    face - lt pink
    pom-pom, eyebrow & whiskers - dk gray

		DMC Balger	Anchor/ Balger	Coats/ Balger
○	= med yellow	444	291	2298
⊕	= dk yellow/filament	742/091	303/091	2303/091
✿	= lt gold	725	306	2307

		DMC	Anchor	Coats
★	= dk gold	783	307	5363
◇	= lt antique gold	3046	887	2410
◆	= med antique gold	680	901	5374

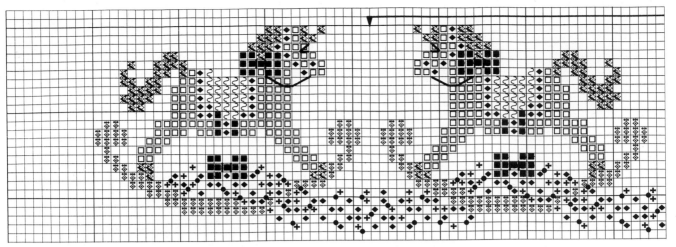

Rocking Horse Reunion

Design area: 66 wide repeat x 24 high

Model: single motif stitched on 14-count white Aida cuff of a
4" x 6" pre-finished red mini stocking

Stitching Note: Use one strand each of lt gray and lt green to
create blend.

		DMC	Anchor	Coats
∂	= pink	894	26	3126
■	= red	666	46	3046
+	= med green	562	210	6031
◆	= dk green	699	923	6228
□	= lt gray/lt green blend	318/564	399/203	8511/6020

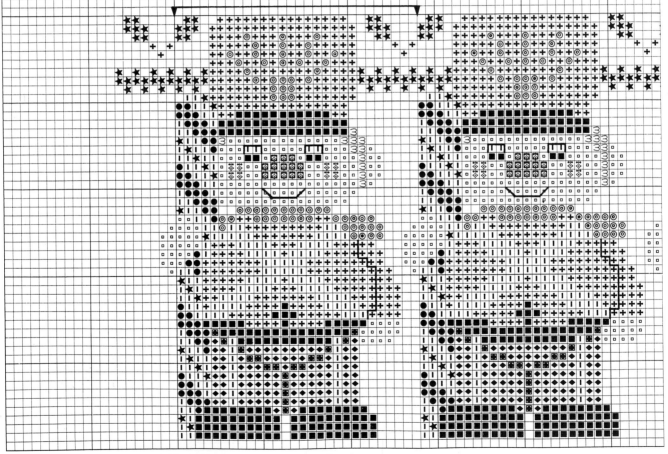

Parade of the Toy Soldiers

Design area: 28 wide repeat x 49 high

Model: stitched on 18-count white Aida cuff of
an 11" x 13" pre-finished plaid stocking

		DMC	Anchor	Coats
I	= white	blanc	2	1001
✳	= lt pink	894	26	3126
◉	= med pink	962	76	3127
●	= med red	666	46	3046
+	= dk red	304	47	3000

Shaded area shows last two rows on previous page.

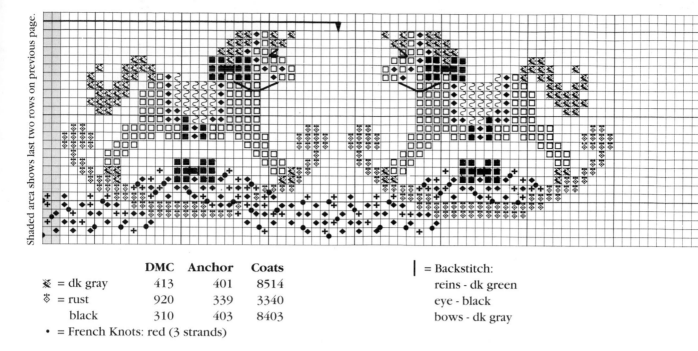

	DMC	Anchor	Coats
⊠ = dk gray	413	401	8514
⬦ = rust	920	339	3340
black	310	403	8403

• = French Knots: red (3 strands)

| = Backstitch:
reins - dk green
eye - black
bows - dk gray

Note: If no symbol is given, that color is used only for decorative stitches or backstitches.

	DMC	Anchor	Coats
▫ = peach	754	778	3006
Ӡ = yellow	725	306	2307
★ = green	701	227	6227
◆ = med blue	798	137	7080
▩ = dk blue	824	164	7182

	DMC	Anchor	Coats
■ = black	310	403	8403

◎ = metallic gold

| = Backstitch:
mouth - dk red (2 strands)
jacket & eyes - black

61

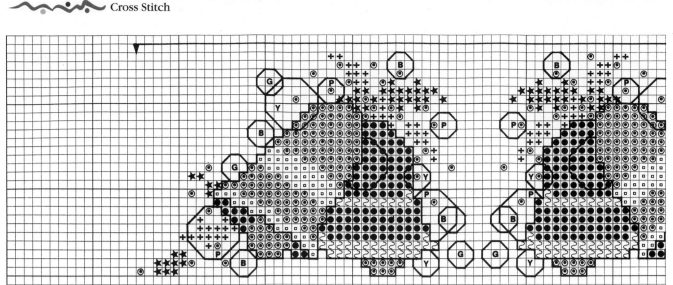

Bells, Bells, Bells

Design area: 78 wide repeat x 26 high
Model: single motif stitched on 14-count white Aida cuff of
a 4" x 6" pre-finished green mini stocking

	DMC	Anchor	Coats
▫ = white	blanc	2	1001
pink	894	26	3126
⊙ = med red	666	46	3046
● = dk red	815	43	3073
yellow	725	306	2307

Note: If no symbol is given, that color is used only for decorative stitches or backstitches.

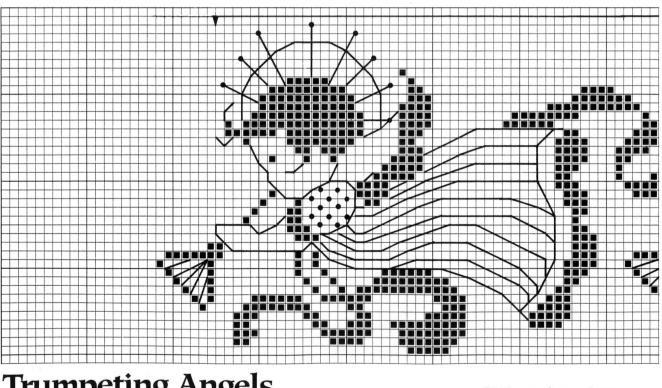

Trumpeting Angels

Design area: 54 wide repeat x 38 high
Model: stitched on 14-count ivory Aida cuff of an 11" x 15"
quilted pre-finished plaid stocking
Stitching Note: This repeat border was designed to be
stitched in any color you wish, using the same floss for all
cross stitches, backstitches, and French knots.

	DMC	Anchor	Coats
■ = red	3705	35	3012
• = French Knots: red			
	= Backstitch: red			

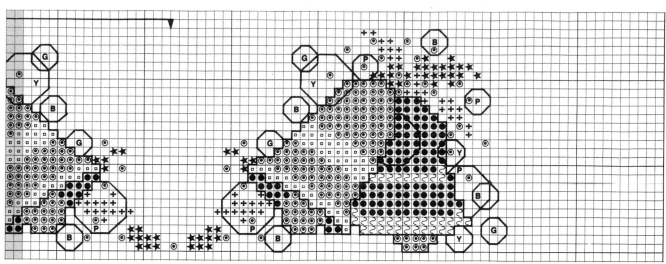

	DMC	Anchor	Coats
lt green	704	256	6238
+ = med green	905	258	6239
★ = dk green	3345	268	6258
blue	813	160	7161
⌒ = gray	318	399	8511

| = Backstitch:
    bells - dk red
    ornament between bells - blue (2 strands)
    remaining ornaments - first letter of color name is
        shown inside each ornament outline (P = pink,
        Y = yellow, G = lt green, B = blue (2 strands)

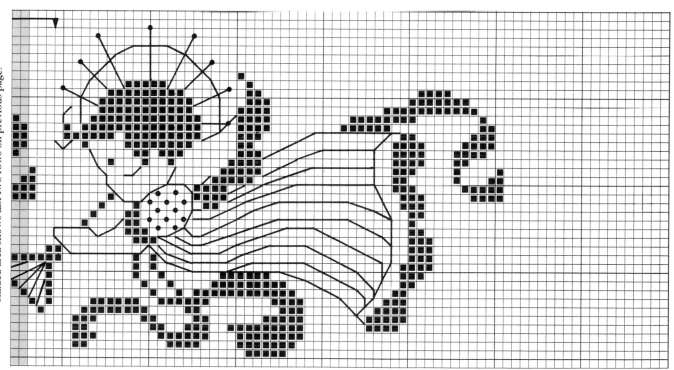

 Cross Stitch

Christmas Cross Stitched Mugs

designed by Bette Ashley

The flavor of hot chocolate or mulled cider will seem sweeter when it is sipped from one of these clever mugs.

Stitching Notes

These designs are planned to fit the 3 1/2" x 4" Stitch-A-Mugs from Crafter's Pride. They have a clear outer shell, an insert strip of white or parchment Aida-patterned vinyl, and an opaque form that snaps inside. The vinyl has 14 squares per inch horizontally and vertically and is treated as if it were a 14-count fabric.

Use the "stab-stitch" method of work, pulling floss completely through with each motion of the needle. A hoop will not be needed, as the vinyl surface holds its shape comfortably as you stitch.

Plan placement on the vinyl strip so ends of strip meet where handle is attached. The strips are 10" x 3 1/2" or approximately 141 squares wide and 49 squares high.

Since the design will be visible on only one side, decide whether the handle should be on the right or the left and position it correctly. Use pins to mark the left and right edges of the design. Slip the vinyl into the shell to check this placement before you start. Vertically center the design.

Santa's Mug

Design size: 46 wide x 39 high
Model: parchment vinyl, parchment mug

		Anchor	Coats	DMC
∘	= white	1	1001	blanc
✕	= peach	868	3868	353
O	= pink	9	3008	352
☆	= med red	46	3046	666
★	= dk red	47	3500	321
◇	= lt green	227	6227	701
◆	= dk green	229	6228	700
⋄⋈	= blue-green	849	7225	932
©	= lt gray	397	8232	762
▲	= very dk gray	236	8999	3799

• = French Knots: very dk gray

❘ = Backstitch: lettering - dk red
    mouth - dk red (2 strands)
    pine branches - dk green
    remaining outlines - very dk gray

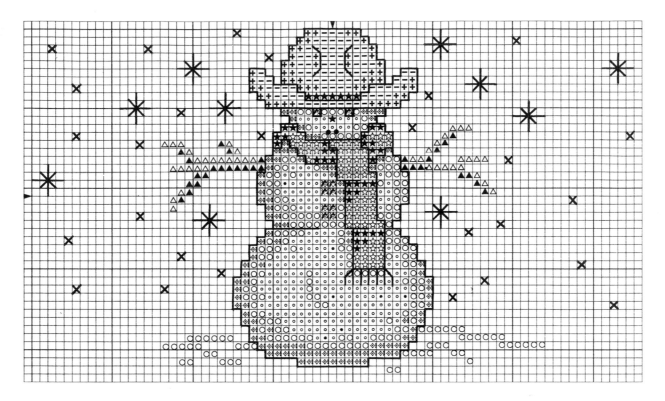

Snowman Mug

Design size: 75 wide x 42 high
Model: parchment vinyl, parchment mug
Stitching Notes: Combine two strands of blending filament with two strands of floss for the white, very lt blue, and med blue cross stitches. Use two strands each of floss and filament for the snowflakes; if desired, stitch additional snowflakes around mug in a random pattern.

		Anchor/ Balger	Coats/ Balger	DMC/ Balger
∘	= white/pearl filament	1/032	1001/032	blanc/032
☆	= med red	47	3500	321
★	= dk red	44	3073	815
O	= very lt blue/ sky blue filament	9159/014	7020/014	3761/014
⬧	= med blue/ blue filament	160/006	7159/006	3325/006
	dk blue	149	7980	311
△	= med rust	371	5470	434
▲	= dk rust	360	5476	898
−	= lt brown	376	2337	3774
+	= dk brown	378	5578	841
✵	= brown-black	382	5382	3371
•	= French Knots: brown - black			
✳	= Double Cross Stitches: med blue floss and sky blue filament			
⏐	= Backstitch: fringe – dk red snowman and scarf – dk blue hat and eyes – black			

Note: If no symbol is given, that color is used only for decorative stitches or backstitches.

The Partridge and the Pear

designed by Sam Hawkins

Set the mood for holiday entertaining with the classic elegance of these Sam Hawkins designs. These unique pieces of stitchery are such a feast for the eyes that your work will be cherished for years to come.

Stitching Notes

These designs were created to be stitched on 14-count prefinished Christmas plaid place mat and napkin.

Treat the width of the gold that is woven into the border area as just another block of threads, stitching right over it as if it were a block of green threads. To help placement of your design, the woven gold is shown as a shaded row on the chart. The edges of the plaid areas are shown by dotted lines.

Use two strands of blending filament with two strands of floss where filament is listed in the Color Key. Choose a metallic gold that matches the woven gold thread.

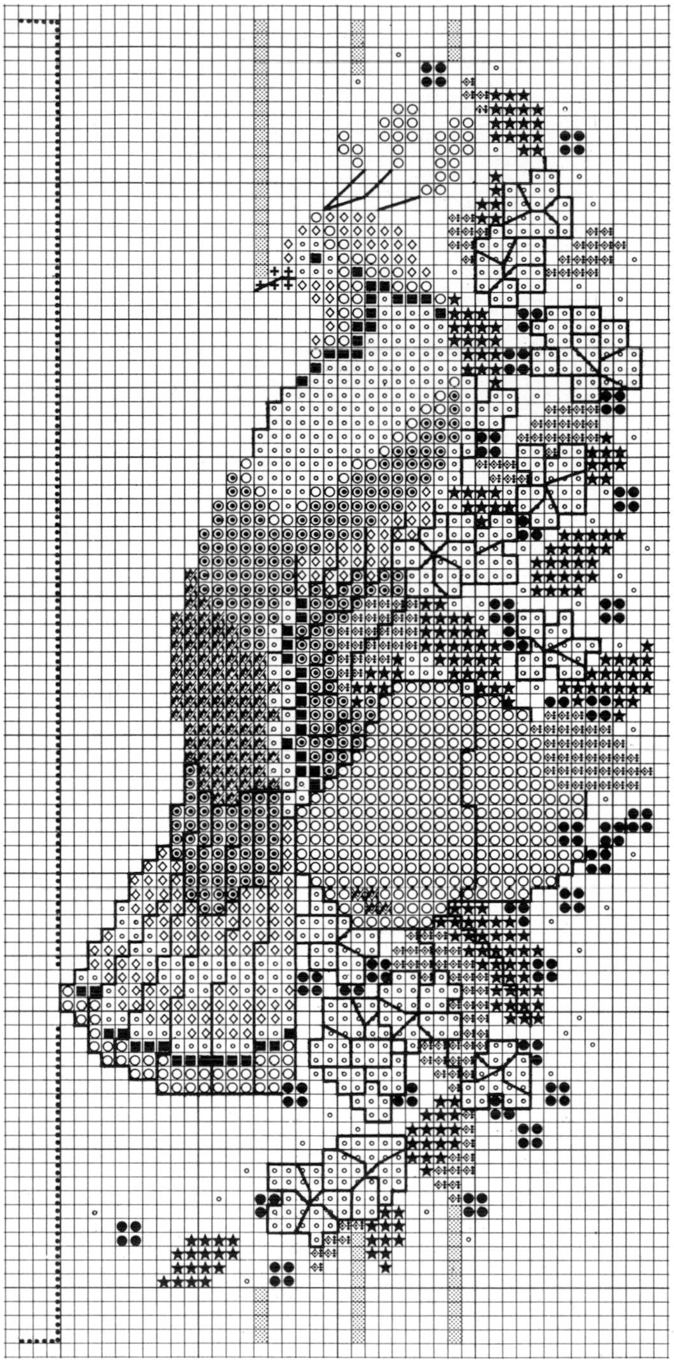

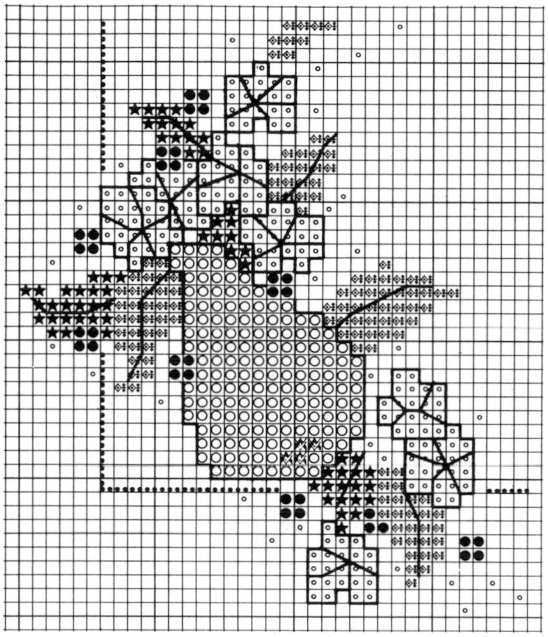

Design Sizes:

Partridge - 43 wide x 90 high to fit place mat

Pear - 37 wide x 43 high to fit napkin

	DMC/ Balger	Anchor/ Balger	Coats/ Balger
◦ = cream/filament	739/032	885/032	5387/032
● = red/filament	309/031	42/031	3000/031
+ = lt orange	402	347	3336
⟡ = med green	320	215	6017
★ = dk green	367	217	6018
◇ = lt brown	437	362	5373
⊙ = med brown	435	369	5365
⋉ = dk brown	433	371	5374
very dk brown	938	381	5477
■ = black-brown	3371	382	5382
○ = metallic gold			
| = Backstitch: flowers - dk brown partridge, pears, leaves - very dk brown			

Note: If no symbol is given, that color is used only for decorative stitches or backstitches.

Fingertip Towels
designed by Sam Hawkins

Once you've dressed up your own bathroom and kitchen with these decorative towels, you'll want to start stitching for friends and relatives.

Stitching Notes

The designs are worked on 10" x 18" fingertip towels with 14-count Aida cloth bands. The bands have 135 wide x 30 high squares available for stitching. Unless otherwise noted in Color Key, backstitching is done with 2 strands of floss.

Season's Greetings

Design size: 111 wide x 29 high
Model: ivory towel

		DMC	Anchor
◦	= white	blanc	2
◇	= lt red	891	35
★	= dk red	321	47
☆	= orange	721	324
−	= yellow	725	306
+	= gold	783	307
✖	= blue	996	433
O	= lt green	704	256
◆	= med green	905	258
■	= dk green	986	246
	brown	801	357

• = French Knots: dot "I" - med green

| = Backstitch:
    pine - dk green
    candle holder, candle wick - brown
    lettering - med green

Note: If no symbol is given, that color is used only for decorative stitches or backstitches.

Candy Canes

Design size: 35 wide x 33 high
Model: blue towel

		DMC	Anchor
◦	= white	blanc	2
★	= red	666	46
	dk red	326	59
◈	= lt green	702	239
■	= dk green	699	923

| = Backstitch:
    candy canes - dk red
    pine - dk green
    berries - red

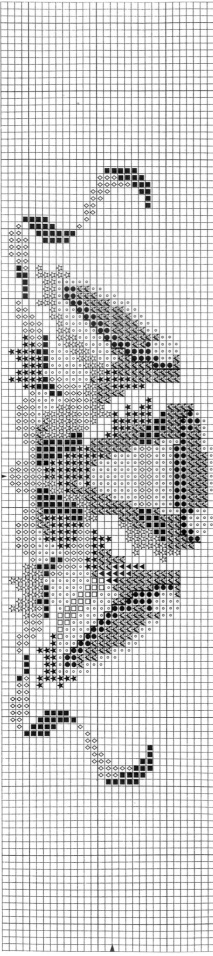

Christmas Bells

Design size: 89 wide x 30 high
Model: ivory towel

		DMC	Anchor
◇	= lt red	321	47
■	= dk red	498	20
○	= lt gold	725	306
✹	= dk gold	782	308
□	= lt blue	519	167
▲	= dk blue	518	168
☆	= lt green	906	256
★	= dk green	904	258
●	= med brown	433	371
	dk brown	801	357
│	= Backstitch:		
	edge of bells - dk brown		

Note: If no symbol is given, that color is used only for decorative stitches or backstitches.

Christmas Trees Welcome

Design size: 87 wide x 28 high
Model: red towel

		DMC	Anchor
○	= pink	894	26
▽	= orange	3340	329
□	= yellow	742	303
☆	= lt green	704	256
■	= dk green	699	923
+	= blue	996	433
✹	= brown	300	352
│	= Backstitch:		
	lattice - dk green		

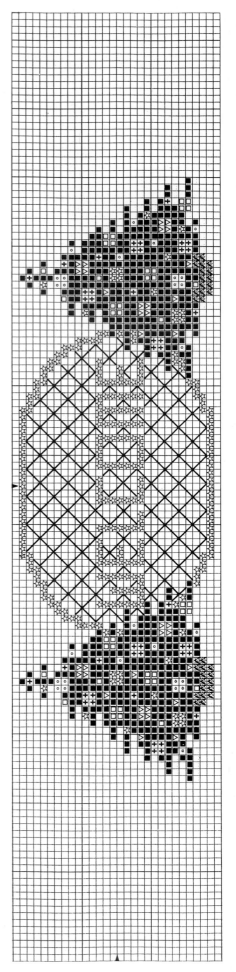

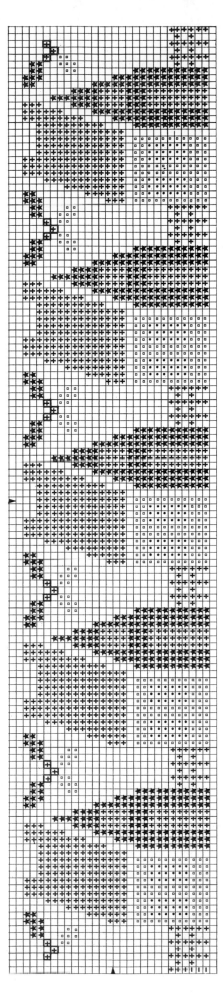

Christmas Village

Design size: 137 wide x 27 high
Model: ivory towel

		DMC	Anchor
•	= lt red	891	35
+	= dk red	304	47
□	= lt green	906	256
★	= dk green	904	258
|	= Backstitch:		
	berries - dk red		

Deck the Halls

Design size: 137 wide x 27 high
Model: ivory towel

		DMC	Anchor
●	= red	321	47
+	= green	700	229
•	= French Knots: note - red		
	lettering - green		
|	= Backstitch:		
	notes, staff - red		
	lettering - green		

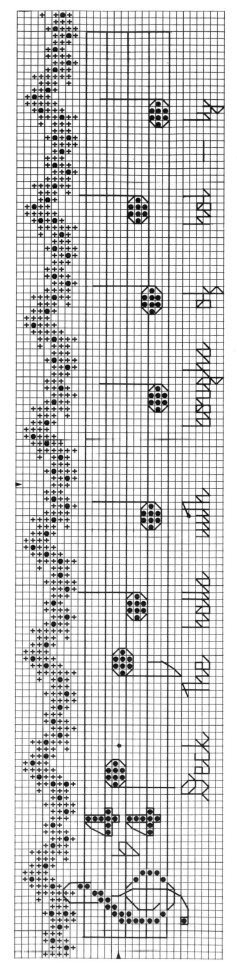

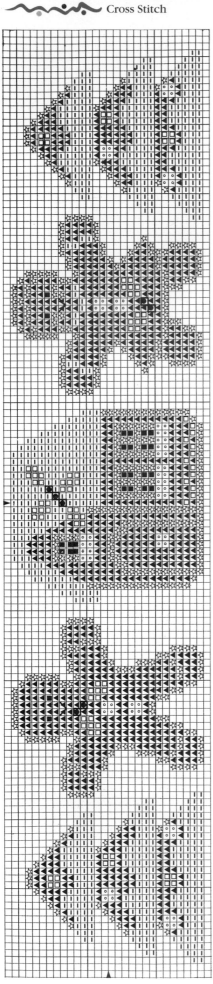

Gingerbread Cookies

Design size: 132 wide x 28 high
Model: green towel

		DMC	Anchor
–	= white	blanc	2
☆	= pink	957	40
●	= red	666	46
∘	= yellow	727	293
□	= lt green	954	203
▲	= brown	436	363
■	= dk brown	898	360
│	= Backstitch:		
	mouth, berries - red		

Goose Parade

Design size: 137 wide x 26 high
Model: red towel

		DMC	Anchor
∘	= white	blanc	2
●	= red	891	35
+	= orange	721	324
◇	= gold	783	307
✕	= green	909	229
■	= brown	801	357
│	= Backstitch:		
	goose, eye - brown		

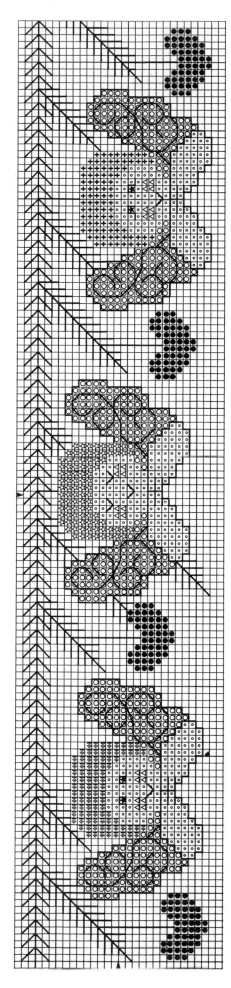

Hearts and Angels

Design size: 136 wide x 27 high
Model: ivory towel

		DMC	Anchor
○	= lt peach	353	8
△	= pink	894	26
●	= red	304	47
◈	= orange	721	324
☆	= yellow	743	297
O	= lt gold	676	891
	green	699	923
	blue	826	161
+	= lt brown	436	363
★	= dk brown	801	357
		= Backstitch:		

left angel's wings - pink
center angel's wings - blue
right angel's wings - orange
around wings, hands, eyes -
   dk brown
mouths, ornament hangers - red
pine - green

Note: If no symbol is given, that color is used only for decorative stitches or backstitches.

Ho, Ho, Ho

Design size: 134 wide x 30 high
Model: green towel

		DMC	Anchor
○	= white	blanc	2
□	= peach	353	8
+	= pink	956	40
●	= red	666	46
※	= green	699	923
■	= black	310	403
		= Backstitch:		

mouth - red
eyes - black

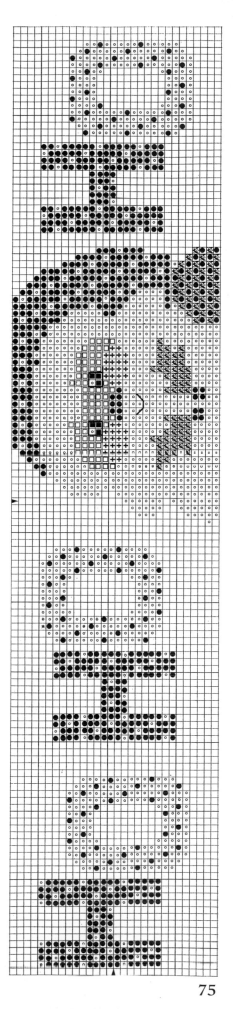

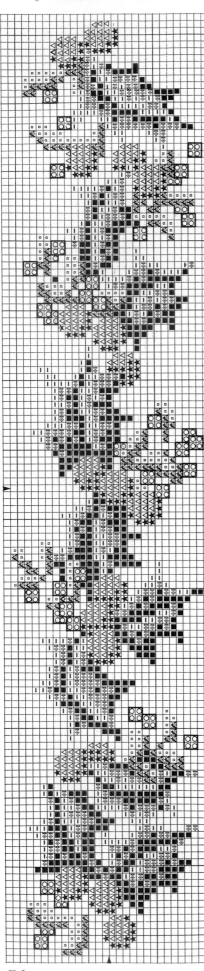

Holly and Mistletoe

Design size: 135 wide x 27 high
Model: lt pink towel

		DMC	Anchor
O	= white	blanc	2
△	= lt red	891	35
★	= dk red	816	44
▫	= lt green	907	255
※	= med green	905	258
−	= lt blue-green	992	187
⬥	= med blue-green	909	229
■	= dk blue-green	890	879
	brown	632	936
|	= Backstitch:		
	berries - brown		

Note: If no symbol is given, that color is used only for decorative stitches or backstitches.

Joy, Love, Peace

Design size: 131 wide x 28 high
Model: green towel

		DMC	Anchor
−	= peach	353	8
+	= pink	603	76
▼	= red*	321	47
☆	= orange	971	316
○	= lt yellow	744	301
□	= gold yellow	742	303
⬥	= lt blue	996	433
●	= dk blue	995	410
△	= green**	907	255
■	= dk brown	838	380

    *we used 1 str 321 with 2 str Balger® Blending Filament red 003

    **we used 1 str 907 with 2 str Balger® Blending Filament green 015

| = Backstitch:
    angel wing, bird wing - dk brown
    vines - green
    hearts - pink
    "LOVE" - dk blue

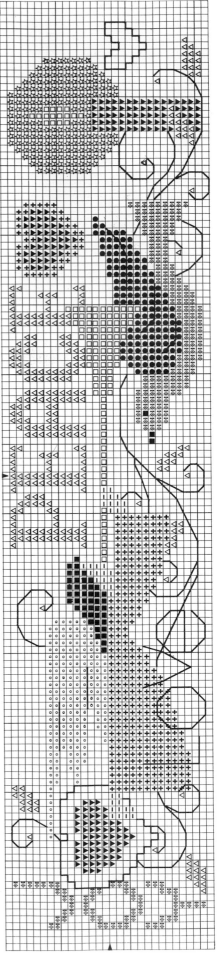

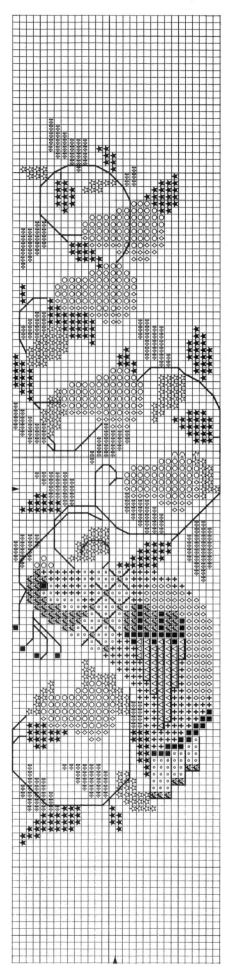

Partridge in a Pear Tree

Design size: 115 wide x 29 high
Model: lt blue towel

		DMC	Anchor
◦	= white	blanc	2
◇	= peach	352	10
O	= yellow	743	297
☆	= lt green	471	266
◈	= med green	905	258
★	= dk green	895	246
✖	= rust	920	339
△	= lt brown	422	373
+	= med brown	434	309
■	= dk brown	938	381
		= Backstitch:		

vine - dk green
eye, feathers on head, wing,
   tail - dk brown
neck pattern - rust

Santa

Design size: 135 wide x 18 high
Model: ivory towel

		DMC	Anchor
●	= red	666	46
+	= gold	783	307
◇	= lt green	906	256
	dk green	699	923
		= Backstitch:		

pine - dk green

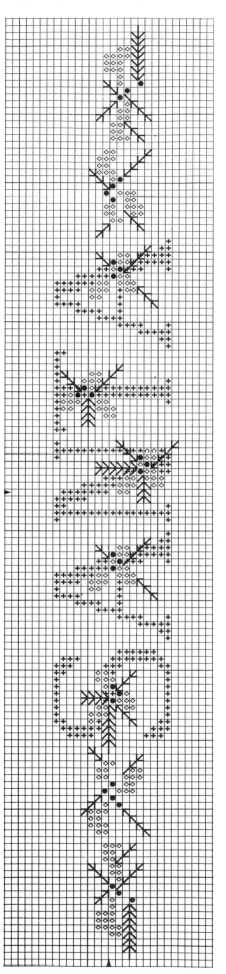

Noel

designed by Polly Carbonari

This sweet little couple celebrates the season with a candle representing the birth of baby Jesus.

Design size: 112 wide x 88 high
Model: stitched on 14-count ivory perforated
plastic, shown in a 10-1/2" x 8-1/2" wood frame

	Anchor	Coats	DMC
▫ = white	1	1001	blanc
O = lt pink	36	3125	3326
◈ = med pink	1024	3071	3328
⊕ = dk pink	1025	3013	347
∕ = med red	46	3500	666
✄ = dk red	44	3073	815
~ = peach	1012	2331	754
☆ = lt yellow	305	2295	743

	Anchor	Coats	DMC
★ = dk yellow	308	5308	781
◇ = med green	876	6876	503
♦ = dk green	212	6211	561
♡ = lt turquoise	185	6185	964
♥ = dk turquoise	188	6187	943
⌃ = lt fuchsia	103	4303	211
= = med fuchsia	86	4086	3608
✳ = dk fuchsia	94	4089	917
■ = gray	236	8514	3799
│ = Backstitch: gray			

Merry Christmas

designed by Jamie Leigh

Geometric patchwork designs stitched with a needle in shades of red and green floss create a classic Christmas greeting.

Design size: 162 wide x 132 high

Model: stitched on 14-count Fiddler's Lite, shown in a 15" x 13-1/2" red frame

		Anchor	Coats	DMC
▫	= cream	1011	2331	948
☆	= very lt red	35	3012	3705
□	= lt red	9046	3500	321
≃	= med red	19	3019	304
✕	= med dk red	1006	3401	304
★	= dk red	44	3073	815

		Anchor	Coats	DMC
■	= very dk red	22	3021	814
✎	= very lt peach	6	3006	754
○	= lt peach	8	3868	353
◈	= med peach	9	3008	352
⊕	= med dk peach	10	3011	351
⊞	= dk peach	11	3111	350
●	= very dk peach	13	2335	347
◇	= very lt blue-green	206	6209	564
△	= lt blue-green	208	6210	563
#	= med blue-green	210	6213	562

Continue stitching from chart on page 82.

Continue stitching from chart on page 83.

	Anchor	Coats	DMC
∞ = med dk blue-green	211	6211	561
♦ = dk blue-green	878	6878	501
▲ = very dk blue-green	879	6880	500
▽ = very lt gray-green	213	6875	504
♡ = lt gray-green	214	6016	368
◉ = med gray-green	216	6876	502
♥ = med dk gray-green	217	6018	367
▼ = dk gray-green	218	6246	319
➴ = very dk gray-green	683	6021	890

‒ ‒ = Running Stitch:
    around each quilt design—med dk red
    inside & outside borders—very dk red

| = Backstitch: very dk blue-green (2 strands)

A	B
C	D

Shaded area shows last two rows on page 81.

Continue stitching from chart on page 84.

A	B
C	D

	Anchor	Coats	DMC
▫ = cream	1011	2331	948
☆ = very lt red	35	3012	3705
□ = lt red	9046	3500	321
≃ = med red	19	3019	304
× = med dk red	1006	3401	304
★ = dk red	44	3073	815
■ = very dk red	22	3021	814
⌇ = very lt peach	6	3006	754
○ = lt peach	8	3868	353
◈ = med peach	9	3008	352
⊕ = med dk peach	10	3011	351
⊞ = dk peach	11	3111	350
● = very dk peach	13	2335	347
◇ = very lt blue-green	206	6209	564
△ = lt blue-green	208	6210	563

	Anchor	Coats	DMC
# = med blue-green	210	6213	562
∞ = med dk blue-green	211	6211	561
◆ = dk blue-green	878	6878	501
▲ = very dk blue-green	879	6880	500
▽ = very lt gray-green	213	6875	504
♡ = lt gray-green	214	6016	368
⊙ = med gray-green	216	6876	502
♥ = med dk gray-green	217	6018	367
▼ = dk gray-green	218	6246	319
✎ = very dk gray-green	683	6021	890

– – = Running Stitch:
    around each quilt design—med dk red
    inside & outside borders—very dk red
| = Backstitch: very dk blue-green (2 strands)

A	B
C	D

Shaded area shows last two rows on page 81.

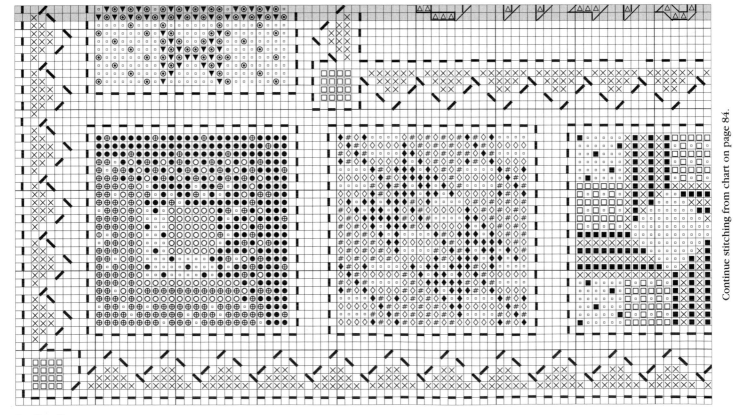

Continue stitching from chart on page 84.

Section C

	Anchor	Coats	DMC
▫ = cream	1011	2331	948
☆ = very lt red	35	3012	3705
□ = lt red	9046	3500	321
≃ = med red	19	3019	304
✕ = med dk red	1006	3401	304
★ = dk red	44	3073	815
■ = very dk red	22	3021	814
✐ = very lt peach	6	3006	754
○ = lt peach	8	3868	353
◈ = med peach	9	3008	352
⊕ = med dk peach	10	3011	351
⊞ = dk peach	11	3111	350
● = very dk peach	13	2335	347
◇ = very lt blue-green	206	6209	564
△ = lt blue-green	208	6210	563

	Anchor	Coats	DMC
# = med blue-green	210	6213	562
∞ = med dk blue-green	211	6211	561
◆ = dk blue-green	878	6878	501
▲ = very dk blue-green	879	6880	500
▽ = very lt gray-green	213	6875	504
♡ = lt gray-green	214	6016	368
⊙ = med gray-green	216	6876	502
♥ = med dk gray-green	217	6018	367
▼ = dk gray-green	218	6246	319
✔ = very dk gray-green	683	6021	890

– – = Running Stitch:

   around each quilt design—med dk red

   inside & outside borders—very dk red

| = Backstitch: very dk blue-green (2 strands)

Shaded area shows last two rows on page 82.

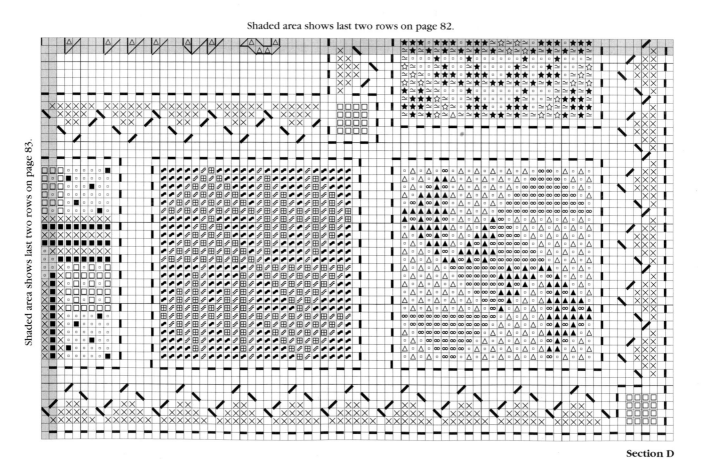

Shaded area shows last two rows on page 83.

Section D

	A	B
	C	D

Merry Mittens and Socks

designed by Polly Carbonari

These festive designs will put your feet in the mood to dance and make your hands ready to applaud this holiday season.

Continue stitching from chart on page 87.

Socks

Design size: 70 wide x 220 high

Model: stitched on 14-count natural Aida cloth, shown in a 7" x 17" red frame

		Anchor	Coats	DMC
□	= white	1	1001	blanc
⬖	= med red	46	3500	666
●	= dk red	44	3073	815
ℱ	= yellow-green	254	6001	3348
◇	= med green	225	6225	702
◆	= dk green	227	6227	701
✠	= very dk green	218	6246	319
✳	= turquoise	186	6185	959
☆	= lt fuchsia	85	4085	3609
★	= med fuchsia	86	4086	3608
	gray	236	8514	3799
|	= Backstitch: gray			

Note: If no symbol is given, that color is used only for decorative stitches or backstitches.

86

Shaded area shows last two rows on page 86.

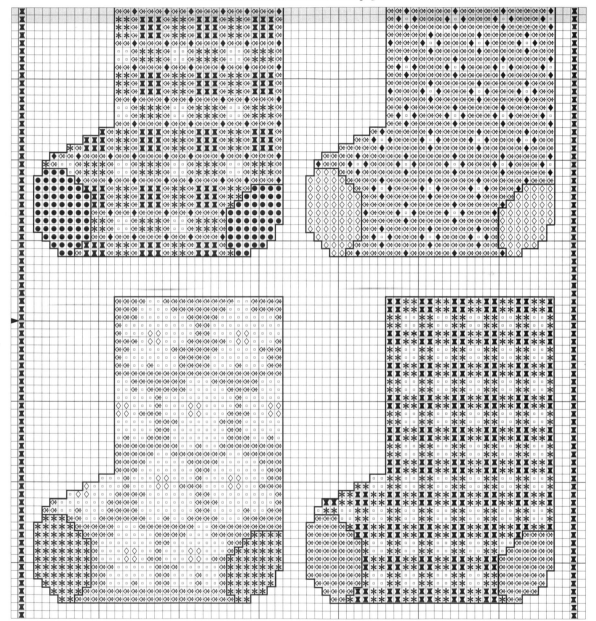

Continue stitching from chart on page 88.

Shaded area shows last two rows on page 87.

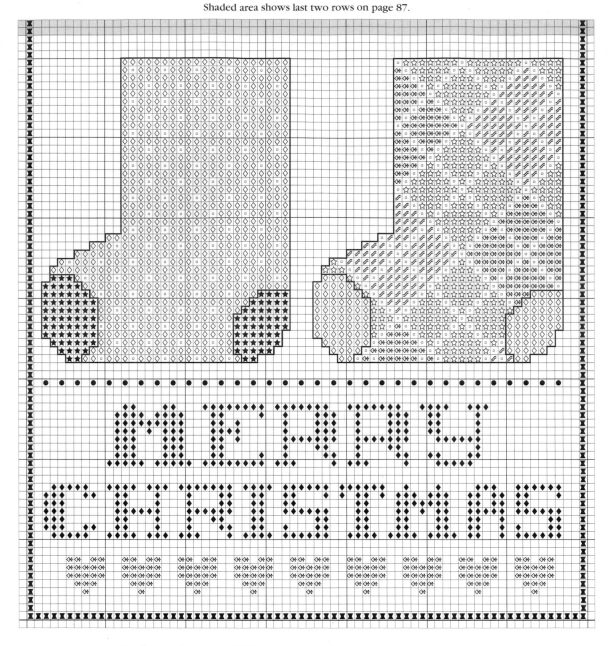

		Anchor	**Coats**	**DMC**
▫	= white	1	1001	blanc
⧉	= med red	46	3500	666
●	= dk red	44	3073	815
⌇	= yellow-green	254	6001	3348
◇	= med green	225	6225	702
◆	= dk green	227	6227	701
⫩	= very dk green	218	6246	319
✳	= turquoise	186	6185	959
☆	= lt fuchsia	85	4085	3609
★	= med fuchsia	86	4086	3608
	gray	236	8514	3799
│	= Backstitch: gray			

Note: If no symbol is given, that color is used only for decorative stitches or backstitches.

Mittens

Design size: 56 wide x 217 high
Model: stitched on driftwood
Yorkshire, shown in a 6" x 17" gray frame

	Anchor	Coats	DMC
□ = white	1	1001	blanc
● = red	47	3047	321
☆ = lt yellow	295	2295	726
★ = med yellow	297	2294	973
✳ = yellow-orange	304	2314	741
O = yellow-green	254	6001	3348
◇ = lt green	241	6225	966
# = med green	226	6239	703
◆ = dk green	227	6227	701
∧ = lt fuchsia	85	4085	3609
✕ = dk fuchsia	87	4087	3607
gray	236	8513	414
	= Backstitch: gray			

Continue stitching from chart on page 90.

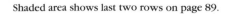

Shaded area shows last two rows on page 89.

	Anchor	Coats	DMC
▫ = white	1	1001	blanc
● = red	47	3047	321
☆ = lt yellow	295	2295	726
★ = med yellow	297	2294	973
✳ = yellow-orange	304	2314	741
O = yellow-green	254	6001	3348
◇ = lt green	241	6225	966
# = med green	226	6239	703
◆ = dk green	227	6227	701
∧ = lt fuchsia	85	4085	3609
✕ = dk fuchsia	87	4087	3607
gray	236	8513	414

| = Backstitch: gray

Note: If no symbol is given, that color is used only for decorative stitches or backstitches.

Plastic Canvas

Plastic Canvas

Plastic canvas is a molded plastic grid with evenly spaced holes. This wonderful product makes it possible to do easy needlepoint stitching on it, while it holds its shape. It is supple enough to stitch on, but strong and resilient enough to join to other pieces. Plastic canvas can be easily cut with scissors and doesn't ravel. These attributes give the crafter a whole range of dimensional design possibilities.

Plastic canvas is an ideal material for Christmas decorations. The holiday projects we've selected are colorful and fun to stitch.

You'll find a whole tree full of ornaments that are great to make for the Christmas bazaar or use as package decorations. There are two clever doorstops that can be set upon the bookshelf or mantel if a doorstop is not needed. Candy cane holders are a neat way to offer a treat to visitors. Our snowy tissue box cover is a festive way to display this necessary convenience during sniffle season. And the delightful little Gingerbread House will add a special note to holiday surroundings.

Plastic Canvas How-To

TYPES OF PLASTIC CANVAS

The canvas is available in several forms. Most commonly used are flat canvas sheets that come in several sizes; in clear or a variety of colors; and in four mesh sizes. Mesh simply means the number of stitches per inch.

The canvas consists of holes into which the threaded needle is inserted and bars over which the stitches are made. Canvas called 7-mesh has 7 stitches, or bars, to the inch.

Most projects are made from clear canvas sold in sheets of about 10-1/2" x 13-1/2" and with 7 bars to the inch.

The canvas is also available in sheets of 11" x 14" with 10 bars to the inch. A project worked on 10-mesh canvas will be considerably smaller than the same project worked on the larger 7-mesh canvas. **Fig 1** shows the same project worked on the two mesh sizes of canvas; 14-mesh canvas is also available.

7-mesh   10-mesh   **Fig 1**

Hint: Always be sure to use the mesh size canvas specified in your project instructions if the finished project must be a certain size (such as to fit over a tissue box).

Plastic canvas is manufactured by several different companies. Not all canvas is exactly the same, so be sure to use just one brand of canvas in a project, or the pieces may not fit together exactly.

The clear 7-mesh canvas comes in three weights: regular, extra stiff, and extra soft. The stiff canvas is ideal for projects needing added strength, while the soft canvas is best for pieces that must be curved or shaped.

TYPES AND SIZES OF CANVAS
regular weight sheets: 10-1/2" x 13-1/2", 12" x 18" and 13-1/2" x 21-1/2"
extra stiff sheets: 12" x 18"
extra soft sheets: 12" x 18"
specialty shapes: 12" x 18" oval (for placemats)
3" and 4" squares
3-1/2" x 4-1/2" diamonds
various sized circles

Other specialty shapes include butterflies, dimensional pieces, purse forms and precut alphabet and numbers. **Fig 2** shows some of the available forms of plastic canvas.

Fig 2

Colored canvas is bright and fun and is often used in projects that leave some areas of canvas unstitched for a special effect. For instance, red and green canvas is frequently used for Christmas projects.

All of the projects in this chapter were worked on plastic canvas sheets, with seven stitches to the inch, called 7-mesh plastic canvas. We have used regular weight canvas, available in sheets measuring 10 1/2" x 13 1/2".

ABOUT THE YARN

Any yarn that covers the canvas well can be used. Experiment with different types of yarn to achieve the coverage and effect you desire. When working with double or triple strands, remember to increase the yarn amounts accordingly. When working with most yarn, use a 36" length for stitching; use an 18" length if yarn tends to fray.

Worsted Weight Yarn, available in many colors in both synthetic and wool fibers, is easy to work with and widely available. This yarn has a tendency to "pill," so it is not good for an item such as a tote bag that will get a lot of wear.

One strand of worsted weight will cover 7-mesh canvas well. It is too heavy for use on 10-mesh.

Sport Weight Yarn is thinner than worsted weight and not available in as many colors. One strand covers nicely on 10-mesh canvas, but you will need two strands for coverage on 7-mesh.

Rug Yarn works well on 7-mesh with one strand but is much too heavy for 10-mesh canvas.

Craft Yarns come in a variety of types and finishes, and most work well on 7-mesh canvas.

Persian Type Yarn is a twisted wool 3-ply yarn used frequently in regular needlepoint. Its greatest advantage is the many lovely colors available, with many shadings within one color family. The plies can be divided so that you can use one or two plies on 10-mesh canvas; for 7-mesh, use three-ply strands. Experiment to see what gives the coverage you like.

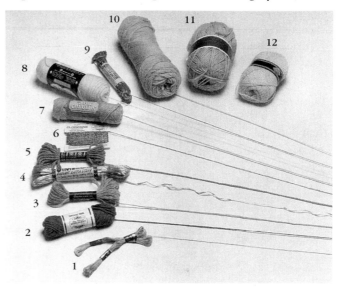

Sample of yarns suitable for plastic canvas:
1 cotton embroidery floss, **2** tapestry yarn, **3** acrylic Persian yarn, **4** rayon raffia, **5** nylon needlecraft yarn, **6** metallic needlepoint thread, **7** acrylic plastic canvas yarn, **8** acrylic sport weight yarn, **9** metallic plastic canvas cord, **10** and **11** worsted weight yarn, and **12** acrylic/wool blend sport weight yarn

Tapestry Yarn is another wool yarn used for regular needlepoint. One strand of tapestry yarn usually covers 10-mesh well; use two or three strands to give good coverage on 7-mesh.

Cotton Embroidery Floss comes in many colors, and is often used for detail work or overstitching. It is too thin to use in large areas on 7-mesh canvas, but on 10-mesh you can use it as desired, with three 6-strand pieces in the needle.

Specialty Yarns can give a unique look to a project. You can get wonderful effects using yarns such as angora, metallic, synthetic raffia, pearl cotton, or narrow ribbon to accent certain projects. Experiment to get the look you like. There are also nylon yarns made especially for plastic canvas work.

Getting Started

THE PATTERN CHARTS AND EQUIPMENT

There is a pattern chart for each stitched piece. Some square or rectangular pieces may not be charted; follow the instructions noted in the individual project. The color keys near the charts indicate the color and type of stitch to use.

You will need a size 16 or 18 tapestry needle for stitching, a grease pencil or felt pen to mark the pattern shape on the canvas, and strong scissors and a sharp craft knife to cut the canvas.

CUTTING THE CANVAS

All of our patterns are measured by **bars**, not holes. Mark the outline of each piece on the plastic canvas and cut them (**Fig 3**), using scissors or craft knife for small areas. Trim any plastic nubs and cut corners on the diagonal (**Fig 4**); be careful not to cut so close that the corner is weakened.

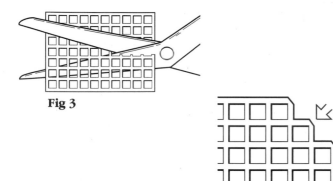

Fig 3

Fig 4

BEGINNING AND ENDING

Do not tie a knot to begin stitching with a new strand. Hold an inch of the end in place and work the first few stitches over the end (**Fig 5**). You may also anchor the end by running it through a few stitches of an adjacent stitched area. End strand by running it through the back of a stitched area and trim it closely.

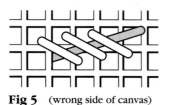

Fig 5   (wrong side of canvas)

Stitching Hints: When possible, work light-colored areas of a design first, leaving dark stitches for later. This keeps the lighter areas free of "fuzz" from the dark colors.

Keep your stitch tension as even as possible, establishing a rhythm as you work. If you pull stitches too tightly, the yarn won't cover well; if stitches are too loose, they will not lie flat on the canvas and will look unattractive.

As you stitch, the yarn in your needle will start to twist. To untwist, drop the needle and let the yarn untwist itself. Do this whenever needed.

THE STITCHES
CONTINENTAL STITCH

Most design areas are worked in Continental Stitch. This forms a flat diagonal stitch on the front of the canvas.

To work rows, bring the needle up through the canvas at odd numbers and down at even numbers (**Fig 6**). The rows can be worked from right to left or left to right; notice the difference in numbering, depending on the direction of the work.

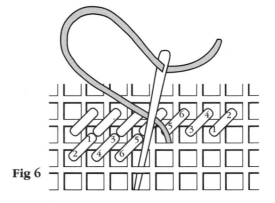

Fig 6

SLANTING GOBELIN

Slanting Gobelin (pronounced like "go") is a long diagonal stitch that can be worked over any number of bars (**Fig 7**). Gobelin Stitches are indicated by long lines showing the exact placement of each stitch with color references in the color key.

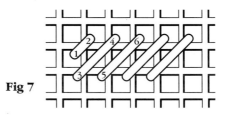

Fig 7

Reverse Slanting Gobelin Stitches slope in the opposite direction (**Fig 8**). Rows can be worked horizontally or vertically; direction will be shown on the chart.

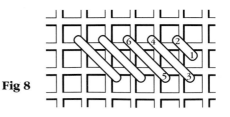

Fig 8

STRAIGHT STITCH

Straight Stitches can be made in any direction and over one or more bars; direction will be noted on the chart. They can be used for details and decorations worked on top of an area of completed stitching. Bring needle up at one end of the stitch and down at the other end (**Fig 9**).

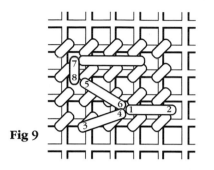
Fig 9

BACKSTITCH

This is a straight stitch used for details and decoration, worked on top of an area of completed stitching (**Fig 10**). It is worked over one bar in any direction. The placement of the Backstitches will be indicated on the chart.

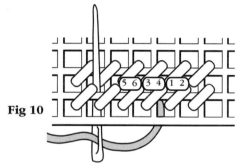
Fig 10

CROSS STITCH

Cross Stitch is used for decorative detail. It is worked over one (**Fig 11**) or more (**Fig 12**) bars; placement will be shown on the chart. Bring needle up at 1, down at 2, up at 3, and down at 4 to complete each stitch.

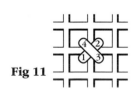
Fig 11

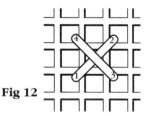
Fig 12

FRENCH KNOT

The French Knot (**Fig 13**) is usually worked after the rest of the piece has been stitched. Bring needle up in center of hole, wrap strand around needle one time, and insert needle back down through same hole.

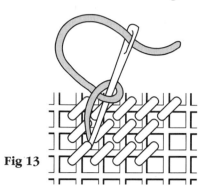
Fig 13

SCOTCH STITCH

This is a square stitch that can be worked in many different sizes. It is shown worked over three bars (**Fig 14**). The exact placement and direction of the stitches is indicated on the chart. Work this stitch in diagonal or horizontal rows.

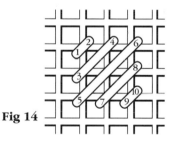
Fig 14

MOSAIC STITCH

This stitch is similar to the Scotch Stitch, but it is worked over just two bars (**Fig 15**).

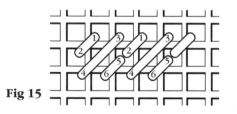
Fig 15

LAZY DAISY

This is a decorative stitch that is worked on top of completed work. The chart will show the exact placement of each stitch (**Fig 16**). Bring needle up at 1, make a loop, and go down into same hole. Bring needle up at 2 inside the loop and pull gently to adjust the size and shape of the loop. Go down at 3 to secure loop. Be sure to anchor end especially well on the wrong side.

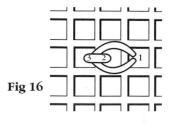

Fig 16

DIAGONAL TURKEY WORK

This stitch is most easily worked from left to right with the canvas held so the stitches will be along the diagonal. Following numbering (**Fig 17**), bring needle down at 1 and up at 2, then back down at 3 and up at 4, slipping needle under yarn; tighten yarn to secure stitch. As you go down again at 5, hold a loop of yarn the size specified in the project instructions. Continue in the diagonal direction, counting space 5 as space 1. Note that loops will lie below the securing stitches. Work second row above first row, starting at left side.

Fig 17

OVERCAST STITCH

This stitch is used in two ways: to finish canvas edges or to join two pieces of canvas. Work from left to right or right to left, whichever is more comfortable.

To finish canvas edges, stitch loosely so strand will cover canvas (**Fig 18**). Take one stitch in each hole along a straight edge or into an inside corner and three stitches when going around an outside corner. If the strand does not cover well, take additional stitches in each hole as needed.

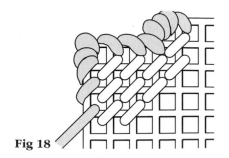

Fig 18

To join two pieces, hold pieces together and line up matching holes. Start joining with a holding stitch through the first hole of the two pieces, then continue joining (**Fig 19**), going through both pieces with each stitch. When ending off strand, tie a knot or weave end in securely.

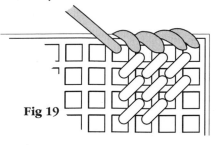

Fig 19

On a curved or angled seam where holes will not match on the two pieces, it will be necessary to take additional stitches to compensate and cover to plastic edge.

LOOP OVERCAST STITCH

This stitch is used to join pieces that have Diagonal Turkey Work. Start joining by working regular Overcast Stitch through first hole. Then form loops by going through each of the following holes two times. First time go through hole and up over index finger and into same hole (**Fig 20**). Second time bring yarn around loop, then on to next hole (**Fig 21**). Repeat these two stitches in each hole where loop is desired.

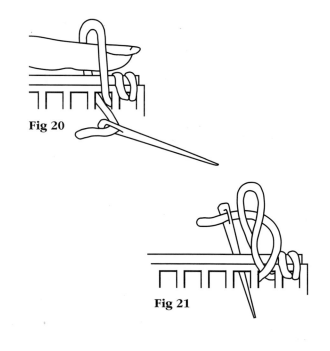

Fig 20

Fig 21

Snowy Santa Tissue Box Cover

designed by Carol Wilson Mansfield

Since each Christmas season also seems to correspond with sniffle season, make this handy tissue box cover and conveniently display it for all of your holiday guests.

MATERIALS

2 sheets 7-mesh plastic canvas
4 white pom-poms, 1/2" diameter
128 clear sunburst beads, 12mm diameter
4 red round or faceted beads, 10mm diameter
monofilament line and sewing needle
tacky craft glue or hot glue
worsted weight yarn:

white	25 yds
pink	4 yds
gold	4 yds
brown	12 yds
red	25 yds
blue	45 yds
green	18 yds

Instructions

Step 1: Cut out four Sides and one Top. Stitch following charts, leaving empty spaces as indicated for beads.

Step 2: Using monofilament line, sew on the snowflake and red beads where indicated on charts. Glue pom-poms to Sides where indicated on chart.

Step 3: Overcast Top opening with blue and bottom edge of each Side with white. Join the four Sides, matching colors of stitches next to edge, and add Top piece as in **Construction Diagram**.

COLOR KEY

white Continental (fill in)
+ = pink Continental
o = gold Continental
☆ = red Continental
★ = blue Continental
⊙ = green Continental
■ = brown Continental
/ = white Slanting Gobelin
❁ = space for snowflake bead
○ = space for red bead
P = pompon placement

Construction Diagram

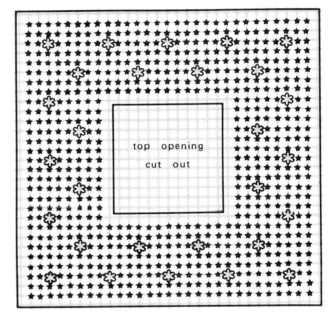

TOP 31 bars wide x 31 high

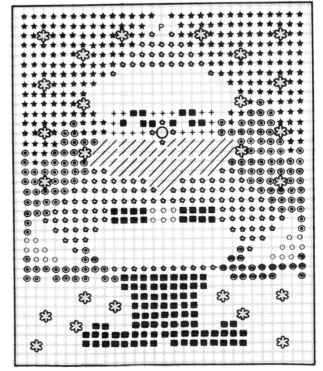

SIDE 31 bars wide x 38 high (make four)

Gingerbread House

designed by Carol Wilson Mansfield

What says Christmas better than gingerbread in the oven? That's why you'll love this Gingerbread House that can be enjoyed year after year—and you'll only have to decorate it with "icing" once. We've used colorful yarns, lace, beads and baubles to simulate candies.

MATERIALS

2 sheets 7-mesh plastic canvas
1 white pom-pom, 1" diameter
3 white starburst sequins
2 white embroidered medallions, about 3/4" diameter
1 1/8 yds lace edging, 1/2" wide
3/4 yd ruffled edging, 1 3/4" wide
Suggested beads:
    4 pink spaghetti beads
    10 pink beads, 10mm diameter
    5 yellow paddle wheel beads, 16mm diameter
    3 amber faceted beads, 8mm diameter
    6 green sunburst beads, 12mm diameter
monofilament line and sewing needle
tacky craft glue or hot glue
worsted weight yarn:

white	60 yds
yellow	8 yds
pink	8 yds
red	12 yds
lavender	4 yds
lt green	12 yds
dk green	3 yds
tan	45 yds
med brown	8 yds
dk brown	32 yds

Instructions

Step 1: Cut out all pieces.

Step 2: Stitch all pieces following charts. Symbols refer to the colors in the color key for this pattern. Work as indicated with Continental and Slanting Gobelin stitches, then add Backstitch details (**Fig 1**).

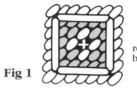

Fig 1

red Backstitches around brown window stitches

Step 3: Glue or sew on beads and embroidered medallions. Symbols on chart show placement; notation at side of pattern is suggested type of decoration.

Step 4: (All overcasting and joining is done with white.) Overcast top edges of four building pieces; overcast sides and lower edges of four roof pieces.

Step 5: Join four building pieces, then add Base, joining with Overcast Stitch on all sides. Join Roofs A and B across top edge, Roofs C and D across top edge. Join four sides of Chimney (three seams), but don't stitch the last seam closed. Overcast top and bottom edges of Chimney assembly and then join the fourth seam.

Step 6: Glue ruffled edging to base of building; glue narrow lace edging to three sides of Roofs A-B and C-D. When thoroughly dry, continue with assembly.

Step 7: Run a narrow line of glue along the top edges of the taller side of building and set Roof A-B in place. Hold with pins until set, then glue on Roof C-D in a similar manner. See **Construction Diagram** for placement.

Step 8: Glue Chimney in place following **Construction Diagram**. Top off with a white pom-pom "marshmallow" glued in place on the chimney top.

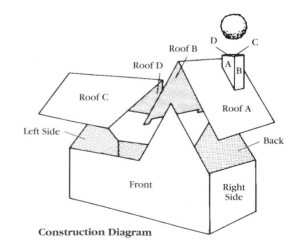

Construction Diagram

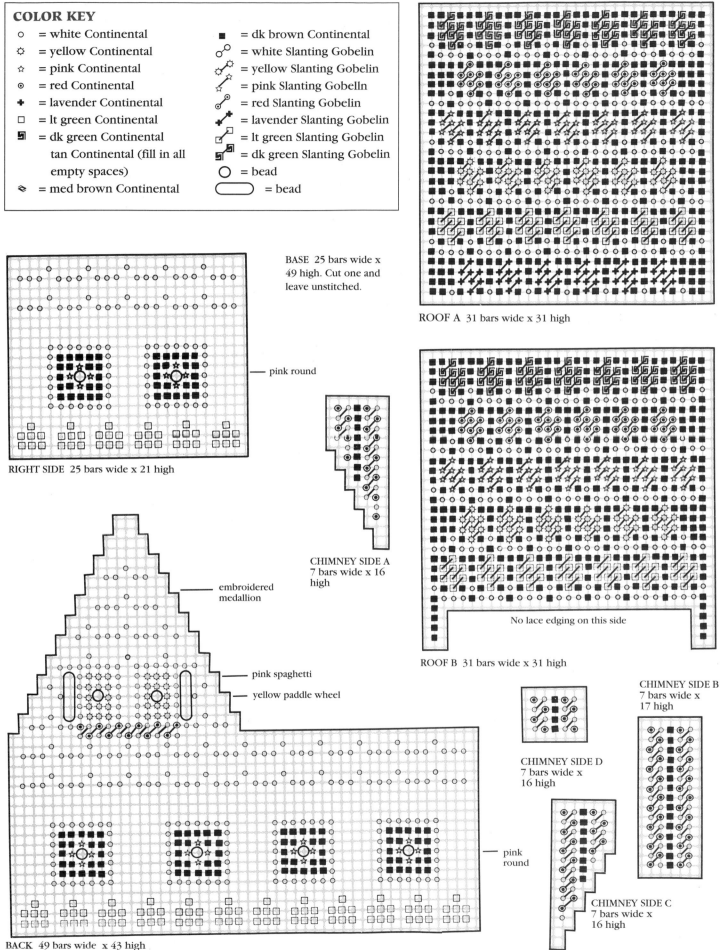

COLOR KEY

- ○ = white Continental
- ✿ = yellow Continental
- ☆ = pink Continental
- ⊙ = red Continental
- ✚ = lavender Continental
- ▢ = lt green Continental
- ⑤ = dk green Continental
- tan Continental (fill in all empty spaces)
- ❖ = med brown Continental
- ■ = dk brown Continental
- ⚲ = white Slanting Gobelin
- ✿⁄ = yellow Slanting Gobelin
- ☆⁄ = pink Slanting Gobeln
- ⊙⁄ = red Slanting Gobelin
- ✚⁄ = lavender Slanting Gobelin
- ▢⁄ = lt green Slanting Gobelin
- ⑤⁄ = dk green Slanting Gobelin
- ○ = bead
- ⬭ = bead

BASE 25 bars wide x 49 high. Cut one and leave unstitched.

ROOF A 31 bars wide x 31 high

RIGHT SIDE 25 bars wide x 21 high

— pink round

CHIMNEY SIDE A 7 bars wide x 16 high

No lace edging on this side

ROOF B 31 bars wide x 31 high

embroidered medallion

pink spaghetti

yellow paddle wheel

CHIMNEY SIDE B 7 bars wide x 17 high

CHIMNEY SIDE D 7 bars wide x 16 high

— pink round

CHIMNEY SIDE C 7 bars wide x 16 high

BACK 49 bars wide x 43 high

99

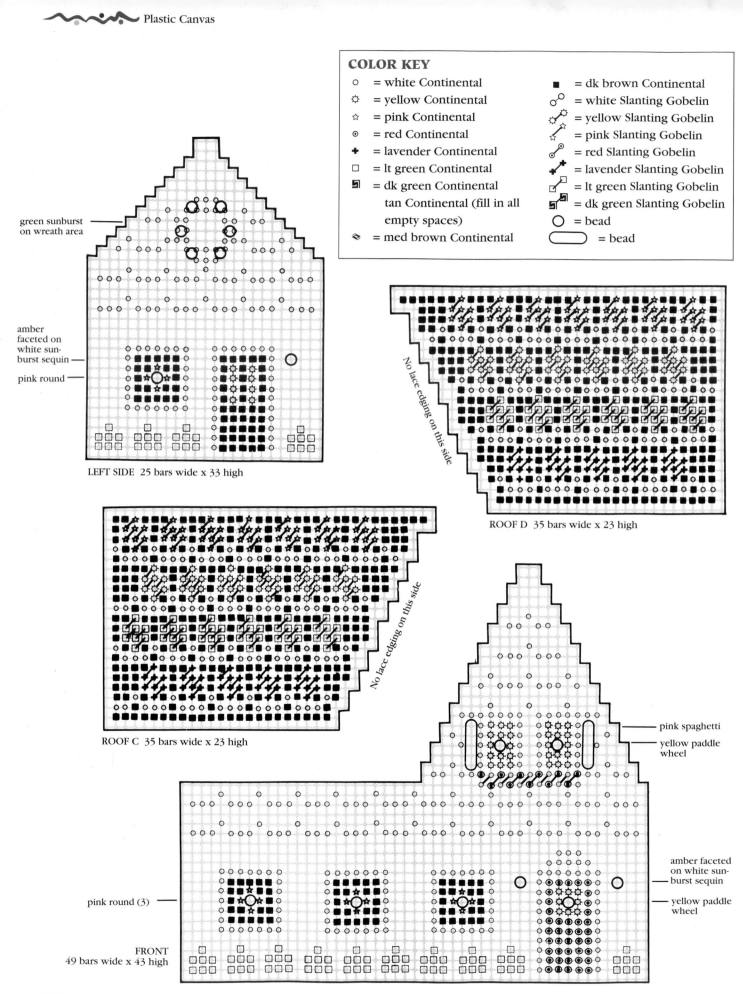

COLOR KEY

○ = white Continental	■ = dk brown Continental
✿ = yellow Continental	⚬ = white Slanting Gobelin
☆ = pink Continental	✿ = yellow Slanting Gobelin
⊙ = red Continental	☆ = pink Slanting Gobelin
✚ = lavender Continental	⚬ = red Slanting Gobelin
□ = lt green Continental	✚ = lavender Slanting Gobelin
⌐ = dk green Continental	□ = lt green Slanting Gobelin
tan Continental (fill in all empty spaces)	⌐ = dk green Slanting Gobelin
❧ = med brown Continental	○ = bead
	⬭ = bead

green sunburst on wreath area

amber faceted on white sunburst sequin

pink round

LEFT SIDE 25 bars wide x 33 high

No lace edging on this side

ROOF D 35 bars wide x 23 high

No lace edging on this side

ROOF C 35 bars wide x 23 high

pink spaghetti
yellow paddle wheel

amber faceted on white sunburst sequin

yellow paddle wheel

pink round (3)

FRONT
49 bars wide x 43 high

Christmas Eve Fireplace Doorstop

designed by Lois Winston

This clever fireplace is just the right size for a Christmas elf. Place a weight inside and use it to prop open a door or use it as a bookend on your shelf.

MATERIALS
2 sheets 7-mesh plastic canvas
black embroidery floss
brick or desired weight (see Note)
tacky craft glue or hot glue
worsted weight yarn:

white	11 yds
off-white	55 yds
red	18 yds
dk red	2 yds
orange	4 yds
yellow	11 yds
gold	6 yds
green	19 yds
tan	10 yds
lt brown	18 yds
med brown	53 yds
dk brown	13 yds
black	10 yds

Note: Wrap an 8" x 4" x 2" brick in plastic wrap. Any heavy material, such as sand, dried beans, or uncooked rice, can be placed in a plastic bag and used instead of a brick.

Instructions

Step 1: Draw outlines and cut out Fireplace, Holly, three Stockings, Cane A, Cane B, two Brick A, two Brick B, and one Brick C.

Step 2: Stitch following charts and excluding black French Knots. Work black floss Backstitches and yellow and red French Knots last, over previous stitching. While stitching presents, overcast gold on dk red present to match gold Continental; overcast white on red present to match white Continental; overcast green and white to match green and white Continental on green and white present.

Step 3: Using green, overcast all edges of Holly and matching edges of tree. Using yellow, overcast star and white edges of candles to create a candlelight halo. Overcast matching edges of dk red present with dk red. Using red, overcast red present, candlesticks, Canes A and B, and red edges of Stockings. Overcast white edges of Stockings with white, tree trunk with med brown, and matching edges of mantle top with tan and lt brown. Attach Stockings to Fireplace with black French Knots where indicated on chart.

Step 4: Use med brown and refer to **Construction Diagram** to join Fireplace to Brick pieces. Join one Brick B to bottom edge of Fireplace; join two Brick A to Brick B and Fireplace side edges, continuing to overcast up side edges of Fireplace. Join Brick C to Brick B and two Brick A. Insert brick or desired weight. Overcast one long edge of other Brick B (which will be glued to wrong side of Fireplace), then join remaining edges to Bricks A and C.

Step 5: Glue overcast edge of Brick B to wrong side of Fireplace. Make small bows of yarn: two yellow, one red, one gold, and one white. Glue yellow bows to Canes, red bow to green and white present, gold bow to dk red present, and white bow to red present. Glue Holly to mantle and Canes to Holly.

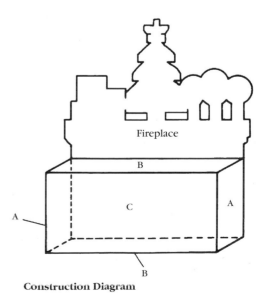

Construction Diagram

COLOR KEY

fill in off-white Continental

▽ = white Continental

⫽ = white Slanting Gobelin

☆ = red Continental

= red French Knot

● = dk red Continental

★ = orange Continental

⌐ = orange Slanting Gobelin

+ = yellow Continental

◇ = yellow Slanting Gobelin

• = yellow French Knot

♡ = gold Continental

○ = green Continental

\ = green Slanting Gobelin

◇ = tan Continental

■ = lt brown Continental

⌐ = lt brown Slanting Gobelin

♥ = med brown Continental

╱ = med brown Slanting Gobelin

□ = dk brown Continental

❮ = dk brown Slanting Gobelin

▲ = black Continental

◆ = black French Knot to attach Stockings

⟋ = black Backstitch (six strands floss)

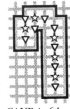

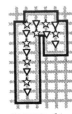

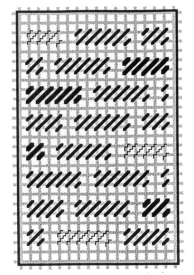

STOCKING 10 bars
wide x 12 high (make 3)

BRICK A 17 bars wide x 27 high
(make 2)

CANE A 6 bars
wide x 10 high

CANE B 6 bars
wide x 10 high

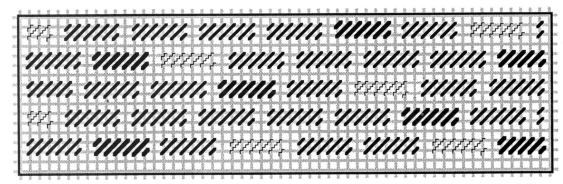

BRICK B 56 bars wide x 17 high (make 2)

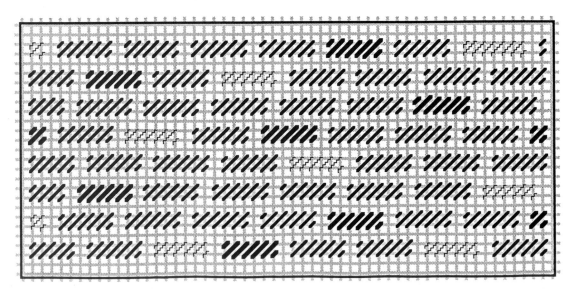

BRICK C 56 bars wide x 27 high

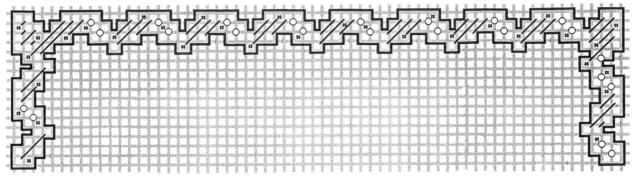

HOLLY 64 bars wide x 17 high

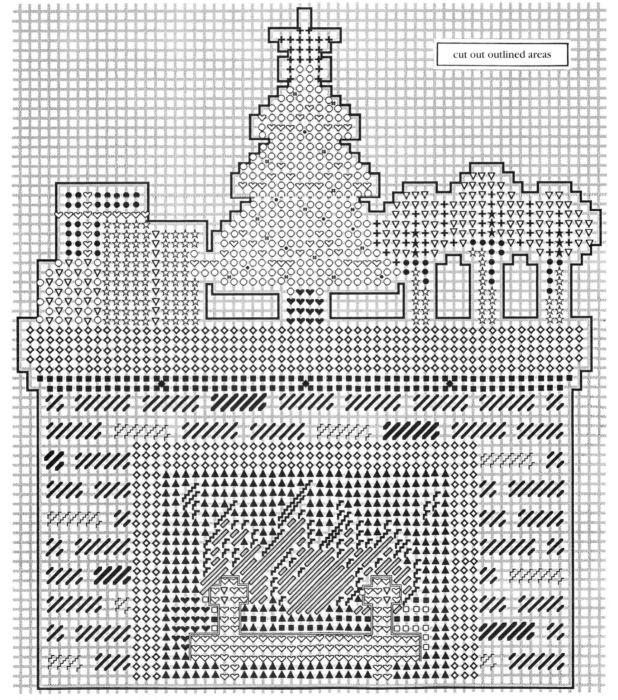

cut out outlined areas

FIREPLACE 61 bars wide x 71 high

103

Santa's Sleigh Doorstop

designed by Jane Cannon Meyers

The Christmas season is full of festive celebrations when we entertain family and friends. This colorful sleigh full of gifts has been cleverly designed for use as a doorstop—but it would be just as nice on a table or shelf.

MATERIALS

6 sheets 7-mesh plastic canvas
7 pre-made package bows in assorted colors, 1 1/2" diameter
brick or desired weight (see Note)
6 gold jingle bells, 15mm
tacky craft glue or hot glue
worsted weight yarn:

white	38 yds
pink	10 yds
burgundy	9 yds
red	6 yds
lt green	10 yds
dk green	177 yds
gold metallic	15 yds
lt blue-green	15 yds
dk blue-green	8 yds
lt blue	19 yds
dk blue	19 yds
black	9 yds

Note: *Wrap an 8" x 4" x 2" brick in plastic wrap. Any heavy material, such as sand, dried beans, or uncooked rice, can be placed in a plastic bag and used instead of a brick.*

Instructions

Step 1: Draw outlines and cut out two Sleighs, Right Side, Left Side, Floor, Base, twelve Present 1, four Present 2 Side, two Present 2 Top/Bottom, six Present 3, four Present 4 Side, two Present 4 Top/Bottom, four Present 5 Side, two Present 5 Top/Bottom, two Present 6 Side A, two Present 6 Side B, and two Present 6 Top/Bottom.

Step 2: Stitch following charts. Stitch one Sleigh using chart; turn other Sleigh piece over so it will be the reverse of first one and fill in with dk green Slanting Gobelin in horizontal rows over two bars. Fill in Floor with dk green Continental. Stitch six Present 1 with dk blue and lt blue Mosaic; then six with dk green and lt green Mosaic (color changes are noted in Color Key). Use two strands gold metallic yarn when stitching Present 3.

Step 3: To assemble Sleigh, refer to **Fig 1**. Overcast long edges of Floor with dk green; join to unstitched bars of Right Side and Left Side with white. Join short edges of unstitched Base to bottom edges of Right Side and Left Side with black. Using dk green, overcast long edges of Right Side, join Left Side to Sleigh front, and

Right Side to Sleigh front along short edge above runner. Join Base to Sleigh front with black. Overcast remaining side and bottom edges of Sleigh front with black. Insert brick or desired weight. Using dk green, overcast short side edge of Sleigh back; join Sleigh back to Left Side and Right Side. Join Base to Sleigh back with black. Overcast remaining side and bottom edges of Sleigh back with dk green. Glue long edges of Floor to Sleigh front and back.

Step 4: Overcast top edges of Sleigh front and back, Right Side, and Left Side with two strands gold metallic yarn. Attach each jingle bell to Sleigh front where indicated on chart with a 10" piece of gold metallic yarn, tie a small bow on inside, and trim ends.

Step 5: To assemble Presents, refer to **Fig 2**.

Present 1: Join edges with white to match white stitching; join all other edges with dark color (dk blue or dk green).

Present 2: Join edges with dk blue-green to match dk blue-green stitching; join all other edges with lt blue-green.

Present 3: Join all edges with white. Use 1 yard gold metallic yarn to tie a package bow. Trim and knot ends.

Present 4: Join edges with white to match white stitching; join all other edges with dk blue.

Present 5: Join edges with burgundy to match burgundy stitching; join all other edges with white.

Present 6: Join all edges with dk green.

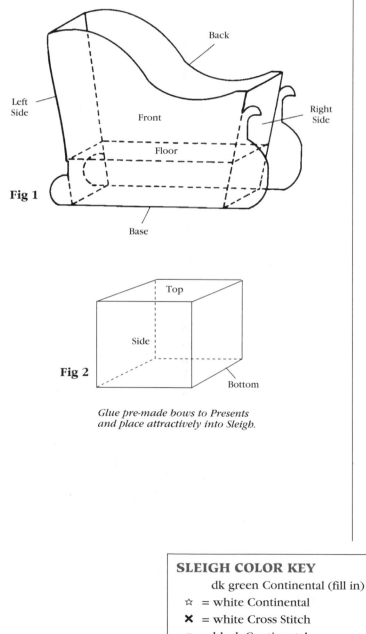

Fig 1

Fig 2

Glue pre-made bows to Presents and place attractively into Sleigh.

SLEIGH COLOR KEY
dk green Continental (fill in)
☆ = white Continental
✖ = white Cross Stitch
■ = black Continental
❀ = bell placement

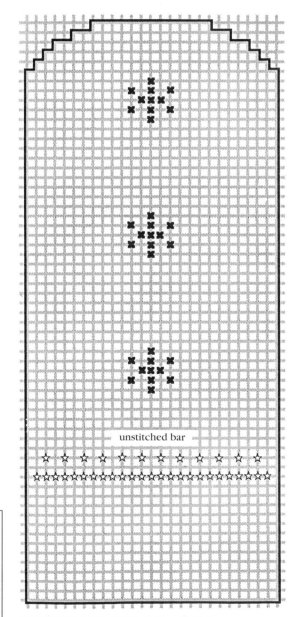

SLEIGH LEFT SIDE 27 bars wide x 61 high

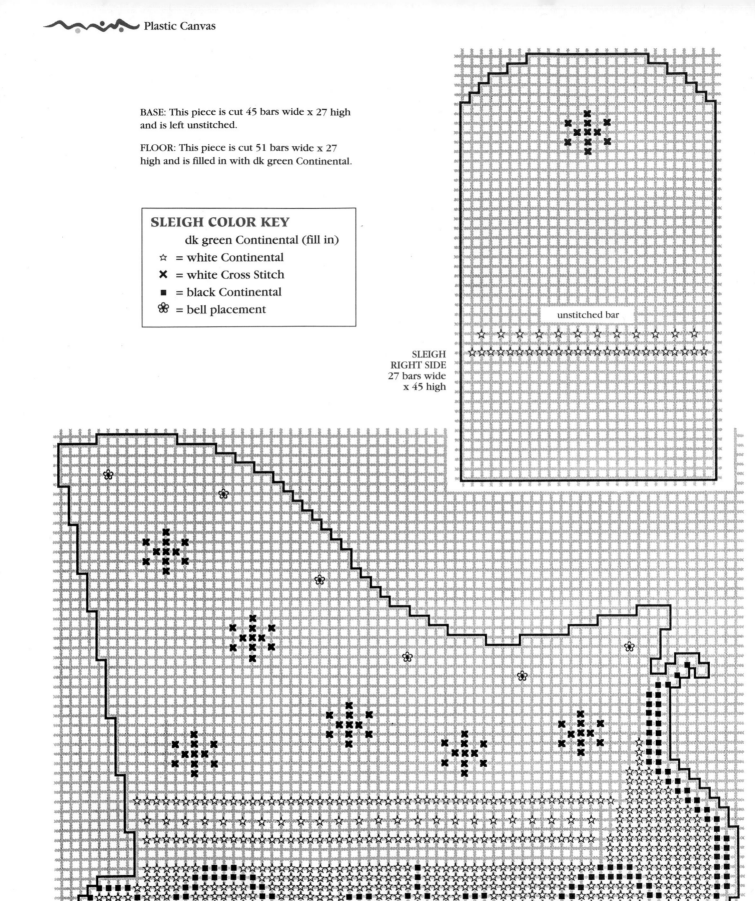

BASE: This piece is cut 45 bars wide x 27 high and is left unstitched.

FLOOR: This piece is cut 51 bars wide x 27 high and is filled in with dk green Continental.

SLEIGH COLOR KEY
dk green Continental (fill in)
☆ = white Continental
✕ = white Cross Stitch
■ = black Continental
✿ = bell placement

unstitched bar

SLEIGH
RIGHT SIDE
27 bars wide
x 45 high

SLEIGH 71 bars wide x 56 high (make 2)

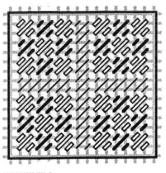

PRESENT 1
16 bars wide x 16 high (make 12)

Note: *Present 1 is stitched in two color combinations and joined for two presents.*

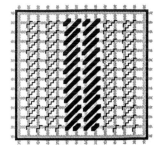

PRESENT 2 SIDE
14 bars wide x 14 high (make 4)

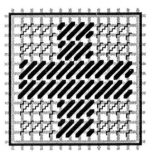

PRESENT 2 TOP/BOTTOM
14 bars wide x 14 high (make 2)

PRESENT COLOR KEY

white Continental (fill in)

\ = white Slanting Gobelin and Mosaic

/// = pink Mosaic

★ = burgundy Continental

♡ = red Continental

● = dk green Continental

⌐ = lt blue-green Slanting Gobelin

◆ = dk blue-green Slanting Gobelin

◇ = lt blue Continental

⬭ = lt color Mosaic (see Step 2)

♥ = dk blue Continental

⟋ = dk color Mosaic (see Step 2)

■ = metallic gold Continental

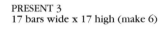

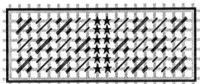

PRESENT 3
17 bars wide x 17 high (make 6)

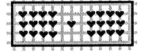

PRESENT 4 SIDE
13 bars wide x 5 high
(make 4)

PRESENT 5 SIDE
20 bars wide x 8 high (make 4)

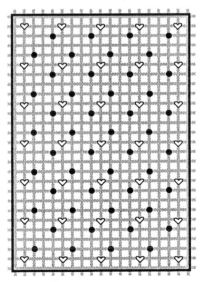

PRESENT 6 SIDE A
19 bars wide x 27 high (make 2)

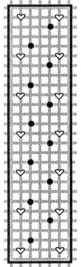

PRESENT 6 SIDE B
7 bars wide x
27 high (make 2)

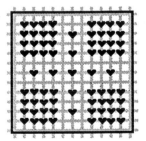

PRESENT 4 TOP/BOTTOM
13 bars wide x 13 high (make 2)

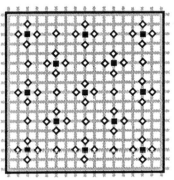

PRESENT 5 TOP/BOTTOM
20 bars wide x 20 high (make 2)

Note: *Present 5 does not show on photo.*

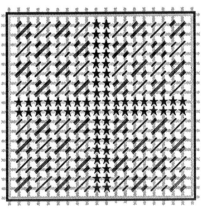

PRESENT 6 TOP/BOTTOM
19 bars wide x 7 high (make 2)

107

Ornament Exchange

designed by Sue Penrod

Everyone loves to decorate the Christmas tree! These three-dimensional ornaments use just one or two small pieces of plastic canvas, some yarn and a few trims. Use them for a special package tie-on, for the gift bazaar, for ornament exchanges or simply hang them on your own tree to enjoy.

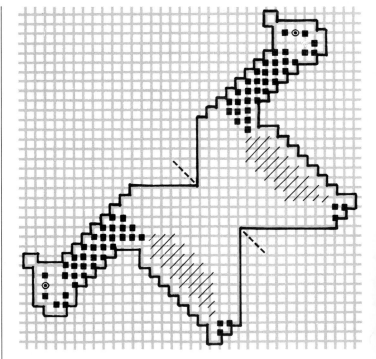

Canada Goose

MATERIALS
1/4 sheet 7-mesh plastic
   canvas
6" red satin ribbon,
   1/8" wide
2 plastic holly leaves,
   3/4" long
2 small red hollyberries
2 black beads, 3mm
   diameter
tacky craft glue or
   hot glue
worsted weight yarn:
   white   5 yds
   grey   3 yds
   black   4 yds

Instructions

Step 1: Draw outline and cut out Canada Goose.

Step 2: Stitch following chart.

Step 3: Bend piece in half, wrong sides together (let it remain rounded). Starting at bottom of Goose, join the edges loosely, using yarn color to match the previous stitching.

Step 4: Glue beads in place in spaces indicated on chart. Tie ribbon around Goose's neck; make a bow and glue in place (see photo). Glue berries and leaves at side of bow.

CANADA GOOSE 35 bars wide x 35 high

COLOR KEY
       white Continental (fill in)
/ = grey Slanting Gobelin
■ = black Continental
⊙ = bead placement

Candy Cane

MATERIALS

1/4 sheet 7-mesh plastic canvas
1/4 yd green satin ribbon, 1/4" wide
worsted weight yarn:
   white   4 yds
   red   3 yds

Instructions

Step 1: Draw outline and cut out Candy Cane.

Step 2: Stitch following chart.

Step 3: Bend piece in half gently, wrong sides together (let it remain rounded). Join all edges loosely with white.

Step 4: Place ribbon around Candy Cane and tie bow as shown in photo.

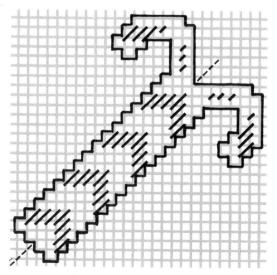

CANDY CANE 26 bars wide x 26 high

COLOR KEY
      white Slanting Gobelin (fill in)
 / = red Slanting Gobelin

Berry and Bell Wreaths

MATERIALS

1/4 sheet 7-mesh plastic canvas
30 red pearl beads, 4mm diameter
2 gold bells, 1/2"
12" red satin ribbon, 1/8" wide
12" red rattail cord
tacky craft glue or hot glue
12 yds green worsted weight yarn

Instructions

Step 1: Draw outline and cut out two Wreaths.

Step 2: Overcast outer and inner edges with green.

Step 3: Fill in Wreaths with green Diagonal Turkey Work, working in direction of lines on chart. Make each loop about 1/2" long.

Step 4: For Berry Wreath, glue pearls in place in clusters of three, referring to photo for placement. Tie ribbon into a bow, trim ends, and glue to Wreath. For Bell Wreath, glue top of each bell into ends of cord. Tie cord into a bow and glue to Wreath.

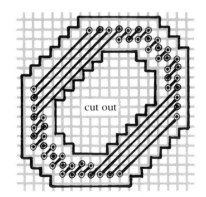

WREATH 18 bars wide x 18 high

COLOR KEY
⊙–⊙ = green Diagonal Turkey Work

Cat

MATERIALS
1/4 sheet 7-mesh
   plastic canvas
3 black beads,
   3mm diameter
1/3 yd green satin
   ribbon, 1/4" wide
17 yds variegated
   yellow worsted
   weight yarn
tacky craft glue
   or hot glue

Instructions

Step 1: Draw outline and cut out Cat.

Step 2: Stitch following chart. Work Continental first, then Diagonal Turkey Work. For whiskers, use two strands of yarn and insert needle at one > and bring it out at second < . Trim whiskers to l/2" long.

Step 3: Overcast marked edges at bottom and legs of Cat. Bend piece in half gently, wrong sides together. Join sides and head of Cat, leaving overcast edges free.

Step 4: Glue beads where indicated on chart for eyes and nose. Place ribbon around neck and tie bow at front; trim ends.

Country Girl

MATERIALS
1/4 sheet 7-mesh plastic
   canvas
6" white satin ribbon,
   1/8" wide
6" green satin ribbon,
   1/8" wide
1 white ribbon rose,
   1/2" diameter
3/8 yd white lace trim,
   3/8" wide
tiny red berries and flowers
tacky craft glue or hot glue
worsted weight yarn:
   white   6 yds
   pink   1 yd
   green   7 yds
   black   1 yd

Instructions

Step 1: Draw outline and cut out Country Girl.

Step 2: Stitch following chart.

Step 3: Overcast edges indicated on chart using pink for hands, green for skirt, white for legs, and black for feet.

Step 4: Fold piece in half, with wrong sides together. Join, starting at back of head and ending at front of skirt hem, using yarn to match previous stitching and leaving hands free.

Step 5: Glue a piece of lace trim around hat; glue a piece of lace trim around each pantaloon leg.

Step 6: Arrange bouquet of red flowers and berries around rose and insert between hands; glue to hold in place. Tie green and white ribbons into bows. Glue green bow in front of bouquet. Glue white bow at back of hat.

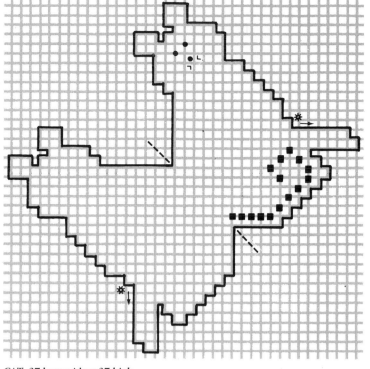

CAT 37 bars wide x 37 high

COLOR KEY
variegated yellow Continental (fill in)
■ = variegated yellow Diagonal Turkey Work
● = bead placement
〉〈 = whisker placement
❋ = overcast

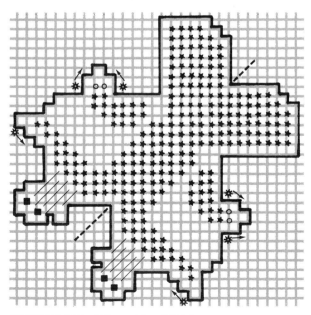

COUNTRY GIRL 30 bars wide x 30 high

COLOR KEY
white Continental (fill in)
╱ = white Slanting Gobelin
○ = pink Continental
★ = green Continental
■ = black Continental
❋ = overcast

Hearts-and-Lace Ball

MATERIALS
1/4 sheet 7-mesh plastic canvas
1 yd gathered lace trim, 1/2" wide
1/3 yd red picot-edge ribbon, 1/4" wide
2" length wire
20 gold beads, 4mm diameter
tacky craft glue or hot glue
worsted weight yarn:
   red   7 yds
   green 7 yds

Instructions

Step 1: Draw outline and cut out Ball.

Step 2: Stitch following chart.

Step 3: Overcast all edges using yarn color to match previous stitching.

Step 4: Glue lace along inside edges so that about 1/4" will show on outside of Ball (see photo).

Step 5: Bring the four ends together forming a ball, and join at bottom point with green.

Step 6: Make a bow with three loops on each side; twist wire around center to hold. Glue bow to top of Ball. Glue beads where indicated on chart.

Rocking Horse

MATERIALS
1/4 sheet 7-mesh plastic canvas
2 black beads, 3mm diameter
1/3 yd red satin ribbon, 1/8" wide
tacky craft glue or hot glue
worsted weight yarn:
   cream 4 yds
   green 7 yds
   rust   10 yds

Instructions

Step 1: Draw outline and cut out Horse.

Step 2: Stitch following chart.

Step 3: Overcast all edges using yarn to match previous stitching.

Step 4: Bend piece in half, wrong sides together (let it remain rounded). Join edges together between the marks indicated on chart using rust yarn, changing to green yarn for saddle. Do not join ears, legs, or rockers together.

Step 5: For tail, make four Loop Overcast stitches 1 1/4" long where indicated on chart. For mane, knot end of yarn and bring needle up from inside of ornament just in front of ears. Make an overcast stitch in front of ears; make seven loose overcast stitches for mane at spaces indicated.

Step 6: With a 6" piece of ribbon, tie a bow around tail loops. Thread remaining ribbon through needle and insert at mouth for bit; tie at mouth, bring to front of saddle and tie in a bow. Glue bow at front of saddle; glue beads in place for eyes.

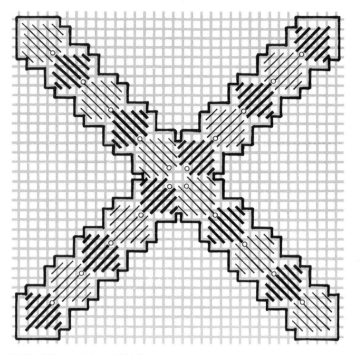

BALL 34 bars wide x 34 high

COLOR KEY
- ⁄ = red Slanting Gobelin
- ❘ = green Slanting Gobelin
- ○ = bead placement

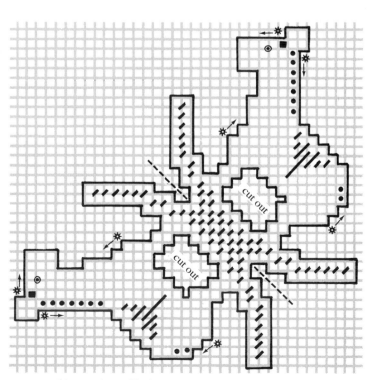

HORSE 36 bars wide x 36 high

COLOR KEY

rust Continental (fill in)
- ❘ = green Continental and Slanting Gobelin
- • = cream mane and tail
- ⊙ = bead placement

Red Basket

MATERIALS
1/4 sheet 7-mesh plastic
 canvas
6" green satin ribbon,
 1/4" wide
5" white lace trim,
 3/8" wide
small teddy bear, 2" high
3 small sprigs greenery
tacky craft glue or
 hot glue
6 yds red worsted
 weight yarn

Instructions

Step 1: Draw outline and cut out Basket.

Step 2: Stitch following chart.

Step 3: Overcast top edges and inside and outside edges of handle.

Step 4: Bend Basket in half, wrong sides together (let it remain rounded). Join right and left sides.

Step 5: Glue lace to inner edge of Basket so that about 1/4" shows above the edge. Arrange bear and greenery inside basket and glue in place. Tie ribbon into bow and glue at center front.

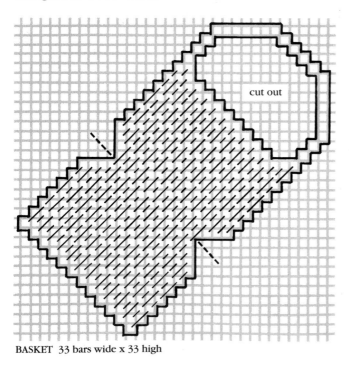

cut out

BASKET 33 bars wide x 33 high

COLOR KEY
 / = red Mosaic

Lacy Heart

MATERIALS
scrap 7-mesh plastic canvas
1/3 yd white lace trim, 5/8" wide
8" green satin ribbon, 1/4" wide
3 flowers with leaves, 5/8" wide
tacky craft glue or hot glue
14 yds white or red worsted weight yarn

Instructions

Step 1: Draw outlines and cut out two Hearts.

Step 2: Stitch following chart, using white or red.

Step 3: Place Hearts with wrong sides together and lace trim between them. Holding all three layers together, join outer edges of Hearts with red, stitching through the lace trim at the same time.

Step 4: Tie ribbon into bow. Arrange flowers, leaves and ribbon at center top of Heart and glue in place.

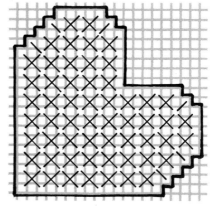

HEART 20 bars wide x 20 high

COLOR KEY
 X = white or red Cross Stitch

114

Square Basket

MATERIALS

1/2 sheet 7-mesh plastic canvas
1/4 yd ivory lace trim, 3/8" wide
1/3 yd ivory picot-edge ribbon, 1/4" wide
4 white ribbon roses, 5/8" diameter
artificial holly
tacky craft glue or hot glue
14 yds blue-green worsted weight yarn

Instructions

Step 1: Draw outline and cut out Basket.

Step 2: Stitch following chart. Stitch handle with Handle Pattern Stitch, working with Basket toward you and end of handle away from you.

Step 3: Starting at bottom corners, join four sides of Basket. Overcast top edges of Basket and edges of handle; join handle end to opposite side of Basket, as in photo.

Step 4: Glue lace trim along top edge of Basket, overlapping ends below handle at one side. Cut ribbon in half and make two bows. Glue a bow at base of handle on each side of Basket.

Step 5: Arrange roses and holly in Basket; glue in place.

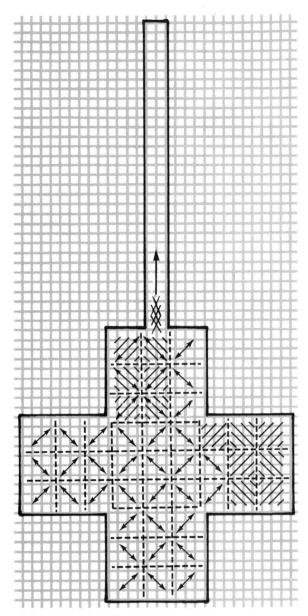

BASKET 29 bars wide x 61 high

COLOR KEY

/ = blue-green Scotch Stitch
   and Handle Pattern Stitch

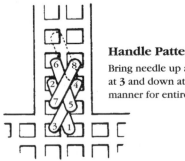

Handle Pattern Stitch

Bring needle up at **1**, down at **2**, up at **3** and down at **4**. Continue in this manner for entire length of handle.

Stocking

MATERIALS
1/4 sheet 7-mesh
  plastic canvas
5" white lace trim,
  3/8" wide
red flowers and
  greenery
tacky craft glue or
  hot glue
worsted weight yarn:
  white 5 yds
  red   10 yds

Instructions

Step 1: Draw outline and cut out Stocking.

Step 2: Stitch following chart.

Step 3: Overcast top cuff edge with white; then bend Stocking gently in half with wrong sides together. Continuing with white, join cuff edges together along side of Stocking. Continue joining edges using yarn color to match previous stitching.

Step 4: Referring to photo, glue lace trim along lower edge of white cuff. Arrange flowers and greenery in top of Stocking and glue in place.

Teddy Bear

MATERIALS
1/4 sheet 7-mesh plastic canvas
2 black beads, 6mm diameter
beige pom-pom, 5/8" diameter
black pom-pom, 5mm diameter
8" plaid (red/green/gold) ribbon, 3/8" wide
2 tiny red berries
tacky craft glue or hot glue
15 yds brown worsted weight yarn

Instructions

Step 1: Draw outline and cut out Bear.

Step 2: Stitch face and legs following chart. Turn piece over and stitch back and belly on the other side with brown Continental.

Step 3: Overcast all edges with brown.

Step 4: Bend belly up on top of back, wrong sides together. Starting at one leg, sew all around edges of Belly, attaching to legs and neck and overcasting Back.

Step 5: Referring to photo, glue small black pom-pom to larger beige pom-pom for muzzle and nose; then glue to Bear where indicated on chart. Glue beads where indicated on chart. Place ribbon around bear's neck and tie a bow. Glue a berry at each side of bow's knot.

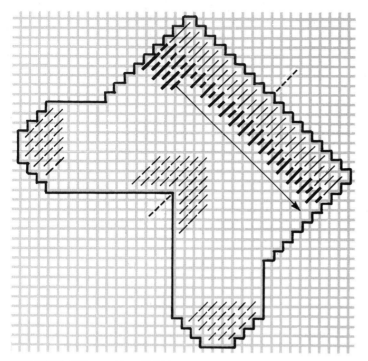

COLOR KEY

/ = red Mosaic (fill in entire stocking)

/ = white Continental and Mosaic

STOCKING 35 bars wide x 35 high

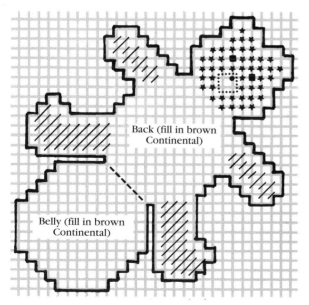

Back (fill in brown Continental)

Belly (fill in brown Continental)

COLOR KEY

★ = brown Continental

/ = brown Slanting Gobelin

■ = bead placement

⋯ = pom-pom placement

BEAR 29 bars wide x 29 high

Tiny Cottage

MATERIALS

1/4 sheet 7-mesh plastic canvas
7" white lace trim, 3/8" wide
tacky craft glue or hot glue
worsted weight yarn:
   white   10 yds
   red   6 yds
   green   2 yds

Instructions

Step 1: Draw outlines and cut out Front and Back.

Step 2: Stitch following chart. Work Straight Stitches last, over previous stitching.

Step 3: Overcast lower edge of each piece with white.

Step 4: Hold pieces with wrong sides together. Using white and red to match previous stitching, join side and roof edges, overcasting the chimney at the same time the roof is joined.

Step 5: Glue lace trim around lower edges.

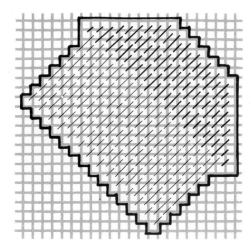

BACK 23 bars wide x 23 high

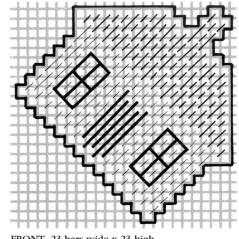

FRONT 23 bars wide x 23 high

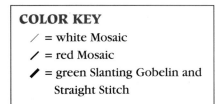

COLOR KEY

/ = white Mosaic

/ = red Mosaic

/ = green Slanting Gobelin and
     Straight Stitch

White Basket

MATERIALS

1/2 sheet 7-mesh plastic canvas
1/3 yd plaid (red/green/gold) ribbon, 3/8" wide
2 Christmas balls, 1/2" diameter
3 pine cones, 7/8" long
artificial holly leaves and berries
tacky craft glue or hot glue
8 yds white worsted weight yarn

Instructions

Step 1: Draw outline and cut out Basket.

Step 2: Stitch following chart.

Step 3: Overcast handle and long straight edges of Basket with white.

Step 4: Join the four corners with white, starting at the base of the Basket; join handle end to opposite side.

Step 5: Arrange pine cones, holly, and Christmas balls in Basket and glue in place.

Step 6: Make a bow with two loops on each side; glue at base of handle.

BASKET 24 bars wide x 52 high

COLOR KEY
X = white Cross Stitch

119

White Goose

MATERIALS

1/4 sheet 7-mesh plastic canvas
8" red satin ribbon, 1/8" wide
2 black beads, 3mm diameter
tacky craft glue or hot glue
worsted weight yarn:
  white   10 yds
  gold   1 yd
  green   2 yds

Instructions

Step 1: Draw outlines and cut out Goose and Wreath.

Step 2: Stitch following charts.

Step 3: Bend Goose in half with wrong sides together (let it remain rounded). Join beak with gold from * to *. Join all other edges with white. Overcast outer and inner edges of Wreath with green.

Step 4: Glue beads to Goose for eyes, as indicated on chart. Thread ribbon through large-eyed needle; take a stitch through one short end of Wreath, bringing ends of ribbon to right side. Tie ribbon into bow; trim ends. Place Wreath around Goose's neck.

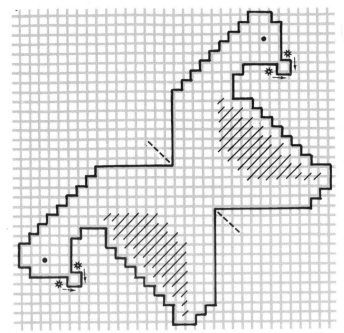

GOOSE 33 bars wide x 33 high

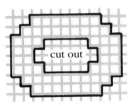

WREATH 12 bars wide x 9 high

COLOR KEY

      green Continental (fill in Wreath)
      white Continental (fill in Goose)
╱ = white Slanting Gobelin
● = bead placement

Woolly Lamb

MATERIALS

1/4 sheet 7-mesh plastic canvas
2 black beads, 3mm diameter
8" blue satin ribbon, 1/4" wide
gold bell, 5/8" high
black pom-pom, 5mm diameter
tacky craft glue or hot glue
worsted weight yarn:
    white or grey   20 yds
    black   5 yds

Instructions

Step 1: Draw outline and cut out Lamb.

Step 2: Stitch face and legs following chart. Make two Loop Overcasting stitches for ears where indicated on chart; make each ear loop about 5/8" long. Make "wool" with rows of Diagonal Turkey Work, making each loop about 1/2" long.

Step 3: Overcast the four legs with black. Bend Lamb in half with wrong sides together; join head with black overcasting. Join woolly areas with either regular overcasting or Loop Overcasting, using yarn to match "wool."

Step 4: Glue beads in place for eyes where indicated on chart. Glue pom-pom in place for nose.

Step 5: Thread ribbon through hole in top of bell and tie a bow. Glue bow and bell in place below chin.

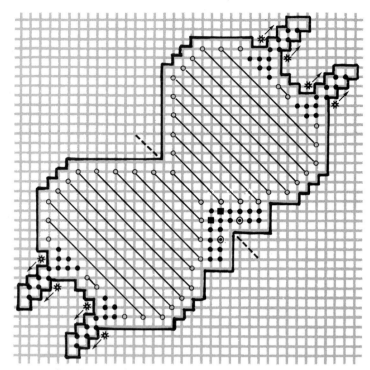

LAMB 36 bars wide x 36 high

COLOR KEY

○–○ = white or grey Diagonal Turkey Work
● = black Continental
■ = black Loop Overcast
⊙ = bead placement
✳ = overcast

Candy Cane Holders

designed by Nancy Dorman

Since Santa and Mrs. Claus love sweets and obviously find joy in giving, they are perfectly at home serving candy canes to each holiday visitor.

MATERIALS

Santa
2 sheets 7-mesh plastic canvas
grey embroidery floss
1 yd gold metallic yarn
tacky craft glue or hot glue
worsted weight yarn:

white	25 yds
med red	30 yds
dk red	2 yds
pink	2 yds
peach	3 yds
green	63 yds
grey	2 yds
black	5 yds

Mrs. Claus
2 sheets 7-mesh plastic canvas
embroidery floss:
  med red
  green
  black
3 yds gold metallic yarn
tacky craft glue or hot glue
worsted weight yarn:

white	30 yds
med red	20 yds
dk red	1 yd
pink	1 yd
peach	4 yds
green	63 yds
black	2 yds

Snowman
2 sheets 7-mesh plastic canvas
tacky craft glue or hot glue
worsted weight yarn:

white	40 yds
red	5 yds
orange	1 yd
green	65 yds
tan	3 yds
brown	4 yds
grey	3 yds
black	5 yds

Instructions

Step 1: For each Candy Cane Holder, draw outlines and cut out two Front/Back, two Sides, one Bottom, and appropriate figure. If you are making Mrs. Claus, draw outline and cut out Gift; for Snowman, draw outline and cut out Broom.

Step 2: Stitch following charts.

Santa: Work Straight Stitches, Backstitches, and French Knot last, over previous stitching. Overcast Santa using white, med red, and black to match previous stitching.

Mrs. Claus: Work Backstitches, Lazy Daisies, and French Knots last, over previous stitching. Overcast Mrs. Claus using white, peach, med red, and black to match previous stitching. Overcast Gift using green and gold metallic to match previous stitching. Tie a 12" length of six strands med red floss around hair and trim ends. Tie a 9" length of six strands green floss in a bow, glue to collar, and trim ends. Tie a 12" length gold metallic in a bow, glue to Gift, and trim ends. Glue Gift to Mrs. Claus between hands.

Snowman: Work Straight Stitches and French Knots last, over previous stitching. Do not work green Straight Stitches on Broom at this time. Overcast Snowman using white, red, green, and black to match previous stitching. Overcast Broom using brown for handle and tan for bristles. Work green Straight Stitches on Broom. Glue Broom to Snowman between hands.

Step 3: Use green to assemble Holder. Join bottom edges of Front, Back, and Sides to Bottom; then join side edges. Overcast top edges of Front, Back, and Sides.

Step 4: Keeping bottom edges even, glue figure to Front. Fill Holder with candy canes or your favorite holiday goodies.

SIDE   17 bars wide x 32 high (make 2)

COLOR KEY

╱ = green Scotch Stitch

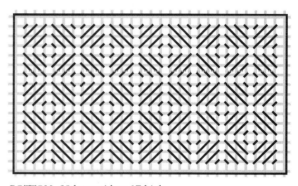

BOTTOM   29 bars wide x 17 high

FRONT/BACK   29 bars wide x 32 high (make 2)

123

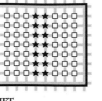

GIFT
10 bars wide x 9 high

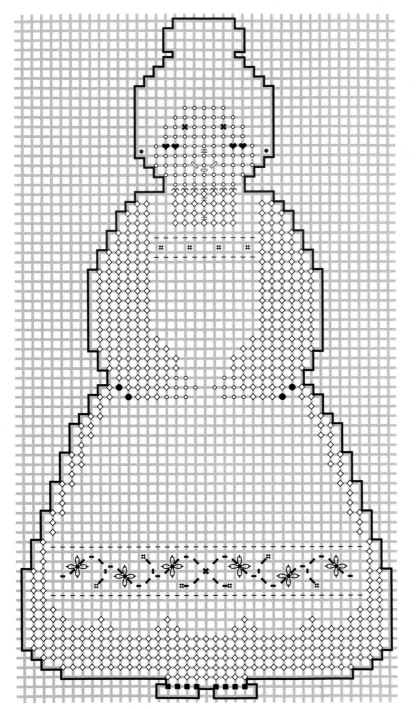

MRS. CLAUS   39 bars x 71 high

COLOR KEY (for Mrs. Claus and Gift)
   white Continental (fill in)
⎁ = white Backstitch
◇ = med red Continental
╱ = med red Backstitch
   (six strands floss)
𝒪 = med red Lazy Daisy
   (six strands floss)
♯ = med red French Knot
   (six strands floss)
● = dk red Continental
♥ = pink Continental
⌀ = pink Backstitch
○ = peach Continental
□ = green Continental
╱ = green Backstitch
   (six strands floss)
■ = black Continental
✕ = black Cross Stitch
⫽ = black Backstitch
   (six strands floss)
★ = gold metallic Continental
⫽ = gold metallic Backstitch
• = gold metallic French Knot

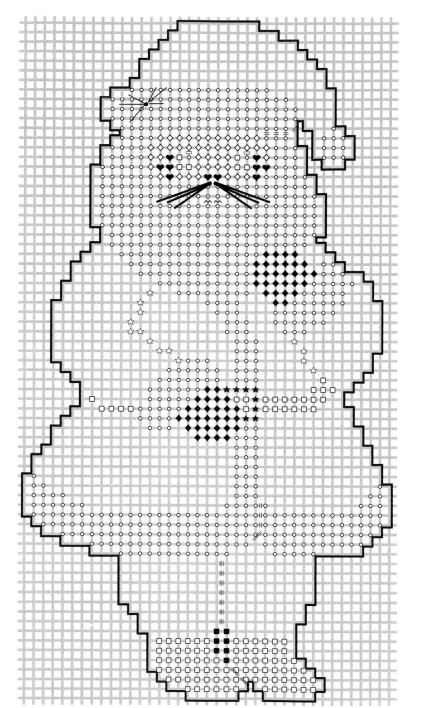

SANTA   39 bars wide x 71 high

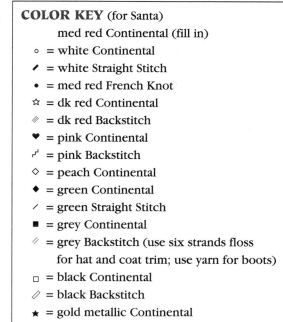

COLOR KEY (for Santa)
      med red Continental (fill in)
  ○ = white Continental
  ✎ = white Straight Stitch
  • = med red French Knot
  ☆ = dk red Continental
  ⫽ = dk red Backstitch
  ♥ = pink Continental
  ⌐ = pink Backstitch
  ◇ = peach Continental
  ◆ = green Continental
  ╱ = green Straight Stitch
  ■ = grey Continental
  ⫽ = grey Backstitch (use six strands floss
      for hat and coat trim; use yarn for boots)
  □ = black Continental
  ⧸ = black Backstitch
  ★ = gold metallic Continental

Crochet

Crochet is a greatly enjoyed needlework pastime that is easier to master than knitting. You can even teach yourself to crochet following the illustrations in this book.

Beginners will want to first try the stitches using yarn and then progress to crochet cotton which requires a little more practice to master. Yarn projects, such as the Hiking Boot Stocking and Baby's First Christmas Afghan, are fun to make, and you will be rewarded with results in a hurry.

With bedspread-weight crochet cotton and a steel crochet hook, you can create beautiful lacy snowflakes, angels and other decorations with the charm of past eras. These wonderful lacy creations are often stiffened to give them a lasting shape so they can stand on their own or hang from the tree.

Our step-by-step instructions will show you how.

Crochet How-To

CHAIN (ch)

Crochet always starts with a basic chain stitch. To begin, make a slip knot on hook (**Fig 1**), leaving a 4" end of yarn.

Step 1: Take hook in right hand, holding it between thumb and third finger (**Fig 2**), and rest index finger near tip of loop.

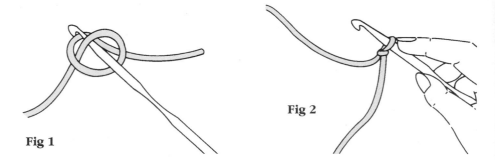

Fig 1

Fig 2

Step 2: Take slip knot in thumb and index finger of left hand and bring yarn over third finger of left hand (**Fig 3a**), catching it loosely at left palm with remaining two fingers (**Fig 3b**).

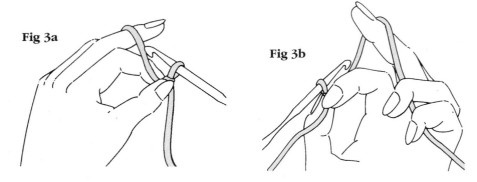

Fig 3a

Fig 3b

Step 3: Bring yarn over hook from back to front (**Fig 4**) and draw through loop on hook: one chain stitch made. Repeat Step 3 for each additional chain desired, moving your left thumb and index finger up close to the hook after each stitch or two (**Fig 5**).

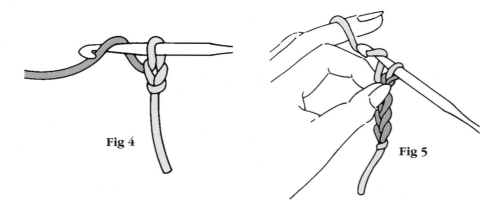

Fig 4

Fig 5

When counting number of chains, do not count the loop on the hook or the starting slip knot.

SINGLE CROCHET (sc)

First, make a chain to desired length.

Step 1: Insert hook in top loop of 2nd chain from hook; hook yarn (bring yarn over hook from back to front) (**Fig 6**). Draw through; you now have 2 loops on hook (**Fig 7**).

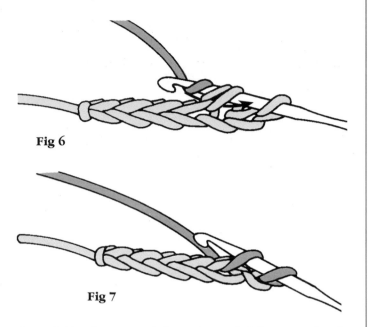

Fig 6

Fig 7

Step 2: Hook yarn and draw through 2 loops on hook (**Fig 8**): one single crochet made. Work a single crochet (repeat Steps 1 and 2) in each remaining chain.

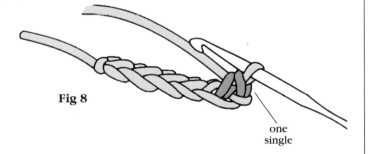

Fig 8

one single

To work additional rows, chain 1 and turn work counterclockwise. Inserting hook under 2 loops of the first stitch below (**Fig 9**), work a single crochet (as before) in each stitch across.

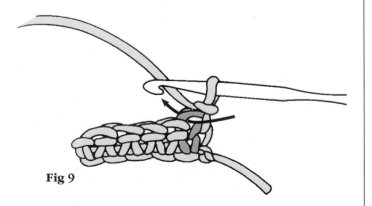

Fig 9

DOUBLE CROCHET (dc)

Double crochet is a taller stitch than single crochet. Begin by making a chain to desired length.

Step 1: Bring yarn once over the hook; insert hook in the top loop of the 4th chain from hook (**Fig 10**). Hook yarn and draw through (**Fig 11**).

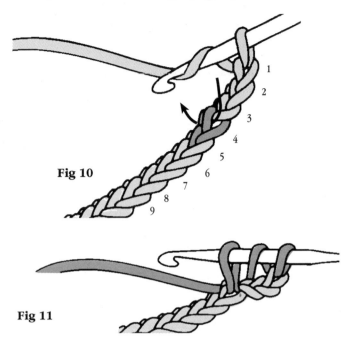

Fig 10

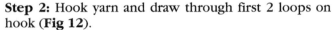

Fig 11

Step 2: Hook yarn and draw through first 2 loops on hook (**Fig 12**).

Fig 12

Step 3: Hook yarn and draw through last 2 loops on hook (**Fig 13**): one double crochet made. Work a double crochet (repeat Steps 1 through 3) in each remaining chain.

Fig 13

129

To work each additional row, make a 3 chain and turn work counterclockwise. Beginning in 2nd stitch (**Fig 14**) (3 chain counts as first double crochet), work a double crochet (as before) in each stitch across (remember to insert hook under 2 top loops of stitch). At end of row, work last double crochet in the top chain of beginning chain-3 (**Fig 15**).

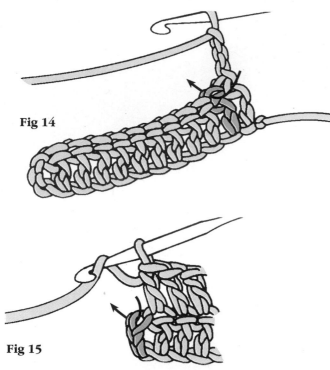

Fig 14

Fig 15

HALF DOUBLE CROCHET (hdc)

This stitch eliminates one step of double crochet—hence its name. It is taller than single crochet, but shorter than double crochet. Begin by making a chain to desired length.

Step 1: Bring yarn over hook; insert hook in top loop of 3rd chain stitch from hook, hook yarn and draw through. There are 3 loops now on hook (**Fig 16**).

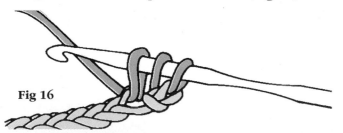

Fig 16

Step 2: Hook yarn and draw through all 3 loops on hook (**Fig 17**): one half double crochet made. Work a half double crochet (repeat Steps 1 and 2) in each remaining chain.

Fig 17

To work each additional row, make a 2 chain and turn work counterclockwise. Beginning in 2nd stitch (2 chain counts as first half double crochet), work a half double crochet (as before) in each stitch across. At end of row, work last half double crochet in the top chain stitch of the beginning chain-2.

TRIPLE CROCHET (trc)

Triple crochet is a tall stitch that works up quickly. First make a chain to desired length.

Step 1: Bring yarn twice over the hook, insert hook in 5th chain from hook (**Fig 18**); hook yarn and draw through. There are now 4 loops on the hook (**Fig 19**).

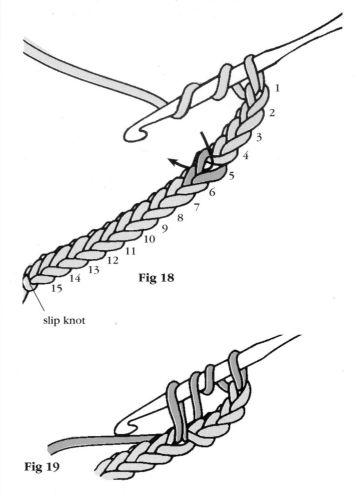

1
2
3
4
5
6
7
8
9
10
11
12
13
14
15

Fig 18

slip knot

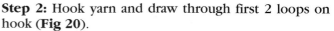

Fig 19

Step 2: Hook yarn and draw through first 2 loops on hook (**Fig 20**).

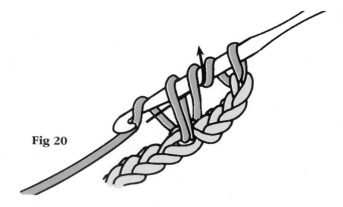

Fig 20

Step 3: Hook yarn and draw through next 2 loops on hook (**Fig 21**).

Fig 21

Step 4: Hook yarn and draw through remaining 2 loops on hook (**Fig 22**): one triple crochet made. Work a triple crochet (repeat Steps 1 through 4) in each remaining chain.

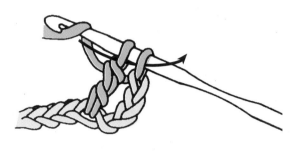

Fig 22

To work each additional row, make a 4 chain and turn work counterclockwise. Beginning in 2nd stitch (4 chain counts as first triple crochet), work a triple crochet (as before) in each stitch across. At end of row, work last triple crochet in top chain stitch of beginning chain-4.

SLIP STITCH (sl st)

This is the shortest crochet stitch and usually is used to join work or to move yarn across a group of stitches without adding height. To practice, make a chain to desired length; then work one row of double crochet.

Step 1: Insert hook in first stitch; hook yarn and draw through both stitch and loop on hook in one motion (**Fig 23**).

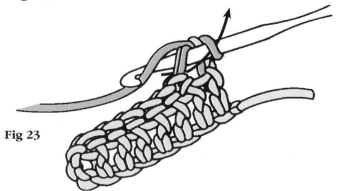

Fig 23

One slip stitch made. Work a slip stitch (repeat Step 1) in each stitch across.

FRONT LOOP, BACK LOOP AND POST

Front loop is the loop toward you at the top of the stitch. **Back loop** is the loop away from you at the top of the stitch. **Post** is the part of the stitch around which other stitches may be worked (**Fig 24**).

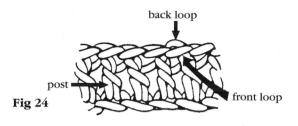

Fig 24

OVERCAST STITCH

Overcast stitch is worked loosely to join crocheted pieces together. Insert the needle through the front and back loop of 2 adjacent stitches (**Fig 25**). Work from right to left.

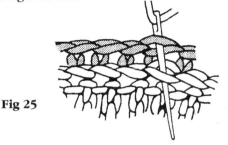

Fig 25

CROCHETING WITH THREAD AND A STEEL HOOK

Don't be afraid to crochet with steel hooks and finer thread. You will be using exactly the same stitches you're familiar with, but at first it will feel clumsy and awkward. But this will pass in a few hours of crocheting, as you adjust your tension and working method to the new tools. Soon you will work much more by feel than when working with the heavier yarns. So be patient with any initial clumsiness and confusion—they won't be with you long.

Steel hooks range in size from 00 (large) to 14 (very fine) and are 5" long, which is shorter than aluminum or plastic hooks. Their shape is different from the other crochet hooks. There is the throat, then the shank, and after the shank the steel begins to widen again before it reaches the finger grip (**Fig 26**). When crocheting, it is important that the stitches do not slide beyond the shank, as this will cause a loose tension and alter the gauge. If you find you are having difficulty at first, put a piece of cellophane tape around the hook to keep the stitches from sliding past the correct area. With practice, you will work in the right place automatically.

throat   shank

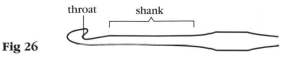

Fig 26

WASHING

If your finished project should need washing, use warm water and a mild soap. Wash gently; do not rub, twist or wring. Rinse well, and gently press water out of piece. Roll piece up in a terry towel, then lay it out to dry as explained in the following blocking instructions.

BLOCKING

This simply means "setting" the finished piece into its final size and shape. To do this, spread the piece out on a flat padded surface (covered with terry toweling), having wrong side facing up. Be sure to shape piece to measurements given with the pattern, having picots, loops, scallops, etc. along the outside edges open and in correct alignment. If necessary, use rust-proof straight pins to hold the edges in place. If piece was not previously washed, dampen it thoroughly with a wet sponge or cloth, or spray it with a commerical spray starch—this will give a firm shape but not stiff. Let dry completely before removing.

If further blocking is necessary, press through a damp cloth with a moderately hot iron on the wrong side (do not rest iron on any decorative raised stitch). When thoroughly dried, remove.

STARCHING AND BLOCKING SUPPLIES

Before starting this procedure, assemble the following necessary supplies.

1. **Stiffening solution**—use one of the following:
(a) Equal amounts of water and commercial stiffening solution used to stiffen crocheted lace (available in your local craft or needlework store), thoroughly mixed.
(b) Equal amounts of white craft glue and water, thoroughly mixed.
(c) Thick solution of commercial boilable starch (liquid or spray starches do not work).

2. **Plastic bag**, the type that locks across the top for mixing solution and soaking crocheted pieces.

3. **Pinning board**, such as a sheet of Styrofoam® (our preference), piece of cardboard or fabric cutting board, to block flat pieces to shape.

4. **Rust-proof straight pins** to pin out and hold project in shape.

5. **Plastic wrap** to cover blocking surface so stiffened project will slide off easily when dry.

6. *For Snowy Village*, **tracing paper** for tracing blocking guides and thick white craft glue for gluing buildings together.

7. *For standing Merrie Angel*, **9"-tall Styrofoam® cone** covered with plastic wrap (secure with **tape**).

STARCHING INSTRUCTIONS

Once you have the supplies ready for starching and blocking, proceed as follows:

Step 1: Cover pinning board and blocking form with plastic wrap and secure in place.

Step 2: Pour stiffening solution into a plastic bag or bowl. Immerse project in solution and work into thread. Remove and press out extra stiffening solution. Do not squeeze—project should be very wet, but there should be no solution in the decorative holes (dab with a dry paper towel to correct this). Any excess stiffening solution can be stored in a locked plastic bag for as long as one week, mixing before next use.

Step 3: With right side up, shape stiffened project, being sure the design is properly aligned with all picots, loops, etc. open; using rust-proof pins, pin design in place as desired. Let project dry thoroughly before removing.

SPECIAL INSTRUCTIONS
FOR SNOWY VILLAGE

Step 1: Using pencil and ruler to be exact, trace blocking guide onto tracing paper. Do not use a copying machine! Copiers may distort the guide lines. (Be sure to trace the total number of blocking guides necessary for doors or windows.)

Step 2: Place blocking guide on blocking surface cover both with plastic wrap and staple, tape or pin to secure them in place.

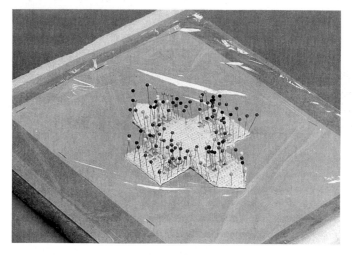

Step 3: With right side up, shape starched project out to same size as blocking guide, being sure to have rows of stitches in correct alignment, and pinning to make neat side edges of building and roof. Make each bottom roof edge a scallop shape.

Step 4: Let dry. With white craft glue, fold and glue building sides together. Fold and glue roof into place.

HINTS:
1. Keep hands clean throughout.
2. Keep spray water bottle handy to wet and reshape.
3. Do not bend stiffened pieces unless slightly damp, as they may crack.

Treetop Angel, Crystal

SIZE:
About 9" tall

MATERIALS:
Bedspread-weight crochet cotton,
  one 225-yd ball white
Size 7 steel crochet hook, or size required for gauge
small amount of polyester fiberfill (for head)

TRIMMINGS:
one 12" white chenille stem (for arms)
starching and blocking supplies, see page 132
poster board for cone (for starching)
eight 1" silver snowflakes (optional)
craft glue

GAUGE:
10 dc = 1"
4 dc rows = 1"

Instructions

HEAD
Ch 2.

Rnd 1: 6 sc in 2nd ch from hook; join in first sc: 6 sc.

Rnd 2: Ch 1, 2 sc in same sc as joining; 2 sc in each rem sc: 12 sc.

Rnd 3: Ch 1, sc in same sc as joining; 2 sc in next sc; * sc in next sc, 2 sc in next sc; rep from * around; join in first sc: 18 sc.

Rnd 4: Rep Rnd 3. At end of rnd: 27 sc.

Rnd 5: Ch 1, sc in same sc as joining; sc in each rem sc; join in first sc.

Rnds 6 through 13: Rep Rnd 5. At end of Rnd 13, stuff head firmly with fiberfill.

Rnd 14: Ch 1, sc in same sc as joining; sc in next sc, sk next sc, * sc in next 2 sc, sk next sc; rep from * around; join in first sc: 18 sc.

Rnd 15: Rep Rnd 14. At end of rnd: 12 sc.

OVERBLOUSE
Rnd 16: Ch 1, sc in same sc as joining; * ch 3, sc in next sc; rep from * 10 times more; ch 3; join in first sc: 12 ch-3 lps.

Rnd 17: Sl st in next ch-3 lp; ch 3 (counts as a dc on this and following rnds), 4 dc in same ch-3 lp; 5 dc in each of next 11 ch-3 lp; join in 3rd ch of beg ch-3: 60 dc.

Rnd 18: Ch 3, dc in each dc; join in 3rd ch of beg ch-3.

Rnd 19: Ch 4 (counts as a dc and ch-1 sp on this and following rnds), * dc in next dc, ch 1; rep from * around; join in 3rd ch of beg ch 4: 60 ch-1 sps.

Rnd 20
sp, ch 1

Rnd 21

Rnd 22
4th ch
next dc;
from ho
weave i

SKIRT
Ch 10, j

Rnd 1:
rnds); 2

Rnd 2:
2 dc): b
(2 dc, c
more; sk

Rnd 3:
in same
shell in
3rd ch o

Rnds 4 t

Rnd 7:
in same
from * 1

Rnd 8: R

Rnd 9:
in same
* 10 time

Gauge

It is essential to achieve the gauge—number of stitches and rows per inch—given in pattern in order to make the correct size.

Before beginning your project, refer to the "Gauge" and make a gauge swatch using the hook and yarn specified. Work several rows; finish off. Place work on a flat surface and measure stitches in center of piece. If you have more stitches to the inch than specified, use a larger size hook. If you have fewer stitches to the inch than specified, use a smaller size hook. Then make another gauge swatch and check your gauge once again. Do not hesitate to change hook size to obtain the specified gauge. Often you will not be able to achieve gauge with the size hook recommended.

Abbreviations

beg	begin(ning)
bl(s)	back loop(s)
ch(s)	chain(s)
dc(s)	double crochet(s)
dec(s)	decrease(-ing)
Fig	figure
fl(s)	front loop(s)
hdc(s)	half double crochet(s)
lp(s)	loop(s)
patt	pattern
prev	previous
rem	remain(ing)
rep	repeat(ing)
rnd(s)	round(s)
sc	single crochet(s)
sk	skip
sl	slip
sl st(s)	slip stitch(es)
sp(s)	space(s)
st(s)	stitch(es)
tog	together
trc(s)	triple crochet(s)
YO	yarn over

Symbols

* An asterisk is used to mark the beginning of a portion of instructions which will be worked more than once; thus, "rep from * twice more" means after working the instructions once, repeat the instructions following the asterisk twice more (3 times in all).

† The dagger identifies a portion of instructions that will be repeated again later in the same row or round.

: The number after a colon at the end of a row or round indicates the number of stitches you should have when the row or round has been completed.

( ) Parentheses are used to enclose instructions which should be worked the exact number of times specified immediately following the parentheses, such as: (dc in next dc, ch 2) twice. They are also used to set off and clarify a group of sts that are to be worked all into the same sp or st, such as: (2 dc, ch 1, 2 dc) in corner sp.

[ ] Brackets and ( ) parentheses are used to provide additional information to clarify instructions.

Sweet Lacy Angels

These enchanting thread crochet angels will be treasu... or Crystal for the crowning touch on your treetop, No... whole choir of angels for the entrance table.

Rnd 10: Sl st in next dc and in next ch-1 sp; beg shell in same sp; ch 2, * in ch-1 sp of next shell work (2 dc, ch 2, 2 dc): ch-2 shell made; ch 2, shell in next shell; ch 2; rep from * 4 times more; in ch-1 sp of next shell work (2 dc, ch 2, 2 dc): ch-2 shell made; ch 2; join in 3rd ch of beg ch-3: 6 shells and 6 ch-2 shells.

Rnd 11: Sl st in next dc and in next ch-1 sp; beg shell in same ch-1 sp; * 11 dc in ch-2 sp of next ch-2 shell: pineapple base made; shell in next shell; rep from * 4 times more; 11 dc in ch-2 sp of next ch-2 shell: pineapple base made; join in 3rd ch of beg ch-3.

Rnd 12: Sl st in next dc and in next ch-1 sp; beg shell in same sp; * sk next 2 dc of same shell, dc in next 11 dc; shell in next shell; rep from * 4 times more; dc in next 11 dc; join in 3rd ch of beg ch-3.

Rnd 13: Rep Rnd 12.

Rnd 14: Sl st in next dc and in next ch-1 sp; beg shell in same sp; * sk next 2 dc of same shell, (dc between next 2 dc) 10 times; shell in next shell; rep from * 4 times more; sk next 2 dc of same shell, (dc between next 2 dc) 10 times; join in 3rd ch of beg ch-3.

Rnd 15: Sl st in next dc and in next ch-1 sp; ch 3, in same sp work (dc, ch 1, 2 dc, ch 1, 2 dc): beg double shell made; * sk next 2 dc of same shell, (dc between next 2 dc) 9 times; in ch-1 sp of next shell work (2 dc, ch 1, 2 dc, ch 1, 2 dc): double shell made; rep from * 4 times more; sk next 2 dc of same shell, (dc between next 2 dc) 9 times; join in 3rd ch of beg ch-3.

Rnd 16: Sl st in next dc and in next ch-1 sp; beg shell in same sp; shell in next ch-1 sp; * sk next 2 dc of same shell, (dc between next 2 dc) 8 times; shell in each of next 2 ch-1 sps; rep from * 4 times more; sk next 2 dc of same shell, (dc between next 2 dc) 8 times; join in 3rd ch of beg ch-3.

Rnd 17: Sl st in next dc and in next ch-1 sp; beg shell in same sp; ch 1, shell in next shell; * sk next 2 dc of same shell, (dc between next 2 dc) 7 times; shell in next shell; ch 1, shell in next shell; rep from * 4 times more; sk next 2 dc of same shell, (dc between next 2 dc) 7 times; join in 3rd ch of beg ch-3.

Rnd 18: Sl st in next dc and in next ch-1 sp; beg shell in same sp; ch 1, shell in next shell; * sk next 2 dc of same shell, (dc between next 2 dc) 6 times; shell in next shell; ch 1, shell in next shell; rep from * 4 times more; sk next 2 dc of same shell, (dc between next 2 dc) 6 times; join in 3rd ch of beg ch-3.

Rnd 19: Sl st in next dc and in next ch-1 sp; beg shell in same sp; ch 2, shell in next shell; * sk next 2 dc of same shell, (dc between next 2 dc) 5 times; shell in next shell; ch 2, shell in next shell; rep from * 4 times more; sk next 2 dc of same shell, (dc between next 2 dc) 5 times; join in 3rd ch of beg ch-3.

Rnd 20: Sl st in next dc and in next ch-1 sp; beg shell in same sp; 9 dc in next ch-2 sp: pineapple base made; shell in next shell; * sk next 2 dc of same shell, (dc between next 2 dc) 4 times; shell in next shell; 9 dc in next ch-2 sp: pineapple base made; shell in next shell; rep from * 4 times more; sk next 2 dc of same shell, (dc between next 2 dc) 4 times; join in 3rd ch of beg ch-3.

Rnd 21: Sl st in next dc and in next ch-1 sp; beg shell in same sp; sk next 2 dc of same shell, dc in next 9 dc, shell in next shell; * sk next 2 dc of same shell, (dc between next 2 dc) 3 times; shell in next shell; sk next 2 dc of same shell, dc in next 9 dc, shell in next shell; rep from * 4 times more; sk next 2 dc of same shell, (dc between next 2 dc) 3 times; join in 3rd ch of beg ch-3.

Rnd 22: Sl st in next dc and in next ch-1 sp; beg shell in same sp; sk next 2 dc of same shell, (dc in next dc, ch 1) 8 times; dc in next dc, shell in next shell; * sk next 2 dc of same shell, (dc between next 2 dc) twice; shell in next shell; sk next 2 dc of same shell, (dc in next dc, ch 1) 8 times; dc in next dc, shell in next shell; rep from * 4 times more; sk next 2 dc of same shell, (dc between next 2 dc) twice; join in 3rd ch of beg ch-3.

Rnd 23: Sl st in next dc and in next ch-1 sp; beg shell in same sp; sk next 2 dc of same shell, (dc in next dc, ch 1) 8 times; dc in next dc, shell in next shell; * sk next 2 dc of same shell, dc between next 2 dc, shell in next shell; sk next 2 dc of same shell, (dc in next dc, ch 1) 8 times; dc in next dc; shell in next shell; rep from * 4 times more; sk next 2 dc of same shell, dc between next 2 dc; join in 3rd ch of beg ch-3.

Rnd 24: Sl st in next dc and in next ch-1 sp; beg shell in same sp; sk next 2 dc of same shell, * (dc in next dc, ch 1) 8 times; dc in next dc, shell in each of next 2 shells; rep from * 4 times more; sk next 2 dc, (dc in next dc, ch 1) 8 times; dc in next dc, shell in next shell; join in 3rd ch of beg ch-3.

Rnd 25: Sl st in next dc and in next ch-1 sp; ch 4 (counts as a dc and a ch-1 sp), dc in same sp: beg V-st made; * † ch 1, sk next 2 dc of same shell, (dc in next dc, ch 1) 9 times; in ch-1 sp of next shell work (dc, ch 1, dc): V-st made; ch 1, between same shell and next shell work (dc, ch 1, dc): V-st made; ch 1 †, in ch-1 sp of next shell work (dc, ch 1, dc): V-st made; rep from * 4 times more; then rep from † to † once; join in 3rd ch of beg ch-4.

Rnd 26: Sl st in next ch-1 sp; beg V-st in same sp; ch 1, * sk next dc of same V-st, (dc in next dc, ch 1) 9 times; (in ch-1 sp of next V-st work V-st, ch 1) 3 times; rep from * 4 times more; (dc in next dc, ch 1) 9 times; (in ch-1 sp of next V-st work V-st, ch 1) twice; join in 3rd ch of beg ch-4: 18 V-sts.

Rnd 27: Ch 1, sc in same ch as joining; * ch 4, sl st in 4th ch from hook: picot made; sk next ch-1 sp, sc in next dc; rep from * around, ending last rep without working last sc; join first sc. Finish off and weave in ends. Set aside.

WINGS (make 2)
Ch 6.

Row 1 (right side): Dc in 4th ch from hook (3 skipped chs count as a dc), ch 1, 2 dc in same ch: shell made; 12 trc in next ch; in next ch work (2 dc, ch 1, 2 dc): shell made: 2 shells and 12 trc; ch 1, turn.

Row 2: Sk first dc, sl st in next dc and in next ch-1 sp; ch 3 (counts as a dc on this and following rows), in same sp work (dc, ch 1, 2 dc): beg shell made; ch 2, sk next 2 dc of same shell, dc in next 12 trc, ch 2, in ch-1 sp of next shell work shell: shell in shell made; ch 1, turn.

Row 3: Sk first dc, sl st in next dc and in next ch-1 sp; beg shell in same sp; ch 2, sk next 2 dc of same shell, (dc in next dc, ch 1) 11 times; dc in next dc, ch 2, shell in next shell: 2 shells and 11 ch-1 sps; ch 1, turn.

Row 4: Sk first dc, sl st in next dc and in next ch-1 sp; beg shell in same sp; ch 3, sk next 2 dc of same shell, (dc in next dc, ch 1) 11 times; dc in next dc, ch 3, shell in next shell; ch 1, turn.

Row 5: Sk first dc, sl st in next dc and in next ch-1 sp; ch 4 (counts as a trc), in same sp work (trc, ch 1, 2 trc): beg trc-shell made; ch 3, sk next 2 dc of same shell, sc in next dc, * ch 3, sc in next dc; rep from * 10 times more; ch 3, in ch-1 sp of next shell work (2 trc, ch 1, 2 trc): trc-shell made; ch 1, turn.

Row 6: Sk first trc, sl st in next trc and in next ch-1 sp; beg trc-shell in same sp; ch 3, sc in next ch-3 lp, * ch 3, sk next ch-3 lp, sc in next ch-3 lp; rep from * 9 times more; ch 3, in ch-1 sp of next trc-shell work trc-shell: trc-shell in trc-shell made; ch 1, turn.

Row 7: Sk first trc, sl st in next trc and in next ch-1 sp; beg trc-shell in same sp; ch 3, sk next ch-3 lp, sc in next ch-3 lp, * ch 4, sc in next ch-3 lp; rep from * 8 times more; ch 3, trc-shell in next trc-shell; ch 1, turn.

Row 8: Sk first trc, sl st in next trc and in next ch-1 sp; beg trc-shell in same sp; ch 3, sc in next ch-4 lp, * ch 4, sc in next ch-4 lp; rep from * 7 times more; ch 3, trc-shell in next trc-shell; ch 1, turn.

Row 9: Sk first trc, sl st in next trc and in next ch-1 sp; beg trc-shell in same sp; ch 3, sc in next ch-4 lp, * ch 4, sc in next ch-4 lp; rep from * 6 times more; ch 3, trc-shell in next trc-shell; ch 1, turn.

Row 10: Sk first trc, sl st in next trc and in next ch-1 sp; beg trc-shell in same sp; ch 3, sc in next ch-4 lp, * ch 5, sc in next ch-4 lp; rep from * 5 times more; ch 3, trc-shell in next trc-shell; ch 1, turn.

Row 11: Sk first trc, sl st in next trc and in next ch-1 sp; beg trc-shell in same sp; ch 3, sc in next ch-5 lp, * ch 5, sc in next ch-5 lp; rep from * 4 times more; ch 3, trc-shell in next trc-shell; ch 1, turn.

Row 12: Sk first trc, sl st in next trc and in next ch-1 sp; beg trc-shell in same sp; ch 3, sc in next ch-5 lp, * ch 5, sc in next ch-5 lp; rep from * 3 times more; ch 3, trc-shell in next trc-shell; ch 1, turn.

Row 13: Sk first trc, sl st in next trc and in next ch-1 sp; beg trc-shell in same sp; ch 3, sc in next ch-5 lp, * ch 6, sc in next ch-5 lp; rep from * twice more; ch 3, trc-shell in next trc-shell; ch 1, turn.

Row 14: Sk first trc, sl st in next trc and in next ch-1 sp; beg trc-shell in same sp; ch 3, sc in next ch-6 lp, (ch 6, sc in next ch-6 lp) twice; ch 3, trc-shell in next trc-shell; ch 1, turn.

Row 15: Sk first trc, sl st in next trc and in next ch-1 sp; beg trc-shell in same sp; ch 3, sc in next ch-6 lp, ch 6, sc in next ch-6 lp, ch 3, trc-shell in next trc-shell; ch 1, turn.

Row 16: Sk first trc, sl st in next trc and in next ch-1 sp; beg trc-shell in same sp; ch 3, sc in next ch-6 lp, ch 3, trc-shell in next trc-shell; ch 1, turn.

Row 17: Sk first trc, sl st in next trc; sc in next ch-1 sp, ch 3, sc in ch-1 sp of next trc-shell: one ch-3 lp; ch 1, turn.

Row 18: Sl st in next ch-3 lp; ch 4 (counts as a trc), in same lp work (2 trc, ch 4, sl st in 4th ch from hook: picot made; 3 trc): picot shell made. Finish off and weave in ends. Set aside.

ARMS
Leaving a 20" end for sewing, ch 70.

Row 1: Sc in 2nd ch from hook and in each rem ch: 69 sc; ch 1, turn.

Row 2: Sc in each sc; ch 1, turn.

Rows 3 through 6: Rep Row 2. At end of Row 6, do not ch 1. Finish off and weave in ends, leaving beg length for sewing.

Cut chenille stem same length as crocheted arm piece. Center chenille stem on crocheted arm piece and join all edges, carefully matching sts. Finish off and weave in end. Bend arm piece into a U-shape and set aside.

HALO
Ch 7, join to form ring.

Rnd 1: Ch 3 (counts as a dc), 15 dc in ring; join in 3rd ch of beg ch-3: 16 dc.

Rnd 2: Ch 7 (counts as a trc and a ch-3 lp), * trc in next dc, ch 3; rep from * 14 times more; join in 4th ch of beg ch-7: 16 trc.

Rnd 3: Ch 1, sc in same ch as joining; * ch 6, sl st in 4th ch from hook: picot made; ch 2, sk next ch-3 lp, sc in next trc; rep from * 15 times more, ending last rep without working last sc; join in first sc: 16 picot. Finish off and weave in ends. Set aside.

HAIR

Ch 6 loosely, join to form ring.

Rnd 1: Ch 1, 3 sc in same ch as joining and in each rem ch; join in first sc: 18 sc.

Rnd 2: Ch 1, sc in same sc as joining and in each rem sc; join in first sc: 18 sc.

Rnd 3: Ch 1, 2 sc in same sc as joining and in each rem sc; join in fl of first sc: 36 sc.

Rnd 4: Ch 1, in same lp as joining work (sc, ch 6, sc), in fl of each rem sc work (sc, ch 6, sc); join in bl of first sc of prev rnd: 36 ch-6 lps.

Rnd 5: Ch 1, sc in same lp as joining; working behind ch-6 lps of prev rnd in rem bl of Rnd 3, sc in each lp; join in first sc: 36 sc.

Rnd 6: Ch 1, sc in same sc as joining and in each rem sc; join in first sc.

Rnd 7: Ch 1, sc in same sc as joining and in each rem sc; join in fl of first sc.

Rnd 8: Ch 1, in same lp as joining work (sc, ch 8, sc); in fl of each sc work (sc, ch 8, sc); join in bl of first sc of prev rnd.

Rnd 9: Ch 1, in same lp as joining work (sc, ch 10, sc); in bl of each sc work (sc, ch 10, sc); join in first sc. Finish off and weave in ends. Set aside.

Starching Instructions

SKIRT

Following Starching Instructions on page 132, moisten skirt in stiffening solution. Make cone blocking shape as follows: Measure Angel's skirt length and add 2". This measurement will be used for the half circle for forming the cone, **Fig 1**. Draw a half circle on poster board and cut out. Shape half circle to form a cone that will be the same width as Angel's skirt (place Angel's skirt on cone to check width of cone); tape to

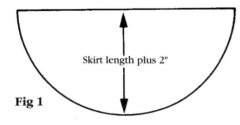

Skirt length plus 2"

Fig 1

hold in place. Trim top "point" of cone evenly to fit top of skirt, **Fig 2.** Cover cone with plastic wrap and secure with tape. Pin skirt to plastic-wrapped cone, keeping shells in straight line. Pin picots on last rnd, shaping scallops on bottom edge.

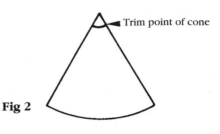

Trim point of cone

Fig 2

HEAD/OVERBLOUSE AND ARMS

Bend arms and place on top of skirt (do not use stiffening solution on arms). Moisten overblouse only, without moistening head, and place on top of arms and skirt. Shape overblouse to fit over arms and top of skirt, and flatten against back of skirt.

HAIR

Moisten hair with stiffening solution and position on head. Pin ends of lps in place; leaving pins in place, slightly lift lps from head to make hair look fuller. Let dry.

WINGS AND HALO

Place wings and halo on pinning board after moistening with stiffening solution and pin to desired shape. Let dry.

Finishing

After all pieces are thoroughly dry, glue arms, head/overblouse, and halo into desired position and let dry.

Hold one wing over a small pan of boiling water; as wing softens, bend edges slightly to curl upwards on side edges and end of wing. Repeat for remaining wing. Wings may be re-steamed until desired shape is achieved. Place wings into desired position, glue and let dry.

SNOWFLAKES (optional)

Thread each snowflake on a piece of crochet thread. Arrange as shown in photo; trim threads. Glue in place in hands.

Treetop Angel, Felicia

designed by Joan Glass

SIZE:
About 9" tall

MATERIALS
Bedspread-weight crochet cotton,
 one 225-yd ball white
Size 7 steel crochet hook, or size required for gauge
small amount of polyester fiberfill (for head)

TRIMMINGS:
one 12" white chenille stem (for arms)
starching and blocking supplies, see page 132
poster board for cone (for starching)
3" x 3" piece of cardboard
small craft paint brush
craft glue

GAUGE:
10 dc = 1"
4 dc rows = 1"

Instructions

HEAD

Ch 4, join to form a ring.

Rnd 1: Ch 3 (counts as a dc on this and following rnds), 9 dc in ring; join in 3rd ch of beg ch-3: 10 dc.

Rnd 2: Ch 3, 2 dc in next dc; * dc in next dc, 2 dc in next dc; rep from * 3 times more; join in 3rd ch of beg ch-3: 15 dc.

Rnd 3: Ch 3, dc in same ch as joining; 2 dc in each dc; join in 3rd ch of beg ch-3: 30 dc.

Rnd 4: Ch 3, dc in each dc; join in 3rd ch of beg ch-3.

Rnds 5 and 6: Rep Rnd 4.

Rnd 7: Ch 1, sc in same ch as joining; dec over next 2 dc (to work dec: draw up lp in each of next 2 sts, YO and draw through all 3 lps on hook: dec made); sc in next dc; (dec as before, sc in next dc) 8 times; dec as before; join in first sc: 20 sc.

Rnd 8: Ch 1, sc in same sc as joining and in each rem sc; join in first sc: 20 sc.

Rnd 9: Ch 1, sc in next sc, * dec; sc in next 2 sc; rep from * 3 times more; dec; join in first sc: 15 sc. Stuff and shape head with polyester fiberfill.

Rnd 10: Ch 1, * dec; sc in next sc; rep from * 3 times more; dec; join in first sc: 10 sc.

Rnd 11: Ch 3, dc in each sc; join in 3rd ch of beg ch-3: 10 dc. Do not finish off.

OVERBLOUSE

Rnd 12: Ch 3, in same ch as joining work (dc, ch 1, 2 dc): beg shell made; * in next dc work (2 dc, ch 1, 2 dc): shell made; rep from * 8 times more; join in 3rd ch of beg ch-3: 10 shells.

Rnd 13: Sl st in next dc and in next ch-1 sp; beg shell in same sp; * in ch-1 sp of next shell work shell: shell in shell made; rep from * 8 times more; join in 3rd ch of beg ch-3.

Rnd 14: Sl st in next dc and in next ch-1 sp; beg shell in same sp; shell in each of next 2 shells; (ch 1, shell in next shell) 3 times; shell in each of next 2 shells; (ch 1, shell in next shell) twice; ch 1; join in 3rd ch of beg ch-3.

Rnd 15: Sl st in next dc and in next ch-1 sp; ch 4 (counts as a trc on this and following rnds), in same sp work (trc, ch 1, 2 trc): beg trc-shell made; in ch-1 sp of next shell work (2 trc, ch 1, 2 trc): trc-shell made; in ch-1 sp of next shell work (2 trc, ch 1, 2 trc): trc-shell made; † ch 1, in ch-1 sp of next shell work (2 trc, ch 1, 2 trc): trc-shell made †; rep from † to † twice more; in ch-1 sp of each of next 2 shells work (2 trc, ch 1, 2 trc): trc-shell made; rep from † to † twice; ch 1; join in 4th ch of beg ch-4: 10 trc-shells.

Rnd 16: Sl st in next trc and in next ch-1 sp; beg trc-shell in same sp; trc-shell in ch-1 sp of each of next 2 trc-shells; † ch 1, trc-shell in next trc-shell †; rep from † to † twice more; trc-shell in ch-1 sp of each of next 2 trc-shells; rep from † to † twice; ch 1; join in 4th ch of beg ch-4.

Rnd 17: Sl st in next trc and in next ch-1 sp; * ch 5, sc between next 2 trc-shells, ch 5, sc in ch-1 sp of next trc-shell; rep from * 9 times more; ch 5, sc between next 2 trc-shells, ch 5; join in 2nd sl st. Finish off and weave in ends. Set aside.

SKIRT
Ch 22, join to form a ring.

Rnd 1: Ch 3 (counts as a dc on this and following rnds); dc in next 10 chs, ch 1, dc in next 11 chs, ch 1; join in 3rd ch of beg ch-3: 22 dc.

Rnd 2: Ch 3, dc in each dc and in each ch-1 sp; join in 3rd ch of beg ch-3: 24 dc.

Rnd 3: Ch 3, dc in each dc; join in 3rd ch of beg ch-3.

Rnd 4: Ch 3, dc in next dc, ch 1, * dc in next 2 dc, ch 1; rep from * 10 times more; join in 3rd ch of beg ch-3.

Rnd 5: Ch 4 (counts as a dc and a ch-1 sp), dc in next dc, ch 1, sk next ch-1 sp, * (dc in next dc, ch 1) twice; sk next ch-1 sp; rep from * 10 times more; join in 3rd ch of beg ch-4.

Rnd 6: Sl st in next ch-1 sp; ch 4 (counts as a trc), in same sp work (trc, ch 2, 2 trc): beg trc-shell made; * sk next 2 ch-1 sps, in next ch-1 sp work (2 trc, ch 2, 2 trc): trc-shell made; rep from * 6 times more; sk next 2 ch-1 sps; join in 4th ch of beg ch-4: 8 trc-shells.

Rnd 7: Sl st in next trc and in next ch-2 sp; beg trc-shell in same sp; * in ch-2 sp of next trc-shell work trc-shell: trc-shell in trc-shell made; rep from * 6 times more; join in 4th ch of beg ch-4.

Rnds 8 and 9: Rep Rnd 7.

Rnd 10: Sl st in next trc and in next ch-2 sp; beg trc-shell in same sp; ch 1, * trc-shell in next trc-shell; ch 1; rep from * 6 times more; join in 4th ch of beg ch-4.

Rnd 11: Sl st in next trc and in next ch-2 sp; beg trc-shell in same sp; ch 2, * trc-shell in next trc-shell; ch 2; rep from * 6 times more; join in 4th ch of beg ch-4.

Rnd 12: Sl st in next trc and in next ch-2 sp; beg trc-shell in same sp; ch 3, * trc-shell in next trc-shell; ch 3; rep from * 6 times more; join in 4th ch of beg ch-4.

Rnd 13: Sl st in next trc and in next ch-2 sp; beg trc-shell in same sp; ch 5, * trc-shell in next trc-shell; ch 5; rep from * 6 times more; join in 4th ch of beg ch-4.

Rnd 14: Sl st in next trc and in next ch-2 sp; beg trc-shell in same sp; ch 7, * trc-shell in next trc-shell; ch 7; rep from * 6 times more; join in 4th ch of beg ch-4.

Rnd 15: Sl st in next trc and in next ch-2 sp; beg trc-shell in same sp; ch 8, * trc-shell in next trc-shell; ch 8; rep from * 6 times more; join in 4th ch of beg ch-4.

Rnd 16: Sl st in next trc and in next ch-2 sp; beg trc-shell in same sp; ch 9; * trc-shell in next trc-shell; ch 9; rep from * 6 times more; join in 4th ch of beg ch-4.

Rnd 17: Sl st in next trc and in next ch-2 sp; beg trc-shell in same sp; ch 4; in 5th ch of next ch-9 lp work trc-shell; ch 4; * trc-shell in next trc-shell; ch 4, in 5th ch of next ch-9 lp work trc-shell; ch 4; rep from * 6 times more; join in 4th ch of beg ch-4: 16 trc-shells.

Rnd 18: Sl st in next trc and in next ch-2 sp; beg trc-shell in same sp; ch 4, * trc-shell in next trc-shell, ch 4; rep from * 14 times more; join in 4th ch of beg ch-4.

Rnds 19 and 20: Rep Rnd 18. At end of Rnd 20, finish off and weave in ends. Set aside.

WINGS (make 2)
Ch 5.

Row 1: Trc in 5th ch from hook (4 skipped chs count as a trc and a ch-1 sp), ch 2, in same ch work (2 trc, ch 2, 2 trc): trc-shell made; ch 1, turn.

Row 2: Sk first trc, sl st in next trc and in next ch-2 sp; ch 4, in same sp work (trc, ch 2, 2 trc): beg trc-shell made; ch 2, in next ch-2 sp work (2 trc, ch 2, 2 trc): trc-shell made; ch 1, turn.

Row 3: Sk first trc, sl st in next trc and in next ch-2 sp; beg trc-shell in same sp; ch 2; in next ch-2 sp work trc-shell; ch 2; trc-shell in ch-2 sp of next trc-shell: trc-shell in trc-shell made; ch 1, turn.

Row 4: Sk first trc, sl st in next trc and in next ch-2 sp; beg trc-shell in same sp; * ch 2, in next ch-2 sp work trc-shell; ch 2; trc-shell in next trc-shell; rep from * once more; ch 1, turn.

Row 5: Sk first trc, sl st in next trc and in next ch-2 sp; beg trc-shell in same sp; * ch 4, sk next ch-2 sp, trc-shell in next trc-shell; rep from * 3 times more; ch 1, turn.

Row 6: Sk first trc, sl st in next trc and in next ch-2 sp; beg trc-shell in same sp; * ch 5, sk next ch-4 lp, trc-shell in next trc-shell; rep from * 3 times more; ch 1, turn.

Row 7: Sk first trc, sl st in next trc and in next ch-2 sp; beg trc-shell in same sp; * ch 1, in 3rd ch of next ch-5 lp work trc-shell; ch 1; trc-shell in next trc-shell; rep from * 3 times more: 9 trc-shells; ch 1, turn.

Row 8: Sk first trc, sl st in next trc and in next ch-2 sp; beg trc-shell in same sp; * ch 1, trc-shell in next trc-shell; rep from * 7 times more; ch 6, turn.

Row 9: * Sc in ch-2 sp of next trc-shell, ch 6, sc in ch-1 sp between same trc-shell and next trc-shell, ch 6; rep from * 7 times more; sc in ch-2 sp of next trc-shell, ch 6, sc in 4th ch of beg ch-4 of same trc-shell, † working on side edge of wing, ch 6, sc in top of trc of trc-shell at end of side row †; rep from † to † 6 times more; ch 4, sc in beg ch of wing, ch 4, sc in top of trc on opposite side edge of wing; rep from † to † 6 times; ch 6; join in last trc of trc-shell at end of side row of wing. Finish off and weave in ends. Set aside.

ARMS
Work same as for Crystal on page 137.

HALO

Ch 5, join to form a ring.

Rnd 1: Ch 3 (counts as a dc on this and following rnds), 11 dc in ring; join in 3rd ch of beg ch-3: 12 dc.

Rnd 2: Ch 6 (counts as a dc and a ch-3 lp); * dc in next dc, ch 3; rep from * 10 times more; join in 3rd ch of beg ch-6: 12 dc and 12 ch-3 lps.

Rnd 3: Ch 9 (counts as a trc and a ch-5 lp); * trc in next dc, ch 5; rep from * 10 times more; join in 4th ch of beg ch-9: 12 trc and 12 ch-5 lps.

Rnd 4: Ch 3, 5 dc in next ch-5 lp; * dc in next trc, 5 dc in next ch-5 lp; rep from * 10 times more; join in 3rd ch of beg ch-3: 72 dc.

Rnd 5: * Ch 5, sk next 2 dc, sc in next dc; rep from * 22 times more; ch 5; join in joining sl st of prev rnd: 24 ch-5 lps. Finish off and weave in ends. Set aside.

Starching Instructions

SKIRT:

Referring to Skirt starching instructions for Tree Top Angel, Crystal, starch skirt and pin to plastic-wrapped cone, keeping shells in vertical and horizontal line. Pin each center of the ch-4 lps between shells of last rnd to point downwards.

HEAD/OVERBLOUSE AND ARMS:

Bend arms and place on top of skirt (do not use stiffening solution on arms). Moisten overblouse only, without moistening head, and place on top of skirt, making sure the front and back of overblouse are positioned correctly. (**Note:** *Center front and center back of Overblouse are where shells are separated by ch-1 sps.*) Shape overblouse to fit over arms and top of skirt and flatten against front and back of skirt. Position head as if praying, and pin at back and front of head to hold position while drying.

WINGS AND HALO:

Place wings and halo on pinning board after moistening with stiffening solution and pin to desired shape. Let dry.

HAIR:

Wrap thread around a 3" x 3" piece of cardboard about 160 times. Slip a 6" thread under the wrapped thread at one end of the cardboard and tie firmly. Cut all lps at opposite end (**Fig 1**). Glue knot of hair to center top of head and let dry thoroughly. Distribute strands evenly around head. Separate 9 strands at one side of center front, paint with stiffening solution, and using end opposite hook of steel crochet hook, roll strands into tight curl, fastening to head with craft glue. Place four curls in front, five curls on each side (placed in a row), and make one wide curl at base of neck on back of head with remaining strands.

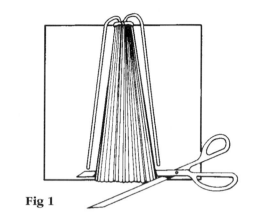

Fig 1

Finishing

When all pieces are thoroughly dry, glue arms, head/overblouse, and halo into desired position and let dry. Hold each wing over a small pan of boiling water and bend beginning 2 rows of wings to a 45° angle. Place wings into desired position on Angel; glue and let dry.

Small Angel, Merrie

SIZE:
About 6" tall
MATERIALS:
Bedspread-weight crochet cotton,
  one 225-yd ball white
Size 7 steel crochet hook, or size required for
  gauge
small amount of polyester fiberfill (for head)
TRIMMINGS:
one 12" white chenille stem (for arms)
size 18 tapestry needle
starching and blocking supplies, see page 132
1 1/2" tall Christmas tree
craft glue
GAUGE:
10 dc = 1"
4 dc rows = 1"

Instructions

HEAD
Ch 2.

Rnd 1: 6 sc in 2nd ch from hook; join in first sc: 6 sc.

Rnd 2: Ch 1, 2 sc in same sc as joining and in each rem sc; join in first sc: 12 sc.

Rnd 3: Rep Rnd 2. At end of rnd: 24 sc.

Rnd 4: Ch 1, sc in same sc as joining and in each rem sc; join in first sc.

Rnds 5 through 11: Rep Rnd 4. Stuff head firmly with polyester fiberfill.

Rnd 12: Ch 1, sc in same sc as joining and in next 2 sc; sk next sc, (sc in next 3 sc, sk next sc) 5 times; join in first sc: 18 sc.

Rnd 13: Ch 1, sc in same sc as joining and in next sc; sk next sc, (sc in next 2 sc, sk next sc) 5 times; join in first sc: 12 sc.

OVERBLOUSE
Rnd 14: Ch 4 (counts as an sc and a ch-3 lp); * sc in next sc, ch 3; rep from * 10 times more; join in first ch of beg ch-4: 12 ch-3 lps.

Note: Mark first lp on following rnds.

Rnd 15: In each rem ch-3 lp work (sc, ch 5, sc): 12 ch-5 lps.

Rnd 16: In each ch-5 lp work (sc, ch 6, sc).

Rnd 17: In each ch-6 lp work (sc, ch 7, sc).

Rnd 18: In each ch-7 lp work (sc, ch 7, sc).

Rnds 19 and 20: Rep Rnd 18.

Rnd 21: Sl st in next ch-7 lp; ch 1, 6 sc in same lp;

ch 3, sl st in first ch: picot made; * 6 sc in next ch-7 lp; ch 3, sl st in first ch: picot made; rep from * 10 times more; join in first sc. Finish off and weave in ends. Set aside.

SKIRT
Ch 12, join to form a ring.

Rnd 1: Ch 3 (counts as a dc), 23 dc in ring; join in 3rd ch of beg ch-3: 24 dc.

Rnd 2: Ch 6 (counts as an sc and a ch-5 lp), sk next dc, sc in next dc, * ch 5, sk next dc, sc in next dc; rep from * 9 times more; ch 5; join in first ch of beg ch-6: 12 ch-5 lps.

Note: Mark first lp on following rnds.

Rnd 3: In each ch-5 lp work (sc, ch 5, sc).

Rnds 4 through 6: Rep Rnd 3.

Rnd 7: In each ch-5 lp work (sc, ch 6, sc).

Rnd 8: In each ch-6 lp work (sc, ch 6, sc).

Rnd 9: In each ch-6 lp work (sc, ch 7, sc).

Rnd 10: In each ch-7 lp work (sc, ch 7, sc).

Rnd 11: In each ch-7 lp work (sc, ch 8, sc).

Rnd 12: In each ch-8 lp work (sc, ch 8, sc).

Rnd 13: In each ch-8 lp work (sc, ch 9, sc).

Rnd 14: In each ch-9 lp work (sc, ch 9, sc).

Rnd 15: Rep Rnd 14.

Rnd 16: * 4 sc in next ch-9 lp; ch 4, sl st in first ch: picot made; 4 sc in same lp; rep from * 11 times more.

Rnd 17: * Sc in next sc, ch 10, sk next 6 sc, sc in next sc; rep from * 11 times more.

Rnd 18: * In each ch-10 lp work (5 sc, picot; 5 sc); join in first sc: 24 picots. Finish off and weave in ends. Set aside.

WINGS (make 2)
Ch 14.

Row 1: Sc in 8th ch from hook (counts as a ch-5 lp), * ch 5, sk next 2 chs, sc in next ch; rep from * once more; 3 ch-5 lps; ch 5, turn.

Row 2 (right side): In each of next 2 ch-5 lps work (sc, ch 5, sc); in next ch-5 lp work (sc, ch 5, sc, ch 2, dc); ch 1, turn.

Row 3: In next ch-2 sp work (sc, ch 5, sc); * in each of next 3 ch-5 lps work (sc, ch 5, sc); in next ch-5 lp work (sc, ch 2, dc); ch 1, turn.

Rows 4 through 11: Rep Row 3. At end of Row 11, do not ch 1; turn.

Row 12: Ch 3, sl st in first ch: picot made; 3 sc in first ch-2 sp; in each of next 3 ch-5 lps work (2 sc, ch 3, sl st in first ch: picot made; 2 sc); in next ch-5 lp work (3 sc, ch 3, sl st in first ch: picot made; sl st). Finish off and weave in ends.

Hold wings with wrong side and row edges together; sew wings along side row edges starting at beg ch and ending with Row 3. Finish off and weave in ends. Set aside.

HAIR
Ch 6, join to form a ring.

Rnd 1: Ch 1, 10 sc in ring; ch 1; do not join.

Rnd 2: 2 sc in bl only of each sc: 20 sc.

Rnd 3: Ch 21, sl st in next sc; * ch 20, sl st in next sc; rep from * 18 times more, ending last rep with sl st in first ch of beg ch-21: 20 ch-20 lps.

Rnd 4: Sl st in first unused lp of Rnd 1; ch 15, in same lp work (sl st, ch 15, sl st); working in rem unused lps, * ch 15, in next lp work (sl st, ch 15, sl st); rep from * 8 times more: 20 ch-15 lps. Finish off and weave in ends.

ARMS
Leaving a 16" end for sewing, ch 50.

Row 1: Sc in 2nd ch from hook and in each rem ch: 49 sc; ch 1, turn.

Row 2: Sc in each sc; ch 1, turn.

Rows 3 through 11: Rep Row 2. At end of Row 11, do not ch 1 or turn. Finish off and weave in end, leaving long end for sewing.

Cut chenille stem same length as crocheted arm piece. Center chenille stem on arm piece and sew short and long crocheted edges carefully matching sts; finish off and weave in end. Bend arm piece into a U-shape and set aside.

HALO
Ch 6, join to form a ring.

Rnd 1: Ch 3 (counts as a dc), 17 dc in ring; join in 3rd ch of beg ch-3: 18 dc.

Rnd 2: Ch 4 (counts as a dc and a ch-1 sp); * dc in next dc, ch 1; rep from * 16 times more; join in 3rd ch of beg ch-4: 18 ch-1 sps.

Rnd 3: * Ch 3, sl st in first ch: picot made; 2 sc in next ch-1 sp; sc in next dc, 2 sc in next ch-1 sp; rep from * 8 times more; join behind base of first picot. Finish off and weave in ends. Set aside.

Starching Instructions

SKIRT
Following Starching Instructions on page 132, moisten skirt in stiffening solution and pin to plastic wrapped cone, keeping sc in straight line. Lift bottom edges with picots away from cone leaving pins in place. To help skirt stand, pin underneath picot in center of lp on last row.

HEAD/OVERBLOUSE AND ARMS
Bend arms and place on top of skirt (do not use stiffening solution on arms). Moisten overblouse only, without moistening head, and place on top of arms and skirt. Shape overblouse to fit over arms and top of skirt, and flatten against back of skirt.

HAIR
Moisten hair with stiffening solution and position on head. Using a pin or toothpick, twist ends of longest loops once, and pin in place. In same manner, pin shorter chain loops in place. Leaving pins in place, lift all loops on pins to make hair appear fuller. Let dry.

WINGS AND HALO
Place wings and halo on pinning board after moistening with stiffening solution and pin to shape, carefully rounding top edges of wings. To curl bottom edges of wings, leave pins in place and lift edges of wings away from pinning board. Let dry thoroughly before removing from pinning board.

Finishing

After all pieces are thoroughly dry, glue arms, head/overblouse, halo, and wings into desired position and let dry. Position arms and glue Christmas tree in place.

Small Angel, Noelle

SIZE:
About 6" tall
MATERIALS:
Bedspread-weight crochet cotton,
  one 225-yd ball white
Size 7 steel crochet hook, or size required for gauge
small amount of polyester fiberfill (for head)
TRIMMINGS:
one 12" white chenille stem (for arms)
starching and blocking supplies, see page 132
4" square piece of gold cardboard (for horn)
craft glue
GAUGE:
10 dc = 1"
4 dc rows = 1"

PATTERN STITCH
Double Triple Crochet (dtrc): YO 3 times, insert hook in next st, draw up lp, (YO and draw through 2 lps on hook) 4 times: dtrc made.

Instructions

HEAD
Work same as for Merrie, page 142, through Rnd 13.

OVERBLOUSE
Rnd 14: Ch 1, sc in same sc as joining; ch 3, * sc in next sc, ch 3; rep from * 10 times more; join in first sc: 12 ch-3 lps.

Rnd 15: Sl st in next ch-3 lp; ch 1, sc in same lp; * ch 6, sl st in 4th ch from hook: picot made; ch 2, sc in next ch-3 lp; rep from * 10 times more; ch 6, sl st in 4th ch from hook; picot made; ch 2; join in first sc.

Rnd 16: Ch 1, sc in same sc as joining; * ch 8, sk next picot, sc in next sc: rep from * 10 times more; ch 3, dtrc (see Pattern Stitch) in first sc: ch-8 lp made.

Rnd 17: Ch 1, sc in joining ch-8 lp, * ch 6, sl st in 4th ch from hook: picot made; ch 2, sc in next ch-8 lp; rep from * 11 times more, ending last rep without working last sc; join in first sc.

Rnds 18 and 19: Rep Rnds 16 and 17.

Rnd 20: Rep Rnd 16.

Rnd 21: Ch 1, 4 sc in joining ch-8 lp; * † ch 4, sl st in 4th ch from hook: picot made; 4 sc in next lp; ch 4, sl st in 4th ch from hook: picot made †; 4 sc in same lp; rep from * 10 times more, then rep from † to † once; join in first sc. Finish off and weave in ends. Set aside.

SKIRT
Ch 10, join to form a ring.

Rnd 1: Ch 3 (counts as a dc), 19 dc in ring; join in 3rd ch of beg ch-3: 20 dc.

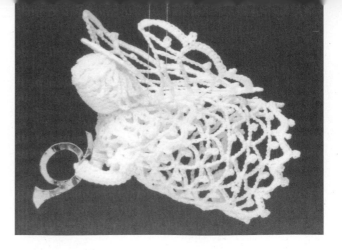

Rnd 2: Ch 1, sc in same ch as joining; * ch 5, sk next dc, sc in next dc; rep from * 8 times more; ch 2, dc in first sc: ch-5 lp made: 10 ch-5 lps.

Rnd 3: Ch 1, sc in joining ch-5 lp, * ch 6, sl st in 4th ch from hook: picot made; ch 2, sc in next ch-5 lp; rep from * 9 times more, ending last rep without working last sc; join in first sc.

Rnd 4: Ch 1, sc in same sc as joining; * ch 8, sk next picot, sc in next sc; rep from * 8 times more; ch 3, dtrc in first sc: ch-8 lp made.

Rnd 5: Ch 1, sc in joining ch-8 lp, * ch 6, picot; ch 2, sc in next ch-8 lp; rep from * 9 times more, ending last rep without working last sc; join in first sc.

Rnds 6 and 7: Rep Rnds 4 and 5.

Rnd 8: Ch 1, sc in same sc as joining; * ch 10, sk next picot, sc in next sc; rep from * 8 times more; ch 5, dtrc in first sc: ch-10 lp made.

Rnd 9: Ch 1, sc in joining ch-10 lp, * ch 7, sl st in 4th ch from hook: picot made; ch 3, sc in next ch-10 lp; rep from * 8 times more; ch 7, sl st in 4th ch from hook: picot made; ch 3; join in first sc.

Rnds 10 through 15: Rep Rnds 8 and 9 three times.

Rnd 16: Rep Rnd 8.

Rnd 17: Ch 1, 5 sc in joining ch-10 lp; * ch 4, sl st in 4th ch from hook: picot made; in next lp work (5 sc, picot as before, 5 sc); rep from * 8 times more; picot as before; 5 sc in next lp; picot as before; join in first sc. Finish off and weave in ends. Set aside.

WINGS (make 2)
Ch 4.

Row 1: 8 dc in 4th ch from hook (3 skipped chs count as a dc): 9 dc; ch 6, turn.

Row 2: Sk first sc, sc in next dc: beg ch-6 lp made; * ch 4, sc in next dc; rep from * 5 times more; ch 3, trc in next dc: ch-6 lp made: 6 ch-4 lps and 2 ch-6 lps; ch 7, turn.

Row 3: Sc in next ch-6 lp: beg ch-7 lp made; * ch 5, sc in next ch-4 lp; rep from * 5 times more; ch 4, trc in next ch-6 lp: ch-7 lp made; ch 8, turn.

Row 4: Sc in next ch-7 lp: beg ch-8 lp made; * ch 6, sc in next ch-5 lp; rep from * 5 times more; ch 5, trc in next ch-7 lp: ch-8 lp made; ch 9, turn.

Row 5: Sc in next ch-8 lp: beg ch-9 lp made; * ch 7, sc in next ch-6 lp; rep from * 5 times more; ch 6, trc in next ch-8 lp: ch-9 lp made; ch 13, turn.

Row 6: Sc in next ch-9 lp: beg ch-13 lp made; * ch 10, sc in next ch-7 lp: ch-10 lp made; rep from * 5 times more; ch 10, trc in next ch-9 lp: ch-13 lp made; ch 12, turn.

Row 7: Sl st in 4th ch from hook: picot made; ch 4, sc in next ch-13 lp: beg picot lp made; * ch 8, sl st in 4th ch from hook: picot made; ch 4, sc in next lp; rep from * 6 times more: 8 picot lps; ch 12, turn.

Row 8: * Sk next picot lp, sc in next sc, ch 12; rep from * 6 times more; sk next 4 chs, next picot, and next 4 chs; sc in next ch: 8 ch-12 lps; ch 1, turn.

Row 9: * 12 sc in next ch-12 lp; ch 4, sl st in 4th ch from hook: picot made; rep from * 6 times more; 12 sc in next ch-12 lp. Finish off and weave in ends. Set aside.

ARMS
Work same as for Merrie on page 143.

HAIR
Ch 6, join to form a ring.

Rnd 1: Ch 1, 10 sc in ring; join in bl of first sc: 10 sc.

Rnd 2: Ch 1, 2 sc in same lp as joining; working in bls only, sc in each rem sc; join in first sc: 20 sc.

Rnd 3: * Ch 20, sl st in next sc; rep from * 18 times more; ch 20; join in first sl st: 20 ch-20 lps.

Rnd 4: In fl of first sc of Rnd 1 work (sl st, ch 15, sl st, ch 15, sl st); * ch 15, in fl of next sc work (sl st, ch 15, sl st); rep from * 8 times more: 20 ch-15 lps. Finish off and weave in ends.

HALO
Ch 6, join to form ring.

Rnd 1: Ch 3 (counts as a dc), 15 dc in ring; join in 3rd ch of beg ch-3: 16 dc.

Rnd 2: Ch 6 (counts as a trc and a ch-2 sp); * trc in next dc, ch 2; rep from * 14 times more; join in 4th ch of beg ch-6. Finish off and weave in ends.

Starching Instructions

SKIRT
To have the proper angle for flying Angel, place a wooden spoon with spoon portion in bottom of a heavy glass, with handle tilted at a 45" angle. On end of spoon handle, shape a form with aluminum foil for the skirt. Remove aluminum form and roll it on the table using pressure to even out any bumps and dips. Place crocheted skirt on form and check the fit.

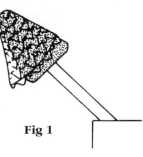

Fig 1

Following Starching Instuctions on page 132, moisten skirt in stiffening solution and place on aluminum form . Adjust and pin skirt to form, keeping shells, picots, rows or stitches in straight line. Keep lower edge of skirt that is on top of form pinned close to form, and let edge on bottom of form hang slightly away (**Fig 1**).

HEAD/OVERBLOUSE AND ARMS
Bend arms at elbows and place on top of skirt. (Do not use stiffening solution on arms.) Pin in place. Moisten overblouse only, without moistening head, and place on top of arms and skirt. Shape overblouse to fit over arms and top of skirt, and flatten against skirt, in back. Tilt head slightly toward back and pin in front of chin to hold in place. Let dry.

HAIR
Moisten hair with stiffening solution and position on head. Using a pin or toothpick, twist ends of the longest lps once, and pin in place. For bangs, twist once and bend ends of lps back and pin in place. For shorter lps, twist once and pin in place. Let dry thoroughly.

WINGS
Place wings on pinning board after moistening with stiffening solution and pin to shape. Let dry. Remove wings from pinning board and moisten with water, using fingertips, on each tip of wings. Pin wings on Angel. Using a 15" length of thread, thread through top outside lp of each side of wing and tie thread ends together, adjusting the wings to desired curvature (**Fig 2**). Let dry thoroughly.

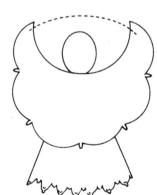

Fig 2

HALO
Place halo on pinning board after moistening with stiffening solution and pin to desired shape.

Finishing
After all pieces are thoroughly dry, glue arms, head/overblouse, halo and wings into desired position and let dry. Trace the horn pattern onto gold cardboard. Cut out. Position arms and glue horn into place.

Horn Pattern

145

Small Angel, Carolee

SIZE:
About 6" tall
MATERIALS:
Bedspread-weight crochet cotton,
   one 225-yd ball white
Size 7 steel crochet hook, or size required for gauge
small amount of polyester fiberfill (for head)
TRIMMINGS:
one 12" white chenille stem (for arms)
starching and blocking supplies, see page 132
2" square piece gold cardboard (for hymnal)
2" wide length cardboard (for wrapping hair)
craft glue
GAUGE:
10 dc = 1"
4 dc rows = 1"

Instructions

HEAD
Work same as for Merrie, page 142, through Rnd 13.

OVERBLOUSE
Rnd 14: Ch 1, 2 sc in same sc as joining; 2 sc in each rem sc; join in first sc: 24 sc.

Rnd 15: Ch 4 (counts as a trc on this and following rnds), in same sc as joining work (trc, ch 1, 2 trc): beg shell made; * ch 3, sk next 3 sc, in next sc work (2 trc, ch 1, 2 trc): shell made; rep from * 4 times more; ch 3; join in 4th ch of beg ch-4: 6 shells.

Rnd 16: Sl st in next trc and in next ch-1 sp; in same sp work beg shell; * ch 3, sc in next ch-3 lp, ch 3, in ch-1 sp of next shell work shell; rep from * 4 times more; ch 3, sc in next ch-3 lp, ch 3; join in 4th ch of beg ch-4: 6 shells.

Rnd 17: Sl st in next trc and in next ch-1 sp; ch 4, in same sp work (2 trc, ch 2, 3 trc): beg 6-trc shell made; * ch 3, in ch-1 sp of next shell work (3 trc, ch 2, 3 trc): 6-trc shell made; rep from * 4 times more; ch 3; join in 4th ch of beg ch-4: six 6-trc shells.

Rnd 18: Sl st in next 2 trc and in next ch-2 sp; in same sp work beg 6-trc shell; * † ch 3, sc in next ch-3 lp, ch 3 †, in ch-2 sp of next shell work 6-trc shell; rep from * 4 times more, then rep from † to † once; join in 4th ch of beg ch-4.

Rnd 19: Ch 1, sc in same ch as joining and in next 2 trc; * 3 sc in next ch-2 sp; sc in next 3 trc, 3 sc in next ch-3 lp; ch 4, sl st in 4th ch from hook: picot made; 3 sc in next ch-3 lp; sc in next 3 trc; rep from * 5 times more, ending last rep without working last 3 sc; join in first sc. Finish off and weave in ends. Set aside.

SKIRT
Ch 12, join to form a ring.

Rnd 1: Ch 3 (counts as a dc), 24 dc in ring; join in 3rd ch of beg ch-3: 25 dc.

Rnd 2: Ch 4 (counts as a trc), in same ch as joining work (trc, ch 1, 2 trc): beg shell made; * ch 4, sk next 4 dc, in next dc work (2 trc, ch 1, 2 trc): shell made; rep from * 3 times more; ch 4; join in 4th ch of beg ch-4: 5 shells.

Rnd 3: Sl st in next trc and in next ch-1 sp; beg shell in same sp; * † ch 4, sc in next ch-4 lp, ch 4 †, in ch-1 sp of next shell work shell: shell in shell made; rep from * 3 times more, then rep from † to † once; join in 4th ch of beg ch-4.

Rnd 4: Sl st in next trc and in next ch-1 sp; beg shell in same sp; * ch 6, shell in next shell; rep from * 3 times more; ch 6; join in 4th ch of beg ch-4.

Rnd 5: Sl st in next trc and in next ch-1 sp; beg shell in same sp; * † ch 4, sc in next ch-6 lp, ch 4 †, shell in next shell; rep from * 3 times more, then rep from † to † once; join in 4th ch of beg ch-4.

Rnds 6 and 7: Rep Rnds 4 and 5.

Rnd 8: Sl st in next trc and in next ch-1 sp; beg shell in same sp; * ch 8, shell in next shell; rep from * 3 times more; ch 8; join in 4th ch of beg ch-4.

Rnd 9: Sl st in next trc and in next ch-1 sp; beg shell in same sp; * † ch 6, sc in next ch-8 lp, ch 6 †, shell in next shell; rep from * 3 times more, then rep from † to † once; join in 4th ch of beg ch-4.

146

Rnd 10: Sl st in next trc and in next ch-1 sp; ch 4, in same ch as joining work (2 trc, ch 2, 3 trc): beg 6-trc shell made; * ch 8, in ch-1 sp of next shell work (3 trc, ch 2, 3 trc): 6-trc shell made; rep from * 3 times more; ch 8; join in 4th ch of beg ch-4.

Rnd 11: Sl st in next 2 trc and in next ch-2 sp; ch 4, in same sp work (3 trc, ch 2, 4 trc): beg 8-trc shell made; * † ch 6, sc in next ch-8 lp, ch 6 †, in ch-2 sp of next shell work (4 trc, ch 2, 4 trc): 8-trc shell made; rep from * 3 times more, then rep from † to † once; join in 4th ch of beg ch-4: five 8-trc shells.

Rnd 12: Sl st in next 3 trc and in next ch-2 sp; beg 8-trc shell in same sp; * † ch 4, sk next ch-6 lp, in next sc work (trc, ch 2, trc, ch 2, trc); ch 4 †, in ch-2 sp of next shell work 8-trc shell; rep from * 3 times more, then rep from † to † once; join in 4th ch of beg ch-4.

Rnd 13: Ch 1, sc in same ch as joining and in next 3 trc; * 3 sc in next ch-2 sp; sc in next 4 trc, 4 sc in next ch-4 lp; sk next trc, 2 sc in next ch-2 sp; ch 4, sl st in 4th ch from hook: picot made; sk next trc, 2 sc in next ch-2 sp; sk next trc, 4 sc in next ch-4 lp; sc in next 4 trc; rep from * 4 times more, ending last rep without working last 4 sc; join in first sc. Finish off and weave in ends. Set aside.

WINGS
RIGHT-HAND SIDE:
Ch 15.

Row 1: Sc in 2nd ch from hook and in each rem ch: 14 sc; ch 4 (counts as first sc and ch-3 lp on following row), turn.

Row 2: Sc in first sc; * ch 3, sk next sc, sc in next sc; rep from * 5 times more; ch 3, sc in next sc: 8 ch-3 lps; ch 6 (counts as first sc and ch-5 lp on following rows), turn.

Row 3: Sc in next ch-3 lp, * ch 5, sc in next lp; rep from * 6 times more: 8 ch-5 lps; ch 6, turn.

Row 4: In next ch-5 lp work (sc, ch 5, sc); * ch 5, sc in next ch-5 lp; rep from * 6 times more: 9 ch-5 lps; ch 6, turn.

Row 5: Sc in next ch-5 lp, * ch 5, sc in next lp; rep from * 7 times more; ch 6, turn.

Row 6: In next ch-5 lp work (sc, ch 5, sc); * ch 5, sc in next lp; rep from * 7 times more; 10 ch-5 lps; ch 6, turn.

Row 7: Sc in next ch-5 lp; * ch 5, sc in next ch-5 lp; rep from * 8 times more; ch 6, turn.

Row 8: Sc in next ch-5 lp; * ch 5, sc in next lp; rep from * 8 times more; ch 7 (counts as first sc and ch-6 lp on following row), turn.

Row 9 (right side): Sc in next ch-5 lp; * ch 6, sc in next lp; rep from * 8 times more (ending at top of wing): 10 ch-6 lps. Finish off and weave in ends.

LEFT-HAND SIDE:
Hold wing with wrong side facing you and beg ch at top; join thread in first unused lp of beg ch.

Row 1: Ch 1, sc in same lp as joining; working in rem unused lps, sc in each rem lp: 14 sc; ch 4, turn.

Rows 2 through 9: Rep Rows 2 through 9 of right-hand side.

WING EDGING:
Hold wing with right side facing you; join thread in side of sc on right-hand side of center of wings; ch 1, sc in same sc as joining and in side of next sc (left-hand side of wing); working along outside edge of wings, 3 sc in next ch-3 lp (side of Row 2); † 7 sc in each of next 3 ch-5 lps; 7 sc in each of next 10 ch-6 lps of Row 9; 7 sc in each of next 3 ch-5 lps; 3 sc in next ch-3 lp (side of Row 2) †; 3 sc in next ch-3 lp (side of Row 2 of right-hand side of wing); rep from † to † once; join in first sc. Finish off and weave in ends. Set aside.

ARMS
Work same as for Merrie, see page 143.

HALO
Ch 6, join to form a ring.

Rnd 1: Ch 3 (counts as a dc), 17 dc in ring; join in 3rd ch of beg ch-3: 18 dc.

Rnd 2: Ch 4 (counts as a trc), in same ch as joining work (trc, ch 2, 2 trc): beg shell made; * ch 2, sk next 2 dc, in next dc work (2 trc, ch 2, 2 trc): shell made; rep from * 4 times more; ch 2, sk next 2 dc; join in 4th ch of beg ch-4: 6 shells.

Rnd 3: Ch 1, sc in same ch as joining; * sc in next trc, sc in next ch-2 sp; ch 4, sl st in 4th ch from hook: picot made; sc in same ch-2 sp; sc in next 2 trc, 2 sc in next ch-2 sp; sc in next trc; rep from * 5 times more, ending last rep without working last sc; join in first sc. Finish off and weave in ends. Set aside.

Starching Instructions
SKIRT
Following Starching Instructions on page 132, moisten skirt with stiffening solution and place on cone. Pin lps in place, and pin picots on bottom edge. Pin shells on last row, and at same time, leaving pins in place, lift shells away from cone.

HEAD/OVERBLOUSE AND ARMS
Bend arms and place on top of skirt. (Do not moisten arms with stiffening solution.) Moisten overblouse only without moistening head, and place on top of arms and skirt. Shape overblouse to fit over arms and top of skirt, and flatten against skirt in back.

HAIR
Wrap thread around a 2" piece of cardboard about 60 times. Slip a 6" thread under the wrapped thread at

one end of cardboard and tie firmly. Cut all lps at opposite end (**Fig 1**). Moisten hair with stiffening solution and place at center top of head. Use pin or toothpick and draw through strands of thread to separate and position, making hair flat against back of head (for ease of wings placement later).

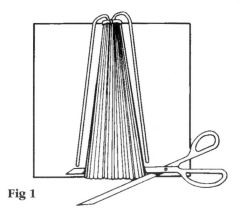

Fig 1

WINGS AND HALO
Place wings and halo on pinning board after moistening with stiffening solution, and pin flat to board.

Finishing

After all pieces are thoroughly dry, glue arms, head/overblouse, halo, and wings into desired position and let dry. For hymnal, draw a 1" x 1 1/2" rectangle on gold cardboard and cut out. Fold cardboard in half on long edge. Position arms and glue hymnbook into place.

Nativity in Filet
designed by Anis Duncan

This magnificent design revives the lovely old art of filet crochet. This is not a difficult project, but does require a good bit of time to complete—time worth investing in a piece sure to become a family heirloom.

SIZE:
About 23" wide x 36" long
MATERIALS:
Bedspread-weight crochet cotton,
   five 225-yd balls white
Size 5 steel crochet hook, or size required for gauge
starching and blocking supplies, see page 132
24" dowel rod, 1/4" diameter
GAUGE:
8 dc = 1"
4 dc rows = 1"

Instructions

FILET CROCHET CHART
Filet design is worked from a chart of squares. On each odd-numbered row (right side of work), work chart from right to left; on each even-numbered row (wrong side of work), work chart from left to right.

On each row of chart:

Work each vertical line as one dc (**Fig 1**). At beg of row, work the first vertical line as ch 3 (counts as a dc). Each following vertical line (dc) is worked in dc (vertical line) in row below, ending by working last vertical line (dc) in top of ch 3 in row below.

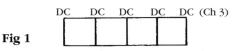

Fig 1

Work each open sp between 2 vertical lines (dc) as one ch (**Fig 2**).

Fig 2

Work each shaded sp between 2 vertical lines (dc) as one dc (**Fig 3**). For each shaded sp, work in row below either into ch-1 sp (open sp) or into dc (shaded sp).

Fig 3

Note: *Remember to work each ch-1 loosely. Beg with Row 5 of chart and work through last row of chart. At end of last row, ch 1, turn.*

TOP EDGING:

Row 1: Sc in each dc across: 183 sc; ch 10, turn.

Row 2: Sk next 2 sc, * sc in next 3 sc, ch 10, sk next sc; rep from * to last sc; sc in next sc. Finish off and weave in all ends.

FINISHING

Following Starching Instructions on page 132, starch hanging.

When dry, insert dowel rod through ch-10 lps at top of hanging.

WALL HANGING

Ch 185 loosely.

Row 1 (right side): Dc in 4th ch (3 skipped chs count as a dc) from hook and in each rem ch: 183 dc; ch 3 (counts as first dc on following rows), turn.

Row 2: Dc in next 2 dc, ch 1 loosely, sk next dc, dc in next dc; * ch 1 loosely, sk next dc, dc in next 3 dc; rep from * to last 6 dc; (ch 1 loosely, sk next dc, dc in next dc) twice; dc in next 2 dc; ch 3, turn.

Row 3: Dc in next 2 dc, (ch 1 loosely, sk next ch-1 sp, dc in next dc) twice; * ch 1 loosely, sk next dc, dc in next dc, ch 1 loosely, sk next ch-1 sp, dc in next dc; rep from * 42 times more; ch 1 loosely, sk next ch-1 sp, dc in next 3 dc; ch 3, turn.

Row 4: Dc in next 2 dc, in next ch-1 sp and in next dc, * ch 1 loosely, sk next ch-1 sp, dc in next dc; rep from * across to last ch-1 sp, dc in next ch-1 sp and in next 3 dc; ch 3, turn.

Now refer to chart in **Fig 4**. You have just completed the first 4 rows; compare your work to the chart. From this point on, you will work only from the chart.

Row 4 -
Row 2 -

Fig 4

-Row 3
-Row 1
Start

149

Hiking Boot Stocking

designed by Carol Wilson Mansfield and Mary Thomas

This hiking boot stocking with a real shoelace is a great gift for the outdoors person in your life. It's made in easy single crochet.

SIZE:
About 7" wide (across top of cuff) x 11" long
  (from folded edge of cuff to base of heel)
MATERIALS:
Craft and rug yarn in 60-yd skeins, 3 skeins rust;
  35 yds steel gray; 6 yds black; 4 yds green; 4 yds red
Size H aluminum crochet hook, or size required
  for gauge
ten 1/2" gold metal D-rings
54" red sport lace
size 18 tapestry needle
GAUGE:
7 sc = 2"
7 sc rows = 2"

Instructions

Starting at top with rust and leaving a 30" end for sewing back seam, ch 45.

Row 1 (right side): Sc in 2nd ch from hook and in each rem ch: 44 sc; ch 1, turn.

Row 2: Sc in each sc; ch 1, turn.

Rows 3 through 8: Rep Row 2.

Note: On following rows use small safety pin or contrasting piece of yarn to mark indicated stitch for attaching D-ring.

Row 9 (marking row): Sc in next 17 sc, mark last sc; sc in next 11 sc, mark last sc; sc in next 16 sc; ch 1, turn.

Rows 10 through 12: Rep Row 2.

Row 13: Sc in next 11 sc, dec over next 2 sc (to work dec: draw up lp in each of next 2 sc, YO and draw through all 3 lps on hook: dec made); sc in next 18 sc, dec as before; sc in next 11 sc: 42 sc; ch 1, turn.

Rows 14 through 16: Rep Row 2.

Row 17 (marking row): Sc in next 16 sc, mark last sc; sc in next 11 sc, mark last sc; sc in next 15 sc; ch 1, turn.

Row 18: Rep Row 2.

Row 19: Sc in next 10 sc, dec; sc in next 18 sc, dec; sc in next 10 sc: 40 sc; ch 1, turn.

Rows 20 through 24: Rep Row 2.

Row 25 (marking row): Sc in next 4 sc, dec; sc in next 5 sc, dec; sc in next 2 sc, mark last sc; sc in next 11 sc, mark last sc; sc in next sc, dec; sc in next 5 sc, dec; sc in next 4 sc: 36 sc; ch 1, turn.

Rows 26 through 30: Rep Row 2. At end of Row 30, do not ch-1. Finish off.

INSTEP:
Hold boot with right side facing you and Row 30 at top; join rust in 7th sc of Row 30.

Row 1: Ch 1, sc in same sc as joining and in next 22 sc: 23 sc; ch 1, turn, leaving rem 6 sc unworked.

Row 2: Sk first sc, sc in next 22 sc: 22 sc; ch 1, turn.

Row 3 (marking row): Sk first sc, sc in next 5 sc, mark last sc; sc in next 11 sc, mark last sc; sc in next 5 sc: 21 sc; ch 1, turn.

Row 4: Sk first sc, sc in each rem sc; ch 1, turn.

Rows 5 through 10: Rep Row 4. At end of Row 10: 14 sc.

Row 11 (marking row): Sc in next 2 sc, mark last sc; sc in next 11 sc, mark last sc; sc in next sc: 14 sc; ch 1, turn.

Row 12: Sc in each sc; ch 1, turn.

Rows 13 through 16: Rep Row 4. At end of Row 16: 10 sc for toe edge. Finish off.

FOOT:
Hold boot with right side facing you and instep at top; join rust in first sc at right outer edge (Row 30).

Row 1 (right side): Ch 1, sc in same sc as joining; 2 sc in next sc; sc in next 4 sc, 2 sc in next sc at inside corner (already worked); working across right edge of instep, 2 sc in first row; sc in next 14 rows, leaving last row unworked; working across toe edge, dec; sc in next 6 sc, dec; working across left edge of instep, sc in next 14 rows, 2 sc in next row and in next sc at inside corner (already worked); sc in next 4 sc, 2 sc in next sc; sc in next sc: 58 sc; ch 1, turn.

Row 2: Sc in each sc; ch 1, turn.

Row 3: Sc in next 25 sc, dec; sc in next 4 sc, dec; sc in next 25 sc: 56 sc; ch 1, turn.

Row 4: Rep Row 2.

Row 5: Sc in next 25 sc, dec 3 times; sc in next 25 sc: 53 sc; ch 1, turn.

Row 6: Rep Row 2.

Row 7: Sc in next sc, dec; sc in next 23 sc; dec; sc in next 22 sc; dec; sc in next sc: 50 sc; ch 1, turn.

Row 8: Sc in next 23 sc, dec twice; sc in next 23 sc: 48 sc; change to black by drawing lp through; cut rust; ch 2, turn.

Row 9: Dc in next 7 sc, hdc in next sc, sc in each sc to last 8 sc, hdc in next sc, dc in next 7 sc. Finish off, leaving an 18" length for sewing.

ASSEMBLING

With tapestry needle and black, sew bottom seam with overcast st (see page 131). With rust, sew heel and back seam in same manner.

CUFF:

Hold boot with wrong side facing you; join gray in seam at top edge.

Note: Cuff is worked in rnds; do not turn.

Rnd 1: Ch 1, sc in next 44 sts; join in first sc: 44 sc.

Rnd 2: Ch 1, sc in same sc as joining and in each rem sc; join in first sc.

Rnd 3: Rep Rnd 2.

Rnd 4: Ch 1, 2 sc in same sc as joining; sc in next 10 sc, * 2 sc in next sc; sc in next 10 sc; rep from * twice more; join in first sc: 48 sc.

Rnds 5 and 6: Rep Rnd 2. At end of Rnd 6, change to green by drawing lp through; do not cut gray.

Rnd 7: Rep Rnd 2. At end of rnd, change to red by drawing lp through; cut green.

Rnd 8: Rep Rnd 2. At end of rnd, change to gray by drawing lp through; cut red.

Rnd 9: Rep Rnd 2. Finish off and weave in all ends.

Turn boot to right side. Fold cuff to right side of boot.

LACE:

With rust, sew one D-ring to each marked st at center front, having curved portion of rings facing center of boot. Lace red sport lace up front of boot through rings and tie into a bow at top.

LOOP:

With gray, ch 15, sl st in 15th ch from hook. Finish off, leaving a 6" end for sewing. Sew loop to top center back of boot.

Snowy Forecast

designed by Mary Thomas

Even if there's no snow this Christmas, you can enjoy the beauty of intricate, lacy snowflakes.
Made from crochet cotton and then stiffened, these snowflakes make perfect tree ornaments,
package tie-ons or decorations to hang in a window.

Snowflake #1

SIZE:
About 3" diameter
MATERIALS:
Bedspread-weight crochet cotton, 10 yds white
Size 7 steel crochet hook

Instructions

Ch 8, join to form a ring.

Rnd 1 (right side): Ch 4 (counts as a trc on this and following rnds), 23 trc in ring; join in 4th ch of beg ch-4: 24 trc.

Rnd 2: Ch 3 (count as a dc), dc in same ch as joining; * † ch 6, sl st in 5th ch from hook: picot made †; rep from † to † twice more; ch 1, sk next 3 trc, 2 dc in next trc; rep from * 4 times more, then rep from † to † 3 times; join in 3rd ch of beg ch-3: six 3-picot lps.

Rnd 3: Ch 4, trc in next dc; * † picot 5 times; ch 1 †, trc in next 2 dc; rep from * 4 times more, then rep from † to † once; join in 4th ch of beg ch-4; ch 20: hanging lp made; sl st in next trc.

Finish off and weave in ends.

Starch and block out to size following Starching Instructions on page 132.

Snowflake #2

SIZE:
About 5 1/4" from point to point
MATERIALS:
Bedspread-weight crochet cotton, 17 yds white
Size 7 steel crochet hook

PATTERN STITCHES
Double triple crochet (dtrc):
YO 3 times, draw up lp in next st or lp, (YO and draw through 2 lps on hook) 4 times: dtrc made.

Triple triple crochet (tr trc):
YO 4 times, draw up lp in next st, (YO and draw through 2 lps on hook) 5 times: tr trc made.

Instructions

Ch 6, join to form a ring.

Rnd 1 (right side): Ch 1, 12 sc in ring; join in first sc: 12 sc.

Rnd 2: Ch 16, sl st in same sc as joining; * ch 16, sl st in next sc; rep from * 9 times more; ch 7; join with a tr trc (see Pattern Stitches) in next sc: 12 ch 16 lps.

Rnd 3: * Ch 6, sc in next ch-16 lp; rep from * 10 times more; ch 3; join with a dc in top of joining tr trc of prev rnd.

Rnd 4: Ch 6 (counts as a dc and ch-3 lp), 3 dc over joining dc of prev rnd; * in next ch-6 lp work (3 dc, ch 3, 3 dc); rep from * 10 times more; 2 dc in next ch-3 lp (next to beg ch-6); join in 3rd ch of beg ch-6.

Rnd 5: Sl st in next ch-3 lp; ch 5 (counts as a dtrc), in same lp work [dtrc (see Pattern Stitches), ch 5, 2 dtrc, ch 11, 2 dtrc, ch 5, 2 dtrc]; * † ch 5, sk next two 3-dc groups, sc in next ch-3 lp, ch 5, sk next two 3-dc groups †, in next ch-3 lp work (2 dtrc, ch 5, 2 dtrc, ch 11, 2 dtrc, ch 2, 2 dtrc); rep from * 4 times more, then rep from † to † once; join in 5th ch of beg ch-5.

Finish off and weave in ends.

Starch and block out to size following Starching Instructions on page 132.

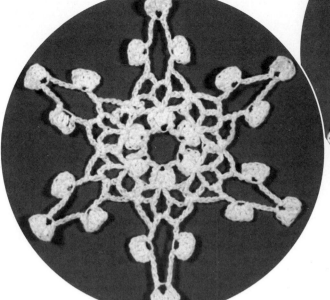

Snowflake #3

SIZE:
About 4 1/2" from point to point
MATERIALS:
Bedspread-weight crochet cotton, 12 yds white
Size 7 steel crochet hook

Instructions

Ch 4.

Rnd 1 (right side)**:** In 4th ch from hook work (3 dc, ch 3, sl st): beg petal made; * ch 6, in 4th ch from hook work (3 dc, ch 3, sl st): petal made; rep from * 4 times more; ch 2; join in same ch as beg petal made, being careful not to twist sts: 6 petals. Finish off.

Rnd 2: Join in 2nd dc of any petal; ch 8 (counts as a dc and a ch-5 lp), in same dc as joining work (dc, ch 5, dc, ch 5, dc); * in 2nd dc of next petal work (dc, ch 5, dc, ch 5, dc, ch 5, dc); rep from * 4 times more; join in 3rd ch of beg ch-8: 18 ch-5 lps.

Rnd 3: Ch 1, sc in next ch-5 lp, * ch 4, dc in next ch-5 lp; ch 6, in 4th ch from hook work (3 dc, ch 3, sl st): beg petal made; † ch 9, in 4th ch from hook work (3 dc, ch 3, sl st): petal made †; rep from † to † once more; ch 2, dc in same ch-5 lp; ch 4, sc in next two ch-5 lps; rep from * around, ending last rep without working last sc; join in first sc.

Finish off and weave in ends.

Starch and block out to size following Starching Instructions on page 132.

Snowflake #4

SIZE:
About 5" from point to point
MATERIALS:
Bedspread-weight crochet cotton, 16 yds white
Size 7 steel crochet hook

Instructions

Ch 6, join to form a ring.

Rnd 1: Ch 3 (counts as a dc on this and following rnds), 17 dc in ring; join in 3rd ch of beg ch-3: 18 dc.

Rnd 2: Ch 3, dc in next dc; * ch 4, sk next dc, dc in next 2 dc; rep from * 4 times more; ch 4, sk next dc; join in 3rd ch of beg ch-3: six 2-dc groups.

Rnd 3: Ch 3, 2 dc in next dc; * ch 5, sk next ch-4 lp, dc in next dc, 2 dc in next dc; rep from * 4 times more; ch 5, sk next ch-4 lp; join in 3rd ch of beg ch-3: six 3-dc groups.

Rnd 4: Ch 3, 2 dc in next dc; dc in next dc, * ch 6, sk next ch-5 lp, dc in next dc, 2 dc in next dc; dc in next dc; rep from * 4 times more; ch 6, sk next ch-5 lp; join in 3rd ch of beg ch-3: six 4-dc groups.

Rnd 5: Ch 3, 2 dc in each of next 3 dc; * ch 6, sk next ch-6 lp, dc in next dc, 2 dc in each of next 3 dc; rep from * 4 times more; ch 6, sk next ch-6 lp; join in 3rd ch of beg ch-3: six 7-dc groups.

Rnd 6: Ch 3, dc in next 2 dc, * ch 6, sk next dc, dc in next 3 dc, ch 6, sk next ch-6 lp, dc in next 3 dc; rep from * 4 times more; ch 6, sk next dc, dc in next 3 dc, ch 6, sk next ch-6 lp; join in 3rd ch of beg ch-3.

Rnd 7: Ch 3, dc in next 2 dc, * ch 3, in next ch-6 lp work (dc, ch 12, dc); ch 3, dc in next 3 dc, ch 3, sc in next ch-6 lp, ch 3, dc in next 3 dc; rep from * 4 times more, ending last rep without working last 3 dc; join in 3rd ch of beg ch-3.

Finish off and weave in ends. Starch and block out to size following Starching Instructions on page 132.

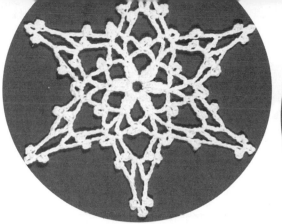

Snowflake #5

SIZE:
About 5" from point to point

MATERIALS:
Bedspread-weight crochet cotton, 12 yds white
Size 7 steel crochet hook

PATTERN STITCHES
Beg Cluster (beg CL):
Ch 4, keeping last lp of each trc on hook, 2 trc in ring, YO and draw through all 3 lps on hook: beg CL made.
Cluster (CL):
Keeping last lp of each trc on hook, 3 trc in ring; YO and draw through all 4 lps on hook: CL made.

Instructions

Ch 8, join to form a ring.

Rnd 1: Beg CL (see Pattern Stitches) in ring; * ch 7, CL (see Pattern Stitches) in ring; rep from * 4 times more; ch 3; join with a trc in top of beg CL: 6 CLs.

Rnd 2: Ch 4, sc in top of joining trc: picot made; * ch 6, sc in top of next CL, ch 6, in 4th ch of next ch-7 lp work (sc, ch 4, sc): picot made; rep from * 4 times more; ch 6, sc in top of next CL, ch 3; join with a trc in top of joining trc of prev rnd.

Rnd 3: * † (Ch 7, sl st in 4th ch from hook) twice: 2 ch-3 picots made; ch 3, sk next picot, sc in next ch-6 lp †; ch 3, sc in next ch-6 lp; rep from * 4 times more, then rep from † to † once; ch 1, sk ch-3 of next lp; join with a dc in top of joining trc of prev rnd.

Rnd 4: Ch 1, in top of joining dc work (sc, ch 4, sc); * † ch 7, sl st in 4th ch from hook: picot made; ch 3, sk next picot, trc in 2nd ch of next ch-3 lp (between picots); ch 7, sl st in 4th ch from hook: picot made; (ch 4, sl st in 4th ch from hook) twice: 2 picots made; ch 3, trc in same ch as prev trc made, ch 7, sl st in 4th ch from hook: picot made; ch 3 †, sk next picot, next ch-3 lp and next sc; in 2nd ch of next ch-3 lp work (sc, ch 4, sc); rep from * 4 times more, then rep from † to † once; join in first sc.

Finish off and weave in ends.

Starch and block out to size following Starching Instructions on page 132.

Snowflake #6

SIZE:
About 5 1/2" from point to point

MATERIALS:
Bedspread-weight crochet cotton, 23 yds white
Size 7 steel crochet hook

Instructions

Rnd 1: * Ch 4, sl st in 4th ch from hook: picot made; rep from * 5 times more; join in ch at base of first picot: 6 picots.

Rnd 2: Ch 3 (counts as a dc on this and following rnds), dc in same ch as joining; * picot twice; 2 dc in ch at base of next picot; rep from * 4 times more; picot twice; join in 3rd ch of beg ch-3.

Rnd 3: Ch 3, 2 dc in next dc; * picot 3 times; sk next 2 picots, dc in next dc, 2 dc in next dc; rep from * 4 times more; picot 3 times; join in 3rd ch of beg ch-3.

Rnd 4: Ch 3, * 2 dc in next dc; dc in next dc; picot 4 times; sk next 3 picots, dc in next dc; rep from * 5 times more, ending last rep without working last dc; join in 3rd ch of beg ch-3.

Rnd 5: Ch 3, * dc in next dc, 2 dc in next dc; dc in next dc; picot 5 times; sk next 4 picots, dc in next dc; rep from * 5 times more, ending last rep without working last dc; join in 3rd ch of beg ch-3.

Rnd 6: Ch 3, * dc in next dc, 2 dc in next dc; dc in next 2 dc; picot 6 times; sk next 5 picots, dc in next dc; rep from * 5 times more, ending last rep without working last dc; join in 3rd ch of beg ch-3.

Rnd 7: Ch 3, dc in next 5 dc, * picot 4 times; sk next 2 picots, trc in next picot, picot 7 times; trc in next picot, picot 4 times; dc in next 6 dc; rep from * 5 times more, ending last rep without working last 6 dc; join in 3rd ch of beg ch-3.

Finish off and weave in ends.

Starch and block out to size following Starching Instructions on page 132.

Picot-Roofed Cottage

SIZE:
About 2 1/2" tall
MATERIALS:
Bedspread-weight crochet cotton, 50 yds white
Size 7 steel crochet hook, or size required for gauge
starching and blocking supplies, see page 132
GAUGE:
8 dc = 1"
4 dc rows = 1"

Note: Both stitch and row gauge must be accurate for pieces to fit blocking guide.

Instructions

COTTAGE FRONT/BACK (make 2)
Ch 19.

Row 1: Sc in 2nd ch from hook and in each rem ch: 18 sc; ch 3 (counts as first dc on following rows), turn.

Row 2: Dc in next 2 sc, ch 3, sk next 3 sc, dc in next 12 sc: 15 dc and one ch-3 lp; ch 3, turn.

Row 3: Dc in next 2 dc, (ch 1, sk next dc, dc in next dc) 3 times; dc in next 3 dc, ch 3, sk next ch-3 lp, dc in next 3 dc: 12 dc, 3 ch-1 sps, and one ch-3 lp; ch 3, turn.

Row 4: Dc in next 2 dc, ch 3, sk next ch-3 lp, dc in next 4 dc, (ch 1, sk next ch-1 sp, sc in next dc) 3 times; dc in next 2 dc; ch 3, turn.

Row 5: Dc in next 2 dc, (dc in next ch-1 sp, dc in next dc) 3 times; dc in next 3 dc, in 2nd ch of next ch-3 lp work (dc, ch 3, dc); dc in next 3 dc; ch 3, turn.

Row 6: Dc in next 2 dc, sk next dc, 3 hdc in next ch-3 lp; sk next dc, dc in next 12 dc; ch 1, turn.

Row 7: Sc in each st. Finish off and weave in ends.

Note: Before proceeding, check piece against blocking guide. If piece is either too small or too large to pin edges to guide lines, check your gauge and rework the piece.

COTTAGE SIDE (make 2)
Ch 14.

Row 1: Sc in 2nd ch from hook and in each rem ch: 13 sc; ch 3 (counts as first dc on following rows), turn.

Row 2: Dc in each sc; ch 3, turn.

Row 3: Dc in next 3 dc, (ch 1, sk next dc, dc in next dc) 3 times; dc in next 3 dc: 10 dc and 3 ch-1 sps; ch 3, turn.

Row 4: Dc in next 3 dc, (ch 1, sk next ch-1 sp, dc in next dc) 3 times; dc in next 3 dc; ch 3, turn.

Row 5: Dc in next 3 dc, (dc in next ch-1 sp, dc in next dc) 3 times; dc in next 3 dc: 13 dc; ch 3, turn.

Row 6: Dc in each dc; ch 1, turn.

Row 7: Sc in each dc; ch 1, turn.

Row 8: Dec over next 2 sc (to work dec: draw up lp in each of next 2 sc, YO and draw through all 3 lps on hook: dec made); sc in next 9 sc, dec as before: 11 sc; ch 1, turn.

Row 9: Dec; sc in next 7 sc, dec: 9 sc; ch 1, turn.

Row 10: Dec; sc in next 5 sc, dec: 7 sc; ch 1, turn.

Row 11: Dec; sc in next 3 sc, dec: 5 sc; ch 1, turn.

Row 12: Dec; sc in next sc, dec: 3 sc; ch 1, turn.

Row 13: Keeping last lp of each sc on hook, sc in next 3 sc, YO and draw through all 4 lps on hook. Finish off and weave in ends.

COTTAGE BASE (make 1)
Ch 14.

Row 1: Sc in 2nd ch from hook and in each rem ch: 13 sc; ch 1, turn.

Row 2: Sc in each sc; ch 1, turn.

Rep Row 2 until piece measures 2" long. At end of last row, do not ch 1. Finish off and weave in ends.

COTTAGE DOOR (make 2)
Ch 4.

Row 1: Sc in 2nd ch from hook and in each rem ch: 3 sc; ch 3 (counts as first dc on following rows), turn.

Row 2: Dc in each sc; ch 1, turn.

Row 3: Sc in each dc; ch 3, turn.

Rows 4 and 5: Rep Rows 2 and 3. At end of Row 5, do not ch 3. Finish off and weave in ends.

COTTAGE JOINING
Note: Right side of work is determined by correct placement as follows:

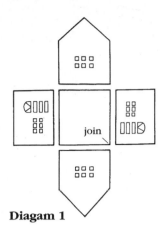

Diagam 1

Place Base on flat surface. With Base in center, place Cottage Sides, Front and Back as shown in **Diagram 1**, carefully placing Front and Back, so that doors will be at opposite ends of the cottage (for front and back doors). With sides tog and carefully matching edges, join Base to Front, Sides and Back in same manner as Church Joining, Row 1 (page 163).

Note: Joining will be worked around base from right to left joining Side, Front, Side, and Back, working in ends of sc rows of base and in unused lps of beg chs of front, sides and back.

PICOT ROOF (make 2)
Ch 22.

Row 1 (right side): Sc in 2nd ch from hook, (ch 5, sk next 4 chs, sc in next ch) 4 times; ch 4 (counts as first dc and ch-1 sp on following rows), turn.

Row 2: * † In 3rd ch of next ch-5 lp work (sc, ch 3, sc): picot made †; ch 5, sk next

sc; rep from * twice more, then rep from † to † once; ch 1, dc in next sc: 4 picots; ch 1, turn.

Row 3: Sc in next dc, * ch 5, sk next picot, in 3rd ch of next ch-5 lp work picot; rep from * twice more; ch 5, sk next picot, sc in 2nd ch of turning ch-4; ch 4, turn.

Row 4: * † In 3rd ch of next ch-5 lp work picot †; ch 5, sk next picot; rep from * twice more, then rep from † to † once; ch 1, dc in next sc; ch 1, turn.

Row 5: Rep Row 3. At end of row, do not ch 4. Finish off and weave in ends.

ROOF JOINING
Hold roof pieces with wrong sides tog and beg ch at top; join thread in first unused lp (base of first sc) of both pieces in top right-hand corner.

Row 1: Ch 1, in same lp as joining work (sc, ch 3, sc): beg picot made; * carefully matching edges, 3 sc in next ch-4 lp; in next lp (base of sc) work (sc, ch 3, sc): picot made; rep from * 3 times more. Finish off and weave in ends.

Finishing

Following Starching Instructions on page 132 and using Blocking Guides for Picot-Roofed Cottage and Picot Roof, starch cottage base with side picots flat along base of cottage and pointing towards sides of cottage. Starch roof with picots in center of roof pointing up. Referring to page 159 for Cottage Door Blocking Guide, starch doors flat. When dry, spray lightly with water until bendable; fold sides along base edge and glue at corners. Glue roof and doors into place.

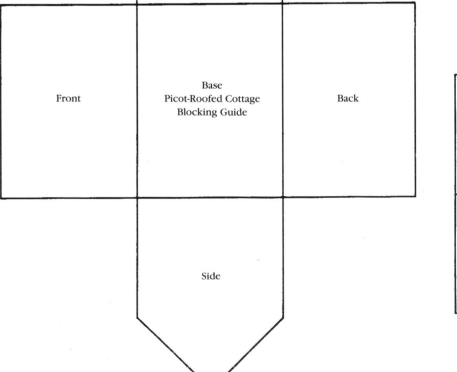

Side

Front

Base
Picot-Roofed Cottage
Blocking Guide

Back

Side

Roof
Picot-Roofed Blocking Guide

center seam

Shell-Roofed Cottage

SIZE:
About 2 1/2" tall
MATERIALS:
Bedspread-weight crochet cotton, 60 yds white
Size 7 steel crochet hook, or size required for gauge
size 18 tapestry needle
starching and blocking supplies, see page 132
GAUGE:
8 dc = 1"
4 dc rows = 1"

Note: Both stitch and row gauge must be accurate for pieces to fit blocking guide.

Instructions

COTTAGE FRONT/BACK (make 2)
Ch 18.

Row 1: Sc in 2nd ch from hook and in each rem ch: 17 sc; ch 3 (counts as first dc on following rows), turn.

Row 2: Dc in next 2 sc, ch 3, sk next 3 sc, dc in next 11 sc: 14 dc and one ch-3 lp; ch 3, turn.

Row 3: Dc in next 2 dc, (ch 2, sk next 2 dc, dc in next dc) twice; dc in next 2 dc, ch 3, sk next ch-3 lp, dc in next 3 dc: 10 dc, 2 ch-2 sps, and one ch-3 lp; ch 3, turn.

Row 4: Dc in next 2 dc, ch 3, sk next ch-3 lp, dc in next 3 dc, (ch 2, sk next ch-2 sp, dc in next dc) twice; dc in next 2 dc; ch 3, turn.

Row 5: Dc in next 2 dc, (2 dc in next ch-2 sp, dc in next dc) twice; dc in next 2 dc, 3 dc in next ch-3 lp; dc in next 3 dc: 17 dc; ch 3, turn.

Row 6: Dc in each dc; ch 3, turn.

Row 7: Dc in each dc. Finish off and weave in ends.

Note: Before proceeding, check piece against blocking guide. If piece is either too small or too large to pin edges to guide lines, check your gauge and rework the piece.

COTTAGE SIDE (make 2)
Ch 14.

Row 1: Sc in 2nd ch from hook and in each rem ch: 13 sc; ch 3 (counts as first dc on following rows), turn.

Row 2: Dc in each sc: 13 dc; ch 3, turn.

Row 3: Dc in next dc, † (ch 1, sk next dc, dc in next dc) twice †; dc in next 2 dc; rep from † to † once; dc in next dc: 9 dc and 4 ch-1 sps; ch 3, turn.

Row 4: Dc in next dc, † (ch 1, sk next ch-1 sp, dc in next dc) twice †; dc in next 2 dc; rep from † to † once; dc in next dc; ch 3, turn.

Row 5: Dc in next dc, † (dc in next ch-1 sp, dc in next dc) twice †; dc in next 2 dc; rep from † to † once; dc in next dc: 13 dc; ch 3, turn.

Row 6: Dc in each dc; ch 1, turn.

Row 7: Rep Row 6.

Row 8: Dec over next 2 dc (to work dec: draw up lp in each of next 2 sts, YO and draw through all 3 lps on hook: dec made); sc in next 9 dc; dec as before: 11 sc; ch 1, turn.

Row 9: Dec; sc in next 7 sc, dec: 9 sc; ch 1, turn.

Row 10: Dec; sc in next 5 sc, dec: 7 sc; ch 1, turn.

Row 11: Dec; sc in next 3 sc, dec: 5 sc; ch 1, turn.

Row 12: Dec; sc in next sc, dec: 3 sc; ch 1, turn.

Row 13: Keeping last lp of each sc on hook, sc in next 3 sc, YO and draw through all 4 lps on hook. Finish off and weave in ends.

COTTAGE BASE (make 1)
Ch 14.

Row 1: Sc in 2nd ch from hook and in each rem ch: 13 sc; ch 1, turn.

Row 2: Sc in each sc; ch 1, turn.

Rep Row 2 until piece measures 2 1/8" long. At end of last row, do not ch 1. Finish off and weave in ends.

COTTAGE DOOR (make 2)
Work same as Cottage Door for Picot-Roofed Cottage, page 158.

COTTAGE JOINING
Note: Right side of work is determined by correct placement as follows:

Place Base on flat surface. With Base in center, place Cottage Sides, Front, and Back as shown in **Diagram 1**, carefully placing doors of Front and Back so that a door will be at opposite ends of the cottage (for front and back doors). With wrong sides tog, carefully matching edges, and using overcast st and size 18 tapestry needle, sew Cottage Sides, Front, and Back to Base. Finish off and weave in ends.

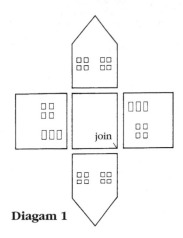

Diagam 1

Note: Joining will be worked around base from right to left joining Side, Front, Side and Back, working in ends of sc rows of base and in unused lps of beg chs of Front, Sides and Back.

SHELL ROOF
(make 1)
FIRST SIDE:
Ch 20.

Row 1: Sc in 2nd ch from hook, * sk next 2 chs, 5 dc in next ch: shell made; sk next 2 chs, sc in next ch; rep from * twice more: 3 shells; ch 3 (counts as first dc on next row), turn.

Row 2: 2 dc in first sc: half shell made; * sk next 2 dc, sc in next dc, sk next 2 dc, shell in next sc; rep from * once; sk next 2 dc, sc in next dc, sk next 2 dc, 3 dc in last sc: half shell made: 2 shells and 2 half shells; ch 1, turn.

Row 3: Sc in next dc, * sk next 2 dc, shell in next sc; sk next 2 dc, sc in next dc; rep from * once more; sk next 2 dc, shell in next sc; sk next 2 dc, sc in next dc; ch 3 (counts as first dc on following rows), turn.

Rows 4 through 7: Rep Rows 2 and 3 twice. At end of Row 7, do not ch 3. Finish off and weave in ends.

SECOND SIDE:
Hold First Side of Roof with Row 1 at top; working in unused lps of beg ch-20, join thread in lp at base of first sc in upper right-hand corner.

Row 1: Ch 1, sc in same ch as joining; * 5 dc in lp at base of next shell: shell made; sc in lp at base of next sc; rep from * twice more: 3 shells; ch 3 (counts as first dc on next row), turn.

Rows 2 through 7: Rep Rows 2 and 3 of First Side of Roof three times. Finish off and weave in ends.

Finishing

Following Starching Instructions on page 132 and using Blocking Guides for Shell-Roofed Cottage, starch cottage Base with attached Sides, Roof, and Doors. When dry, dampen base edges slightly; fold and glue sides at corners. Glue roof and doors in place.

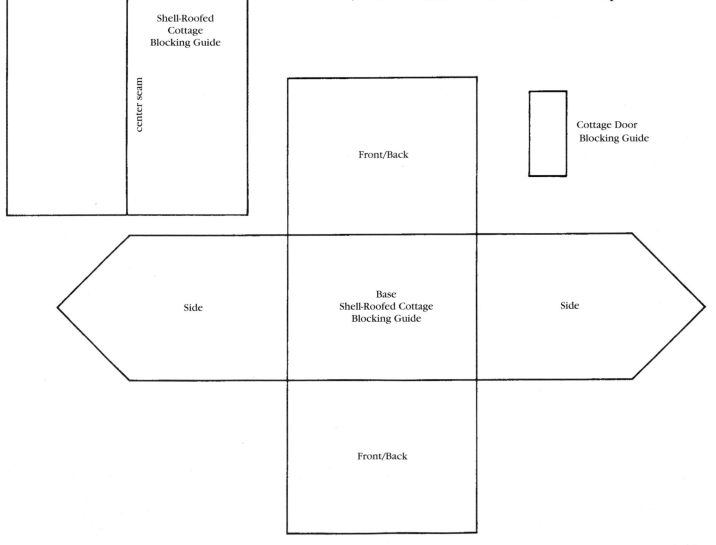

Church

SIZE:
About 7 1/2" tall
MATERIALS:
Bedspread-weight crochet cotton, 175 yds white
Size 7 steel crochet hook, or size required for gauge
starching and blocking supplies, see page 132
GAUGE:
8 dc = 1"
4 dc rows = 1"

Note: Both stitch and row gauge must be accurate for pieces to fit blocking guide.

Instructions

CHURCH FRONT (make 1)
Ch 20.

Row 1: Sc in 2nd ch from hook and in each rem ch: 19 sc; ch 3 (counts as first dc on following rows), turn.

Row 2: Dc in next 4 sc, ch 4, sk next 4 sc, dc in next sc, ch 4, sk next 4 sc, dc in next 5 sc: 11 dc and 2 ch-4 sps; ch 3, turn.

Row 3: Dc in next 4 dc, ch 4, sk next ch-4 lp, dc in next dc, ch 4, sk next ch-4 lp, dc in next 5 dc; ch 3, turn.

Rows 4 through 7: Rep Row 3.

Row 8: Dc in next 4 dc, 4 dc in next ch-4 lp, dc in next dc, 4 dc in next ch-4 lp; dc in next 5 dc: 19 dc; ch 3, turn.

Row 9: Dc in each dc; ch 3, turn.

Row 10: Dec over next 2 dc [to work dec: (YO, draw up lp in next dc, YO and draw through 2 lps on hook) twice; YO and draw through all 3 lps on hook: dec made]; dc in next 3 dc, ch 7, sk next 7 dc, dc in next 4 dc, dec as before: 10 dc and 1 ch-7 lp; ch 3, turn.

Row 11: Dec; dc in next dc, ch 9, sk next dc, next ch-7 lp, and next dc; dc in next 2 dc; dec: 6 dc and 1 ch-9 lp; ch 3, turn.

Row 12: Dec; ch 9, sk next ch-9 lp, dc in next dc, dec: 4 dc and 1 ch-9 lp; ch 3, turn.

Row 13: Dec over next dc and first ch of next ch-9 lp; ch 7, sk next 7 chs, dc in next ch, dec: 4 dc and 1 ch-7 lp; ch 3, turn.

Row 14: Dec over next dc and first ch of next ch-7 lp; dc in next 6 chs, dec: 9 dc; ch 3, turn.

Row 15: Dec; dc in next 4 dc, dec: 7 dc; ch 3, turn.

Row 16: Dec; dc in next 2 dc, dec: 5 dc; ch 3, turn.

Row 17: Dec twice: 3 dc; ch 1, turn.

Row 18: Keeping last lp of each sc on hook, sc in next 3 dc, YO and draw through all 4 lps on hook. Finish off and weave in ends.

Note: Before proceeding, check piece against blocking guide. If piece is either too small or too large to pin edges to guide lines, check your gauge and rework the piece.

CHURCH BACK (make 1)
Ch 20.

Row 1: Sc in 2nd ch from hook and in each rem ch: 19 sc; ch 3 (counts as first dc on following rows), turn.

Row 2: Dc in each sc: 19 dc; ch 3, turn.

Row 3: Dc in next 3 dc, ch 4, sk next 4 dc, dc in next 3 dc, ch 4, sk next 4 dc, dc in next 4 dc: 11 dc and 2 ch-4 lps; ch 3, turn.

Row 4: Dc in next 3 dc, ch 4, sk next ch-4 lp, dc in next 3 dc, ch 4, sk next ch-4 lp, dc in next 4 dc; ch 3, turn.

Rows 5 and 6: Rep Row 4.

Row 7: Dc in next 2 dc, 2 dc in next dc; ch 2, sk next ch-4 lp, 2 dc in next dc; dc in next dc, 2 dc in next dc; ch 2, sk next ch-4 lp, 2 dc in next dc; dc in next 3 dc: 15 dc and 2 ch-2 sps; ch 3, turn.

Row 8: Dc in each dc and in each ch: 19 dc; ch 3, turn.

Rows 9 through 18: Rep Rows 9 through 18 of Church Front.

162

CHURCH SIDE (make 2)

Ch 27.

Row 1: Sc in 2nd ch from hook and in each rem ch: 26 sc; ch 3 (counts as first dc on following rows), turn.

Row 2: Dc in each sc: 26 dc; ch 3, turn.

Row 3: (Dc in next 3 dc, ch 4, sk next 4 dc) 3 times; dc in next 4 dc: 14 dc and 3 ch-4 lps; ch 3, turn.

Row 4: (Dc in next 3 dc, ch 4, sk next ch-4 lp) 3 times; dc in next 4 dc; ch 3, turn.

Rows 5 and 6: Rep Row 4.

Row 7: Dc in next 2 dc, * 2 dc in next dc; ch 2, sk next ch-4 lp, 2 dc in next dc; dc in next dc; rep from * twice more; dc in next 2 dc: 20 dc and 3 ch-2 sps; ch 3, turn.

Row 8: Dc in next 4 dc, * 2 dc in next ch-2 sp; dc in next 5 dc; rep from * twice more: 26 dc; ch 3, turn.

Row 9: Dc in each dc. Finish off and weave in ends.

CHURCH BASE (make 1)

Ch 20.

Row 1: Sc in 2nd ch from hook and in each rem ch: 19 sc; ch 1, turn.

Row 2: Sc in each sc; ch 1, turn.

Rep Row 2 until piece measures 3" long. At end of last row, do not ch 1. Finish off and weave in ends.

CHURCH JOINING

Note: Right side of work is determined by the following placement.

Place Church Base on flat surface. With Base in center, place Church Front, Sides, and Back as in **Diagram 1** with doors and windows in correct direction. With wrong sides tog, join thread in bottom right-hand corner of Base and Side.

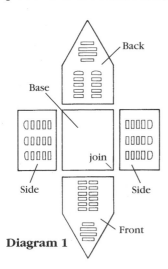

Diagram 1

Note: Joining will be worked around Base from right to left joining Side, Front, Side, and Back, working in ends of sc rows of Base and in unused lps of beg chs of Front, Sides and Back.

Row 1: Ch 4, sl st in 4th ch from hook: picot made; * working through both side and base and keeping edges even, † sc in next 3 sts; ch 4, sl st in 4th ch from hook: picot made †; rep from † to † across to next outside corner, adjusting sts if necessary on next to last rep to end row with picot; rep from * 3 times more; join in first sc. Finish off and weave in ends.

STEEPLE SIDE (make 2)

Ch 13.

Row 1: Dc in 4th ch from hook (3 skipped chs count as a dc) and in each rem ch: 11 dc; ch 3 (counts as first dc on following rows), turn.

Row 2: Dc in each dc; ch 3, turn.

Row 3: Dec over next 2 dc [to work dec: (YO, draw up lp in next dc, YO and draw through 2 lps on hook) twice; YO and draw through all 3 lps on hook: dec made]; dc in next 6 dc, dec as before: 9 dc; ch 3, turn.

Row 4: Dc in each dc; ch 3, turn.

Row 5: Dec; dc in next 4 dc, dec: 7 dc; ch 3, turn.

Rows 6 and 7: Rep Row 4.

Row 8: Dec; dc in next 2 dc, dec: 5 dc; ch 3, turn.

Row 9: Rep Row 4.

Row 10: Dec; dc in next 2 dc: 4 dc; ch 3, turn.

Row 11: Dec; dc in next dc: 3 dc; ch 3, turn.

Row 12: Dec: 2 dc; ch 3, turn.

Row 13: Dc in next dc: 2 dc. Finish off and weave in ends.

STEEPLE FRONT/BACK (make 2)

FIRST SECTION:

Ch 3.

Row 1: Dc in 2nd ch from hook; ch 3 (counts as first dc on following rows), turn.

Row 2: Dc in first dc: 2 dc; ch 3, turn.

Row 3: Dc in first dc and in next dc: 3 dc. Finish off and weave in ends.

SECOND SECTION:

Ch 3.

Work same as Rows 1 through 3 of First Section. At end of Row 3, do not finish off; ch 3, turn.

Row 4: Dc in next 2 dc, ch 1; join to First Section as follows: dc in last dc of Row 3 of First Section and in next 2 dc: 6 dc and one ch-1 sp; ch 3, turn.

Row 5: Working across both sections, dc in next 2 dc, in next ch-1 lp, and in next 3 dc: 7 dc; ch 3, turn.

Row 6: Dec; dc in next 2 dc; dec: 5 dc; ch 3, turn.

Row 7: Dc in each dc; ch 3, turn.

Row 8: Dec; dc in next 2 dc: 4 dc; ch 3, turn.

Row 9: Dc in next dc, dec: 3 dc; ch 3, turn.

Row 10: Dec: 2 dc; ch 3, turn.

Row 11: Dc in next dc; ch 3, turn.

Row 12: Dc in next dc. Finish off and weave in ends.

STEEPLE JOINING

Referring to Steeple Starching Guide for Steeple shape, hold Steeple Side with side on top; join thread in side of dc of Row 1. Work 3 sc in side of Row 1; ch 4, sl st in 4th ch from hook: picot made. Hold Steeple Front to Steeple Side with wrong sides tog and matching side edges, sc in unused ch-1 of Row 1 of Steeple Front and side of next dc of Steeple Side; continuing to join pieces, work 2 sc and picot. Continue to join Steeple Side and Front tog by working 3 sc and picot to top of Steeple and end with 3 sc at Steeple top (do not work picot in last sts). Finish off and weave in ends.

Join Steeple Back to joined piece in same manner as above. Join rem Steeple Side to Steeple Back.

Hold Steeple with Front on bottom and Side at top; join in side of dc of Row 1 of Steeple Side; work 3 sc and picot; rep along this edge in same manner. Do not join this edge, as Steeple will be placed flat when starched.

DOOR (make 2)
Ch 15.

Row 1: Dc in 4th ch from hook, dc in next 10 chs; in last ch work (dc, ch 3, dc, ch 3, dc); working in unused lps on opposite side of beg ch, dc in next 11 lps; ch 3, sl st in same lp. Finish off and weave in ends.

GOTHIC SIDE WINDOW (make 6)
Ch 6.

Rnd 1: Sc in 2nd ch from hook and in each rem ch: 5 sc; ch 18; turn; join in first sc; ch 1, turn.

Rnd 2: Sl st in next 7 chs; over next 4 chs work (sc, hdc, dc, 3 trc, ch 4, sl st in bl of trc just made: picot made; 2 trc, dc, hdc, sc); sl st in next 7 chs and in side of next sc. Finish off and weave in ends.

ROSE WINDOW MEDALLION (make 2)
Ch 5, join to form a ring.

Rnd 1: (Ch 4, sc in ring) 5 times: 5 ch-4 lps.

Rnd 2: * In next ch-5 lp work (sc, 3 dc, sc): petal made; rep from * 4 times more; join in back of first sc of prev rnd: 5 petals.

Rnd 3: * Ch 5, working behind petals of prev rnd, sc in back of next sc of Rnd 1: ch-5 lp made; rep from * 4 times more, ending last rep without working last sc; join in sl st joining of prev rnd: 5 ch-5 lps.

Rnd 4: Ch 1, * in next ch-5 lp work (sc, 5 dc, sc): petal made; rep from * 4 times more; join in back of beg ch-1: 5 petals. Finish off and weave in ends.

ROOF (make 2)
Ch 32.

Row 1: Dc in 5th ch from hook, * † ch 2, sk next 5 chs, 4 dc in next ch †; ch 2, dc in next ch; rep from * twice more, then rep from † to † once; ch 4, turn.

Row 2: Dc in first dc, ch 2, sk next 3 dc, next ch-2 sp, and next dc; * in next ch-2 sp work (4 dc, ch 2, dc); ch 2, sk next 4 dc, next ch-2 sp, and next dc; rep from * twice more; 4 dc in next ch-4 lp; ch 4, turn.

Rep Row 2 until piece measures 3" long. Finish off and weave in ends.

ROOF JOINING

To determine right side of work, hold roof pieces tog with beg ch of each at top; join thread in first unused lp in top right-hand corner of both pieces.

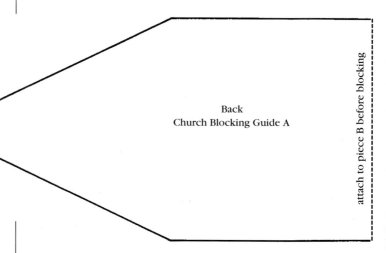

Back
Church Blocking Guide A

attach to piece B before blocking

Note: You will be working through lps of both pieces.

Row 1: Ch 4, sl st in 4th from hook: picot made; working in rem unused lps, * sc in next 3 lps; ch 4, sl st in 4th ch from hook: picot made; rep from * across adjusting sts, if necessary, on next to last rep to end row with picot; sl st in last sc. Finish off and weave in ends.

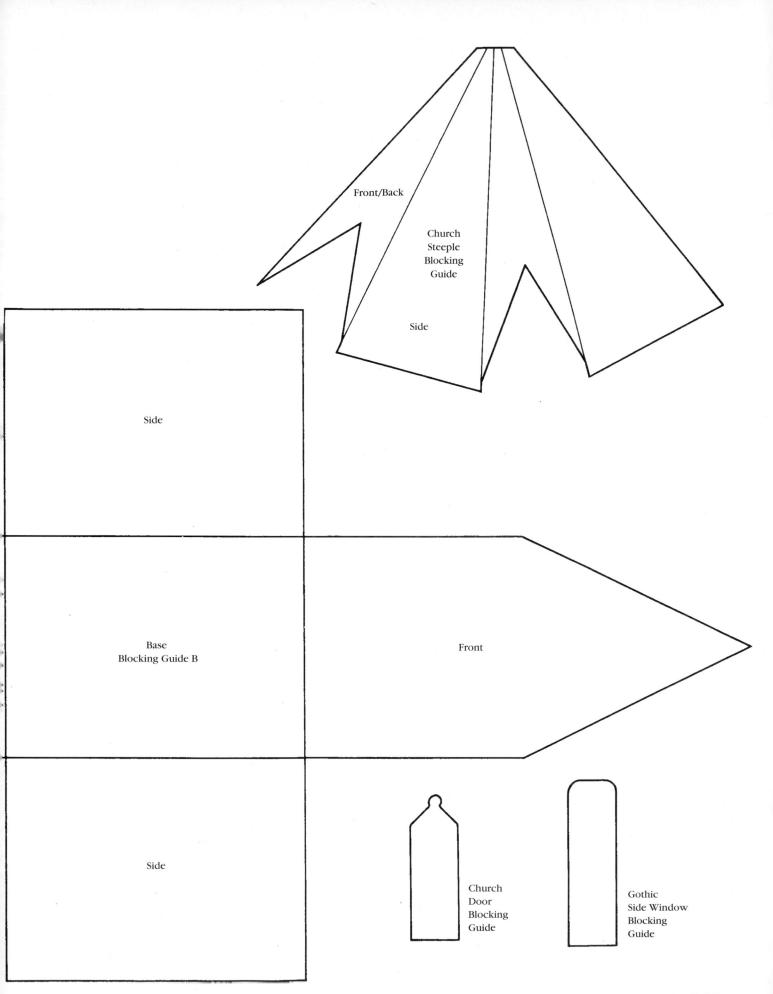

Front/Back

Church
Steeple
Blocking
Guide

Side

Side

Base
Blocking Guide B

Front

Side

Church
Door
Blocking
Guide

Gothic
Side Window
Blocking
Guide

Finishing

Following Starching Instructions on page 132 and using Blocking Guides for Church, starch Church as follows:

(a) Be sure picots are flat along Church base and pointing towards sides of Church.

(b) Be sure each window opening on sides of Church should be 1/2" wide.

(c) Be sure that Church front and back windows are not larger than rose window medallions.

Starch roof with picots in center of roof pointing up (pin, if necessary). Starch doors and gothic windows. Do not starch rose window medallions.

Starch steeple making sure that rows of stitches are straight across, all picots are pointing up, and there are no noticeable "holes" in work along joinings of front, back, and sides.

When dry, dampen sides where joined to base slightly and fold; glue sides at corners. Glue roof, doors, windows, and window medallions in place.

```
┌────────────────────────────────┐
│                                │
│                                │
│                                │
│                                │
│            Roof                │
│        Blocking Guide          │
│                                │
│                                │
├────────────────────────────────┤
│           center seam          │
│                                │
│                                │
│                                │
│                                │
│                                │
│                                │
│                                │
│                                │
│                                │
│                                │
│                                │
│                                │
└────────────────────────────────┘
```

Bandstand

SIZE:
About 2 1/2" tall
MATERIALS:
Bedspread-weight crochet cotton, 40 yds white
Size 7 steel crochet hook, or size required for gauge
4" square of poster board
starching and blocking supplies, see page 132
GAUGE:
8 dc = 1"
4 dc rows = 1"

Note: *Both stitch and row gauge must be accurate for pieces to fit blocking guide.*

Instructions

ROOF (make 1)

Ch 6, join to form a ring.

Rnd 1: Ch 1, 8 sc in ring; join in first sc: 8 sc.

Rnd 2: Ch 3 (counts as first dc on this and following rnds), dc in same sc as joining; 2 dc in each rem sc; join in 3rd ch of beg ch-3: 16 dc.

Rnd 3: Ch 3, dc in next dc, ch 2, (dc in next 2 dc, ch 2) 7 times; join in 3rd ch of beg ch-3: 16 dc and 8 ch-2 sps.

Rnd 4: Ch 3, dc in next dc, 2 dc in next ch-2 sp; (dc in next 2 dc, 2 dc in next ch-2 sp) 7 times; join in 3rd ch of beg ch-3: 32 dc.

Rnd 5: Ch 3, dc in next 2 dc, ch 3, sk next dc, (dc in next 3 dc, ch 3, sk next dc) 7 times; join in 3rd ch of beg ch-3: 24 dc and 8 ch-3 lps.

Rnd 6: Ch 3, dc in next 2 dc, in next ch-3 lp work (dc, 3 trc, dc); * dc in next 3 dc, in next ch-3 lp work (dc, 3 trc, dc); rep from * 6 times more; join in 3rd ch of beg ch-3: 40 dc and 24 trc.

Rnd 7: Ch 1, sc in same ch as joining and in next dc; * ch 4, sl st in 4th ch from hook: picot made; sc in next 2 dc and in next 2 trc; ch 4, sl st in 4th ch from hook: picot made; sc in next trc and in next 3 dc; rep from * 7 times more, ending last rep without working last sc; join in first sc: 64 sc and 16 picots. Finish off and weave in ends.

BANDSTAND BASE (make 1)
Ch 12.

Row 1: Sc in 2nd ch from hook and in each rem ch: 11 sc; ch 1, turn.

Row 2: 2 sc in next sc; sc in next 9 sc, 2 sc in next sc: 13 sc; ch 1, turn.

Row 3: 2 sc in next sc, sc in next 11 sc, 2 sc in last sc: 15 sc; ch 1, turn.

Row 4: 2 sc in next sc; sc in next 13 sc, 2 sc in last sc: 17 sc; ch 1, turn.

Row 5: 2 sc in next sc; sc in next 15 sc, 2 sc in last sc: 19 sc; ch 1, turn.

Row 6: Sc in each sc; ch 1, turn.

Rows 7 through 17: Rep Row 6.

Row 18: Dec over next 2 sc (to work dec: draw up lp in each of next 2 sc, YO and draw through all 3 lps on hook: dec made); sc in next 15 sc; dec as before: 17 sc; ch 1, turn.

Row 19: Dec; sc in next 13 sc, dec: 15 sc; ch 1, turn.

Row 20: Dec; sc in next 11 sc, dec: 13 sc; ch 1, turn.

Row 21 (right side)**:** Dec; sc in next 9 sc, dec: 11 sc; ch 3 (counts as first dc in following row), turn.

SIDE A:
Row 22 (wrong side)**:** Working in front lps only, dc in next 10 sc: 11 dc; ch 1, turn.

Row 23 (right side)**:** Sc in each dc: 11 sc; ch 3, turn.

Row 24 (wrong side)**:** Trc in next sc: corner made; ch 5, trc in 3rd ch from hook: corner made; ch 8, trc in 3rd ch from hook: corner made; ch 2, sk next 7 sc of Row 23, keeping last lp of each trc on hook, trc in next 2 sc, YO and draw through all 3 lps on hook: corner made.

Finish off and weave in ends.

Note: Place marker on wrong side of work.

SIDE B:
On wrong side and to left of Side A just worked, join thread in top lp of Corner C (**Diagram 1**).

Row 1 (wrong side)**:** Ch 3 (counts as a dc), sk side of edge sc of Row 17; dc in side of edge sc of each of next 10 rows: 11 dc; ch 1, turn.

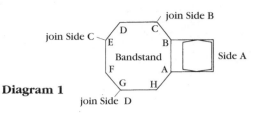

Diagram 1

Rows 2 and 3: Rep Rows 23 and 24 of Side A.

SIDE C:
On wrong side and to left of Side B just worked, join thread in Corner E (**Diagram 1**) in unused lps of beg ch of Base.

Row 1 (wrong side)**:** Ch 3 (counts as a dc), dc in next 10 chs: 11 dc; ch 1, turn.

Rows 2 and 3: Rep Rows 23 and 24 of Side A.

SIDE D:
On wrong side and to left of Side C just worked, join thread in top lp of Corner G (**Diagram 1**).

Row 1: Ch 3 (counts as a dc), sk side of edge sc of Row 6, dc in side of edge sc of each of next 10 rows: 11 dc; ch 1, turn.

Rows 2 and 3: Rep Rows 23 and 24 of Side A.

Bandstand Blocking Guide

Finishing

Following Starching Instructions on page 132 and using Blocking Guides for Bandstand, starch base with sides. For roof, make blocking shape as follows: Draw a circle with a 4" diameter on poster board and cut out. Cut one side only of diameter from outer edge to center, leaving opposite side uncut (**Diagram 2**). Overlap cut edges of circle about 2 1/2" (place roof on roof shape to check width of roof shape); tape to hold in place. Cover roof shape with plastic wrap and secure wrap with tape. Place starched roof on roof shape in an octagonal shape, making 8 "points" where picots are (these will be used as guides for joining sides). When pieces are dry, dampen base where sides are joined; fold sides and glue into position at "points."

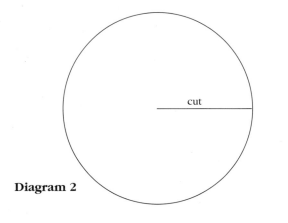

Diagram 2

Mansion

SIZE:
About 3" tall

MATERIALS:
Bedspread-weight crochet cotton, 75 yds white
Size 7 steel crochet hook, or size required for gauge
Size 18 tapestry needle
starching and blocking supplies, see page 132

GAUGE:
8 dc = 1"
4 dc rows = 1"

Note: *Both stitch and row gauge must be accurate for pieces to fit blocking guide.*

Instructions

MANSION FRONT (make 1)
Ch 20.

Row 1: Sc in 2nd ch from hook and in each rem ch: 19 sc; ch 3 (counts as first dc on following rows), turn.

Row 2: Dc in next 7 sc, ch 3, sk next 3 sc, dc in next 8 sc: 16 dc and one ch-3 lp; ch 3, turn.

Row 3: Dc in next 2 dc, † (ch 1, sk next dc, dc in next dc) twice †; dc in next dc, ch 3, sk next ch-3 lp, dc in next 2 dc; rep from † to † once; dc in next 2 dc: 12 dc, 4 ch-1 sps and one ch-3 lp; ch 3, turn.

Row 4: Dc in next 2 dc, † (ch 1, sk next ch-1 sp, dc in next dc) twice †; dc in next dc, ch 3, sk next ch-3 lp, dc in next 2 dc; rep from † to † once; dc in next 2 dc; ch 3, turn.

Row 5: Dc in next 2 dc, † (dc in next ch-1 sp, dc in next dc) twice †; dc in next dc, ch 5, sk next ch-3 lp, dc in next 2 dc; rep from † to † once; dc in next 2 dc: 16 dc and one ch-5 lp; ch 3, turn.

Row 6: Dc in next 2 dc, † (ch 1, sk next dc, dc in next dc) twice †; dc in next dc, in next ch-5 lp work (hdc, sc, hdc); dc in next 2 dc; rep from † to † once; dc in next 2 dc: 12 dc, 4 ch-1 sps, 2 hdc, and one sc; ch 3, turn.

Row 7: Dc in next 2 dc, † (dc in next ch-1 sp, dc in next dc) twice †; dc in next 6 sts; rep from † to † once; dc in next 2 dc: 19 dc; ch 3, turn.

Row 8: Dc in each dc; ch 1, turn.

Row 9: Sc in each dc. Finish off and weave in ends.

Note: Before proceeding, check piece against blocking guide. If piece is either too small or too large to pin edges to guide lines, check your gauge and rework the piece.

MANSION SIDE (make 3)
Ch 20.

Row 1: Sc in 2nd ch from hook and in each rem ch: 19 sc; ch 3 (counts as first dc on following rows), turn.

Row 2: Dc in each sc; ch 3, turn.

Row 3: Dc in next 3 dc, † (ch 1, sk next dc, dc in next dc) twice †; dc in next dc, ch 1, sk next dc, dc in next 2 dc; rep from † to † once; dc in next 3 dc: 14 dc and 5 ch-1 sps; ch 3, turn.

Row 4: Dc in next 3 dc, † (ch 1, sk next ch-1 sp, dc in next dc) twice †; dc in next dc, ch 1, sk next ch-1 sp, dc in next 2 dc; rep from † to † once; dc in next 3 dc; ch 3, turn.

Row 5: Dc in next 3 dc, † (dc in next ch-1 sp, dc in next dc) twice †; dc in next dc, in next ch-1 sp, and in next 2 dc; rep from † to † once; dc in next 3 dc: 19 dc; ch 3, turn.

Row 6: Rep Row 3.

Row 7: Rep Row 5.

Row 8: Dc in each dc; ch 1, turn.

Row 9: Sc in each dc. Finish off and weave in ends.

MANSION BASE (make 1)
Ch 20.

Row 1: Sc in 2nd ch from hook and in each rem ch: 19 sc; ch 1, turn.

Row 2: Sc in each sc; ch 1, turn.

Rep Row 2 until piece measures 2 3/8" long. At end of last row, do not ch 1. Finish off and weave in ends.

MANSION DOOR (make 1)
Ch 6.

Rnd 1: Sc in 2nd ch from hook and in each rem ch: 5 sc; ch 18; join in first sc; ch 1, turn.

Rnd 2: Sl st in next 7 chs, over (not in) next 4 chs work (sc, hdc, 3 dc, hdc, sc); sl st in next 7 chs and in side of next sc. Finish off and weave in ends.

MEDALLION (make 1)
Ch 2.

Rnd 1: Sc in 2nd ch from hook, (ch 2, sc in same ch) 4 times; ch 2; join in first sc. Finish off and weave in ends.

MANSION JOINING
Note: Right side of work is determined by following placement below.

Place Mansion Base on flat surface. With Base in center, place Front to the right of Base, with beg ch next to base. Place rem Mansion Sides around sides of Base with beg ch row next to base. With right sides tog and carefully matching edges, with size 18 tapestry needle and overcast st, sew Base, Front and Sides tog as follows: Work around base from right to left joining Front, Side, Back and Side to base, working in ends of sc rows of Base and in unused lps of beg chs of Front, Sides and Back. Finish off and weave in ends.

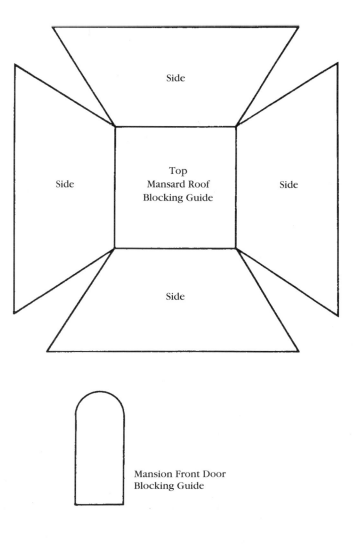

169

MANSARD ROOF SIDE (make 4)
Ch 14.

Row 1: Sc in 5th ch from hook, (ch 4, sk next 2 chs, sc in next ch) 3 times: 4 ch-4 lps; ch 4, turn.

Row 2: Sk first sc, sc in next ch-4 lp, (ch 4, sk next sc, sc in next ch-4 lp) twice; ch 2, sk next sc, dc in next ch-4 lp; ch 5, turn.

Row 3: Sc in next ch-2 sp, (ch 5, sc in next ch-4 lp) twice; ch 3, dc in next ch-4 lp; ch 6, turn.

Row 4: Sc in next ch-3 lp, (ch 6, sc in next ch-5 lp) twice; ch 4, dc in next ch-5 lp; ch 7, turn.

Row 5: Sc in next ch-4 lp, (ch 7, sc in next ch-6 lp) twice; ch 5, dc in next ch-6 lp. Finish off and weave in ends.

MANSARD ROOF TOP (make 1)
Ch 14.

Row 1: Sc in 5th ch from hook, (ch 4, sk next 2 chs, sc in next ch) 3 times: 4 ch-4 lps; ch 4, turn.

Row 2: Sc in next ch-4 lp, (ch 4, sc in next ch-4 lp) twice; ch 2, dc in next ch-4 lp; ch 4, turn.

Row 3: Sc in next ch-2 sp, (ch 4, sc in next ch-4 lp) twice; ch 2, dc in next ch-4 lp; ch 4, turn.

Rows 4 through 6: Rep Row 3. At end of Row 6, ch 3, turn.

Row 7: Sc in next ch-2 sp, (ch 3, sc in next ch-4 lp) twice; ch 2, dc in next ch-4 lp. Finish off and weave in ends.

ROOF JOINING
Hold Roof Top and one Roof Side with wrong sides tog. With Roof Top facing you and matching edges, join thread in right-hand corner; work (3 sc, ch 4, sl st in 4th ch from hook: picot made) 3 times, ending with picot in left-hand corner.

Turn Roof Top to next unjoined left-hand edge, hold unjoined Roof Side to Roof Top with wrong sides tog; join in same manner as above. Rep until all 4 Roof Sides are joined, ending by joining in first sc. Finish off and weave in ends.

FINISHING
Following Starching Instructions on page 132 and using Blocking Guides for Mansion, starch mansion base with sides, roof, and door. Do not starch medallion. When dry, dampen edges of base slightly; fold and glue sides at corners. Glue roof, door, and medallion in place.

Side

Side

Base
Mansion Blocking Guide

Side

Side

Fir Tree

SIZE:
About 3" tall
MATERIALS:
Bedspread-weight crochet cotton, 45 yds white
Size 7 steel crochet hook, or size required for gauge
6" square piece of poster board
starching and blocking supplies, see page 132
GAUGE:
8 dc = 1"
4 dc rows = 1"

Instructions

Ch 2.

Rnd 1: 4 sc in 2nd ch from hook; join in first sc: 4 sc.

Rnd 2: Ch 3 (counts as a dc), dc in same sc as joining; 2 dc in each rem sc; join in 3rd ch of beg ch-3: 8 dc.

Note: Work in bl only of each st for all following rnds.

Rnd 3: Ch 4 (counts as a trc on this and following rnds), 2 trc in next dc; (trc in next dc, 2 trc in next dc) 3 times; join in 4th ch of beg ch-4: 12 trc.

Rnd 4: Ch 4, 2 trc in next trc; (trc in next trc, 2 trc in next trc) 5 times; join in 4th ch of beg ch-4: 18 trc.

Rnd 5: Ch 4, trc in next trc, 2 trc in next trc; (trc in next 2 trc, 2 trc in next trc) 5 times; join in 4th ch of beg ch-4: 24 trc.

Rnd 6: Ch 4, trc in next 2 trc, 2 trc in next trc; (trc in next 3 trc, 2 trc in next trc) 5 times; join in 4th ch of beg ch-4: 30 trc.

Rnd 7: Ch 4, trc in next 3 trc, 2 trc in next trc; (trc in next 4 trc, 2 trc in next trc) 5 times; join in 4th ch of beg ch-4: 36 trc.

Rnd 8: Ch 4, trc in next 7 trc, 2 trc in next trc; (trc in next 8 trc, 2 trc in next trc) 3 times; join in 4th ch of beg ch-4: 40 trc.

Rnd 9: Ch 4, trc in next 8 trc, 2 trc in next trc; (trc in next 9 trc, 2 trc in next trc) 3 times; join in 4th ch of beg ch-4: 44 trc.

TREE BRANCHES

Step 1: Ch 1, turn tree with bottom edge at right-hand side and top of tree at left side; work 3 sl sts in first trc (beg ch-4) of Rnd 9; sl st in fl of first trc of Rnd 8; ch 1. Hold tree with point of tree away from you.

Left: Fir Tree   Right: Baby Pine, page 172

Note: In all following rnds, all sts will be worked in fls only. The wrong side of work will face up when branches are completed.

Rnd 1: Sc in same trc; * in next trc work (2 dc, ch 2, 2 dc); sc in next trc; branch made; rep from * around, ending last rep without working last sc; join in first sc.

Continue to work up the tree as in Step 1 and Rnd 1 in unused fls of sts for each prev rnd (7 rnds of branches in all—number of branches for each rnd will vary). At end of top rnd, finish off and weave in ends.

Finishing

Following Starching Instructions on page 132, starch tree. For blocking shape, make cone shape as follows: Draw a half circle with a 6" diameter on poster board and cut out. Shape half circle to form a cone that will be the same width as tree (place tree on cone to check width of cone); tape to hold in place. Cover cone with plastic wrap and secure wrap with tape. Moisten tree in stiffening solution and place on cone. Pin bottom edge of tree evenly to cone. Hold tree upside down; using pin, draw branches away from cone to make branches in horizontal position. Hold tree right side up; using a downward motion with fingertips, arrange branches evenly around tree. Let dry.

Baby Pine

SIZE:
About 1 3/8" tall
MATERIALS:
Bedspread-weight crochet cotton, 15 yds white
Size 7 steel crochet hook, or size required for gauge
6" square piece of poster board
starching and blocking supplies, see page 132
GAUGE:
8 dc = 1"
4 dc rows = 1"

Instructions

Ch 2.

Rnds 1 through 5: Rep Rnds 1 through 5 of Fir Tree, page 171. At end of Rnd 5, do not finish off.

BABY PINE BRANCHES
Step 1: Ch 1, turn baby pine with bottom edge at right-hand side and top of baby pine at left side; work 3 sl sts in first trc (beg ch-4) of Rnd 5; sl st in fl of first trc of Rnd 4; ch 1.

Hold baby pine with top of pine away from you.

Note: In all following rnds, all sts will be worked in fls only. The wrong side of work will face up when branches are completed.

Rnd 1: Sc in same trc; * in next trc work (2 dc, ch 2, 2 dc), sc in next trc: branch made; rep from * around, ending last rep without working last sc; join in first sc.

Continue to work up the baby pine as in Step 1 and Rnd 1 for unused front lps of sts for each prev rnd (3 rnds of branches in all—number of branches for each rnd will vary). At end of top rnd, finish off and weave in ends.

Finishing

Following Starching Instructions on page 132, starch tree. For blocking shape, make cone shape as follows: Draw a half circle with a 6" diameter on poster board and cut out. Shape half circle to form a cone that will be the same width as tree (place tree on cone to check width of cone); tape to hold in place. Cover cone with plastic wrap and secure wrap with tape. Moisten tree in stiffening solution and place on cone. Pin bottom edge of baby pine evenly around cone. For each branch, place pin in center of branch (ch-2 sp), lift branch slightly, and pin branch to cone making branch appear "rounded."

When all branches have been pinned to cone, let dry.

Baby's First Christmas Afghan

designed by Jean Leinhauser

There's no better way to help a baby celebrate its first Christmas than with this beautiful red afghan, trimmed with a deep, lacy white ruffle! The size is perfect for a lap afghan as a gift for an adult, too.

SIZE:
About 41" square with edging

MATERIALS:
Worsted weight yarn, 31 oz (2170 yds) red; 12 oz (840 yds) white

Size G aluminum crochet hook, or size required for gauge

GAUGE:
4 dc = 1"

Instructions

With red, ch 133.

Row 1 (right side): Dc in 4th ch from hook (3 skipped chs count as a dc) and in each rem ch: 131 dc; ch 3 (counts as first dc on following rows), turn.

Row 2: Dc in next 2 dc, * sk next 2 dc, in next dc work (2 dc, ch 2, 2 dc): shell made; sk next 2 dc, dc in next 3 dc; rep from * across; ch 3, turn.

Row 3: Dc in next 2 dc, * in next ch-2 sp of next shell work (2 dc, ch 2, 2 dc): shell in shell made; sk next 2 dc of same shell, dc in next 3 dc; rep from * across; ch 3, turn.

Row 4: Dc in next 2 dc, * shell in next shell; sk next 2 dc of same shell, dc in next 3 dc; rep from * across; ch 3, turn.

Rep Row 4 until afghan measures about 36" long.

Last Row: Dc in next 2 dc, * sc in next 2 dc, in next ch-2 sp, and in next 2 dc; dc in next 3 dc; rep from * across. Finish off and weave in ends.

EDGING

Hold afghan upside down with right side facing you and beg ch at top; join white in first unused lp of beg ch in upper right-hand corner.

Rnd 1: Ch 1, 3 sc in same lp as joining: corner made; working in rem unused lps, sc in each lp across to last lp; 3 sc in next lp: corner made; working across next side, 2 sc in each edge dc to last edge dc; 3 sc in next edge dc: corner made; working across next side, sc in each st across to last st; 3 sc in next st: corner made; working across next side, 2 sc in each edge dc; join in first sc.

Rnd 2: Ch 5 (counts as a dc and ch-2 sp), dc in same sc as joining; sk next sc, * in next sc work (dc, ch 2, dc); sk next sc; rep from * around; join in 3rd ch of beg ch-5.

Rnd 3: Sl st in next ch-2 sp; ch 3 (counts as a dc), in same sp work (dc, ch 3, 2 dc); in each rem ch-2 sp work (2 dc, ch 3, 2 dc); join in 3rd ch of beg ch-3.

Rnd 4: Sl st in next dc and in next ch-3 lp; ch 1, in same lp work (sc, hdc, dc; ch 4, sl st in 4th ch from hook: picot made; dc, hdc, sc); ch 1, * in next ch-3 lp work (sc, hdc, dc; ch 4, sl st in 4th ch from hook: picot made; dc, hdc, sc); ch 1; rep from * around; join in first sc. Finish off and weave in all ends.

Knitting

*While we would
never dream of
giving up all
the time-saving
conveniences of
modern life, we are still
fascinated by the relaxing
needlecraft of knitting.*

*Knitting is one of the very
oldest needlework skills.
Knitted sweaters, hats,
scarves and gloves have
been made for centuries.
Shepherds used wool to
knit while watching their
sheep. Fishermen devised
patterns that were symbolic
of the lives they led. Fair
Isle patterns developed in
Scandinavian countries
where warm clothing is a
necessity.*

*Today's patterns reflect
the history of this craft.
In this section we've in-
cluded an afghan, a pillow
and a Christmas stock-
ing utilizing Fisherman
stitches. There's also a
colorful stocking created
with Fair Isle patterns.
And in the tradition of
knitted fashions that keep
you warm, there are little
feminine booties for baby
that look like Mary Jane
shoes and a bright
red pair of tube socks
for cold winter nights.*

Knitting

Knitting How-To

CASTING ON (CO)

Only one knitting needle is used with this method. First, measure off a length of yarn that allows about 1" for each stitch you are going to cast on. Make a slip knot on needle at this point as follows. Make a yarn loop, insert needle into loop and draw up yarn from free end to make a loop on needle (**Fig 1**). Pull yarn firmly, but not tightly, to form a slip knot on needle (**Fig 2**). This slip knot counts as your first stitch. Now work as follows:

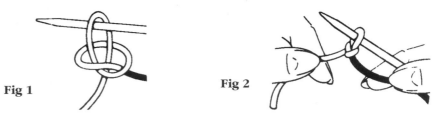

Fig 1   **Fig 2**

Step 1: Hold needle with slip knot in right hand, with yarn from skein to your right and measured length of yarn to your left. With left hand, make a yarn loop (**Fig 3**) and insert needle into loop (**Fig 4**).

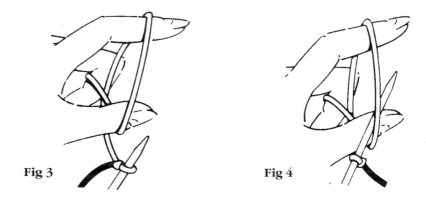

Fig 3   **Fig 4**

Step 2: Still holding loop in left hand, with right hand pick up yarn from skein and bring it from back to front around the needle (**Fig 5**).

Step 3: Bring needle through loop and toward you; at the same time, pull gently on yarn end to tighten loop (**Fig 6**). Make it snug but not tight below needle.

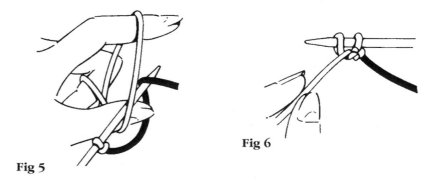

Fig 5   **Fig 6**

You now have one cast-on stitch. Repeat Steps 1 through 3 for each additional stitch desired.

THE KNIT STITCH (K)

Step 1: Hold the needle with cast-on stitches in your left hand. Insert point of right needle into first stitch under the left needle (**Fig 7**).

Step 2: With right index finger, bring yarn under and over point of right needle (**Fig 8**).

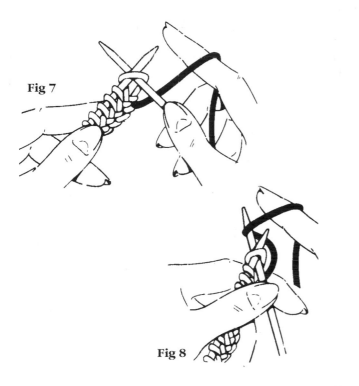

Fig 7

Fig 8

Step 3: Draw yarn through stitch with right needle point (**Fig 9**).

Step 4: Slip the loop on the left needle off, so the new stitch is entirely on the right needle (**Fig 10**).

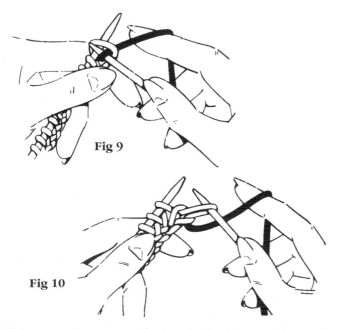

Fig 9

Fig 10

This completes one knit stitch. Repeat Steps 1 through 3 for each knit stitch.

THE PURL STITCH (P)

The reverse of the knit stitch is called the purl stitch. Instead of inserting the needle point from left to right under the left needle as you did for the knit stitch, you will now insert it from right to left, in front of the left needle.

Step 1: Insert right needle from right to left, into first stitch, and in front of left needle (**Fig 11**).

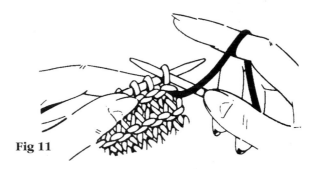

Fig 11

Step 2: Holding yarn in front of work (side toward you), bring it around right needle counterclockwise (**Fig 12**).

Fig 12

Step 3: With right needle, draw yarn back through stitch (**Fig 13**).

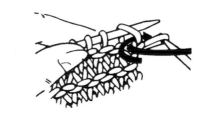

Fig 13

Slide stitch off left needle, leaving new stitch on right needle (**Fig 14**).

Fig 14

One purl stitch is now completed. Repeat Steps 1 through 3 for each purl stitch.

BINDING OFF

To bind off on the knit side:

Step 1: Knit the first 2 stitches. Then insert left needle into the first of the 2 stitches (**Fig 15**), and pull it over the second stitch and completely off the needle (**Fig 16**). You have now bound off one stitch.

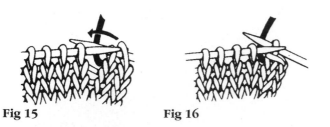

Fig 15   Fig 16

Step 2: Knit one more stitch; insert left needle into first stitch on right needle and pull it over the new stitch and completely off the needle (**Fig 17**). Another stitch is now bound off.

Fig 17

Repeat Step 2 until all stitches are bound off and one loop remains on right-hand needle. "Finish off" or "end off" the yarn (cut yarn and draw end through last loop).

To bind off on the purl side:

Step 1: Purl the first 2 stitches. Now insert left needle into the first stitch on right needle, and pull it over the second stitch and completely off the needle. You have now bound off one stitch.

Step 2: Purl one more stitch; insert left needle into first stitch on right needle and pull it over the new stitch and completely off the needle. Another stitch is bound off.

Repeat Step 2 until all stitches are bound off. "Finish off" or "end off" the yarn (cut yarn and draw end through last loop).

YARN OVER (YO)

To make a yarn over before a knit stitch, bring yarn to front of work as if you were going to purl, then take it over the right needle to the back into the position for knitting; then knit the next stitch (**Fig 18**).

Fig 18

To make a yarn over before a purl stitch, bring yarn around right needle from front to back, then back around into position for purling; purl the next stitch (**Fig 19**).

Fig 19

COLOR CHANGES

Always bring the new color from underneath the old to prevent holes in your knitting.

PICKING UP STITCHES

To pick up a stitch, hold work with right side facing you. Hold yarn in your left hand behind the work and a knitting needle in your right hand. Insert the needle into the work from front to back, one stitch from the edge; yarn over as if to knit, and draw the yarn through (**Fig 20**).

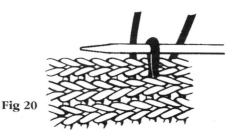

Fig 20

To space the stitches evenly, pick up 3 stitches in 3 consecutive edge stitches and then skip 1 edge stitch. Continue picking up stitches in this manner.

Abbreviations

BC	back cross
beg	begin(ning)
bl(s)	back loop(s)
BO	bind off
CB	cable back
CF	cable front
CO	cast on
dec	decrease(-ing)
dpn(s)	double pointed needle(s)
FC	front cross
Fig	figure
inc	increase(-ing)
K	knit
lp(s)	loop(s)
P	purl
patt	pattern
prev	previous
PSSO	pass slip stitch over
rem	remain(ing)
rep	repeat(ing)
rnd(s)	round(s)
sk	skip
sl	slip
sl st(s)	slip stitch(es)
st(s)	stitch(es)
tog	together
YO	yarn over

Symbols & Terms

* An asterisk is used to mark the beginning of a portion of instructions which will be worked more than once; thus, "rep from * twice more" means after working the instructions once, repeat the instructions following the asterisk twice more (3 times in all).

† The dagger identifies a portion of instructions that will be repeated again later in the same row or round.

: The number after a colon at the end of a row or round indicates the number of stitches you should have when the row or round has been completed.

( ) Parentheses are used to enclose instructions which should be worked the exact number of times specified immediately following the parentheses, such as: (K1, P1) twice. They are also used to set off and clarify a group of sts that are to be worked all into the same sp or st.

[ ] Brackets and ( ) parentheses are used to provide additional information to clarify instructions.

Work even: This term in instructions means to continue working in the pattern as established, without increasing or decreasing.

Gauge

It is essential to achieve the gauge—number of stitches and rows per inch—given in pattern in order to make the correct size.

Before beginning your project, refer to the "Gauge" and make a gauge swatch using the needle and yarn specified. Work several rows; cast off. Place work on a flat surface and measure stitches in center of piece. If you have more stitches to the inch than specified, use a larger size needle. If you have fewer stitches to the inch than specified, use a smaller size needle. Then make another gauge swatch and check your gauge once again. Do not hesitate to change needle size to obtain the specified gauge. Often you will not be able to achieve gauge with the size needle recommended.

Fisherman Afghan and Pillow

designed by Barbara Retzke

In the islands off the west coast of Ireland, knitted pattern stitches are symbolic of the fisherman's life. This afghan and pillow feature pattern stitches such as Ladder of Life, which symbolizes man's climb to eternal happiness, and Lobster Claw, which represents one of the many forms of life under the sea.

Afghan

SIZE:
About 40" x 56"

MATERIALS:
Bulky weight yarn, 42 oz (1680 yds) ecru
Size 13, 10" straight knitting needles,
   or size required for gauge
Cable needle

Materials Note: Two strands of worsted weight yarn may be substituted for bulky weight yarn.

GAUGE:
In stock st, 3 sts = 1"
4 rows = 1"

PATTERN STITCHES
Seed Stitch (worked on uneven number of sts):

Row 1: K1, * P1, K1; rep from * across.

Rep Row 1 for patt.

Honeycomb (multiple of 8 sts):

Row 1 (right side): * Sl 2 sts onto cable needle and hold at back of work; knit next 2 sts, then K2 sts from cable needle; sl next 2 sts onto cable needle and hold at front of work; knit next 2 sts, then K2 sts from cable needle; rep from * across.

Row 2: Purl.

Row 3: Knit.

Row 4: Purl.

Row 5: * Sl 2 sts onto cable needle and hold at front of work; knit next 2 sts, then K2 sts from cable needle; sl next 2 sts onto cable needle and hold at back of work; knit next 2 sts, then K2 sts from cable needle; rep from * across.

Rows 6 through 8: Rep Rows 2 through 4.

Rep Rows 1 through 8 for patt.

Instructions

CENTER PANEL
Cast on 39 sts loosely.

Work 7 rows in seed st.

Next Row: Inc 7 sts as follows: * (K1, P1) twice; inc in next st; rep from * 6 times more; (K1, P1) twice: 46 sts.

Row 1: K1, P1, K1; work Honeycomb Patt Row 1 to last 3 sts; K1, P1, K1.

Row 2: K1, P1, K1; work Honeycomb Patt Row 2 to last 3 sts; K1, P1, K1.

Row 3: K1, P1, K1; work Honeycomb Patt Row 3 to last 3 sts; K1, P1, K1.

Row 4: K1, P1, K1; work Honeycomb Patt Row 4 to last 3 sts; K1, P1, K1.

Row 5: K1, P1, K1; work Honeycomb Patt Row 5 to last 3 sts; K1, P1, K1.

Row 6: K1, P1, K1; work Honeycomb Patt Row 6 to last 3 sts; K1, P1, K1.

Row 7: K1, P1, K1; work Honeycomb Patt Row 7 to last 3 sts; K1, P1, K1.

Row 8: K1, P1, K1; work Honeycomb Patt Row 8 to last 3 sts; K1, P1, K1.

Rep Rows 1 through 8 twenty-five times more or until piece measures about 54"; then rep Row 1 once more.

Next Row: Dec 7 sts as follows: K1, (P1, K1) 3 times; * P2 tog, K1, P1, K1; rep from * 6 times more; (P1, K1) twice: 39 sts.

Work 6 rows in seed st.

Bind off loosely in seed st.

Finish off and weave in all yarn ends.

SIDE PANEL (make 2)
Cast on 39 sts loosely.

Work 7 rows in seed st.

Next Row: Inc 4 sts as follows: * (K1, P1) 4 times; inc in next st; rep from * 3 times more; K1, P1, K1: 43 sts.

PATTERN ROWS:
Row 1: (K1, P1) twice; K5, P4, K7; P1, K1, P1; K7, P4, K5; (P1, K1) twice.

Row 2: K1, P1, K2; P5, K1, P2; K1, P7; K1, P1, K1; P7, K1; P2, K1, P5; K2, P1, K1.

Row 3: K1, P1, K1; P10, † yarn to back, sl next 2 sts onto cable needle and hold at back of work; K1, then K2 from cable needle; K1, sl next st onto cable needle and hold at front of work; K2, then K1 from cable needle †; P1, K1, P1; rep from † to † once; P10; K1, P1, K1.

Row 4: Rep Row 2.

Rep Rows 1 through 4 fifty-one times more, or until piece measures about 2" less than Center Panel; then rep Row 1 once more.

Next Row: Dec 4 sts as follows: * (K1, P1) 3 times; K2 tog, P1; rep from * 3 times more; K1, (P1, K1) 3 times: 39 sts.

Work 6 more rows in seed st.

Bind off loosely in seed st.

Weave or sew panels tog, being sure that cast on edge of each panel is at same end of afghan.

Pillow

designed by Barbara Retzke

SIZE:
Pieces measure about 11" square
MATERIALS:
Worsted weight yarn, 4 oz (280 yds) ecru
Size 6, 10" straight knitting needles,
   or size required for gauge
12" square knife-edge pillow form
Cable needle
Size 18 tapestry needle
GAUGE:
In stock st, 5 sts = 1"

Instructions (make 2)

Cast on 59 sts.

Work in seed st (see Pattern Stitches, page 180) for 6 rows.

Next Row: (Kl, P1) 3 times; * inc in next st, P1, (K1, P1) twice; rep from * to last 5 sts; K1, (P1, K1) twice: 67 sts.

PATTERN ROWS:
Row 1: (K1, P1) 3 times; (K7, P2) twice; (K5, P2) 3 times; K7, P2, K7, (P1, K1) 3 times.

Row 2: (K1, P1) twice; (K2, P7) twice; (K2, P5) 3 times; (K2, P7) twice; K2, (P1, K1) twice.

Row 3: (K1, P1) 3 times; † sl next 2 sts onto cable needle and hold at back of work; knit next st, then K2 from cable needle; K1, sl next st onto cable needle and hold at front of work; knit next 2 sts, then K1 from cable needle †; P2; rep from † to † once; P 23; rep from † to † once; P2; rep from † to † once; (P1, K1) 3 times.

Row 4: Rep Row 2.

Rep Rows 1 through 4 until piece measures about 10".

Next Row: (K1, P1) 3 times; * K2 tog, P1, (K1, P1) twice; rep from * to last 5 sts; K1, (P1, K1) twice: 59 sts.

Work 5 more rows in seed st.

Bind off in seed st.

Finishing

Hold front and back with wrong sides together and cast-on edges at same end of pillow; with tapestry needle and yarn, sew around three sides. Insert pillow form and sew remaining side closed.

Fair Isle Stocking

*designed by Carol Wilson Mansfield
and Mary Thomas*

Create this classic Christmas stocking with striking festive colors. We've given detailed instructions on working the Fair Isle patterns that carry the color changes across the back of the work.

SIZE:
About 6 1/2" wide (across top) x 13 1/2" long
   (from top edge to base of heel)

MATERIALS:
Worsted weight yarn, 2 oz (140 yds) green;
   1 oz (70 yds) lt green; 1 oz (70 yds) white;
   1/2 oz (35 yds) red
Size 8, 10" straight knitting needles,
   or size required for gauge
Size 8, 7" double pointed needles (dpn),

GAUGE:
In stock st, 9 sts = 2"
6 rows = 1"

Instructions

Beg at top, with green and straight needles, cast on 61 sts.

HEM

Row 1: Knit.

Row 2: Purl.

Rows 3 through 10: Rep Rows 1 and 2 four times.

Rows 11 and 12: Knit.

TECHNIQUES FOR WORKING FAIR ISLE DESIGN

The design is worked from charts in stock st, making color changes as indicated. Colors used are shown on the charts. Each square on the charts represents one stitch and each horizontal row of squares represents one row of knitting. The charts are worked from the bottom to the top. Unless otherwise specified, the first and all odd-numbered rows are knitted from * A to B; rep from * across, ending by working from A to C. The 2nd row and all even-numbered rows are purled from C to A once; then from * B to A; rep * from across.

To join a new color, tie it to prev color at beg of row, leaving about 4" end for weaving in later through backs of several sts on wrong side of work. Never weave in more than one end at a time. To finish off a color, cut yarn, leaving about a 4" end. Tie in end and then leave end for weaving in later.

When working the design, only 2 colors are used in a row; therefore, color not being used is carried LOOSELY across back of work so as not to "pucker" or distort the design, or alter the width of the stocking. If the color is carried across more than 3 sts, lock the color in place with the working yarn every 2nd or 3rd st to prevent loose strands at back of work as follows: bring color being carried over needle as shown in **Fig 1**; then knit/purl st with working color only (carried color will be locked in place when next st is completed). When color is carried in this manner, the wrong side of work will look like **Fig 2**.

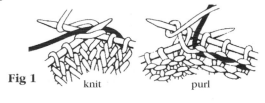

Fig 1   knit   purl

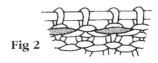

Fig 2

When colors are carried, it is not necessary to twist (or change) colors at point of color changes, except sometimes at the beg or end of a row. Colors are twisted (or changed) by bringing the yarn you have just used in front and over to the left of the color you are going to use next, bringing the new color up from underneath (**Fig 3**).

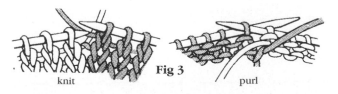

knit   Fig 3   purl

FAIR ISLE DESIGN

Rows 1 through 4: Beg with a knit row, follow chart in **Fig 4** and work Rows 1 through 4.

Rows 5 through 10: Following chart in **Fig 5**, work Rows 1 through 6.

COLOR KEY
Figs 1-10

■	forest green
▨	light green
■	red
□	white

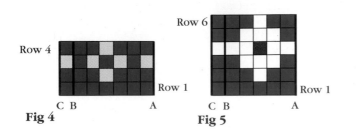

Fig 4

Fig 5

Rows 11 through 18: Following chart in **Fig 6**, work Rows 1 through 8.

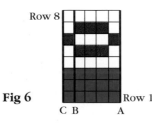

Fig 6

Rows 19 through 36: Following chart in **Fig 7**, work Rows 1 through 18.

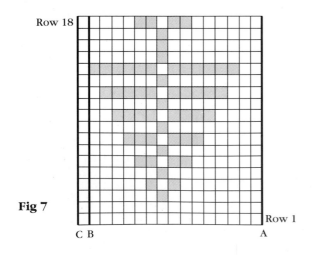

Fig 7

Row 37 (dec row): With white, (K13, K2 tog) 4 times; K1: 57 sts.

Row 38: With white, purl.

Rows 39 through 58: Following chart in **Fig 8**, work Rows 1 through 20.

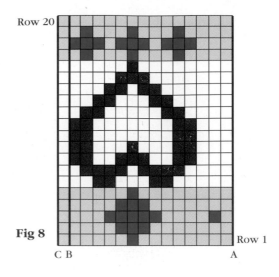

Fig 8

Row 59 (dec row): With white, (K12, K2 tog) 4 times; K1: 53 sts.

Row 60: With white, purl.

Rows 61 through 64: Following chart in **Fig 9**, work Rows 1 through 4.

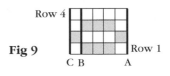

Fig 9

Row 65 (dec row): With white, (K16, K2 tog) twice; K 17: 51 sts.

Row 66 (dividing row): With white and one dpn, purl first 13 sts and leave these sts on dpn for first half of heel (to be worked later). Now with straight needle, purl next 25 sts (for instep). With 2nd dpn, purl rem 13 sts (for 2nd half of heel). Cut white, leaving about a 4" end.

INSTEP

Leaving 13 heel sts on each end on dpns, continue with straight needles and work instep on center 25 sts as follows:

Beg with Row 1 of chart in **Fig 10** and work through Row 30. (*Note: Odd-numbered rows of chart are knitted across from A to B; even-numbered rows are purled across from B to A.*) When all 30 rows of chart have been completed, cut yarn, leaving sts on needle (to be worked later for toe).

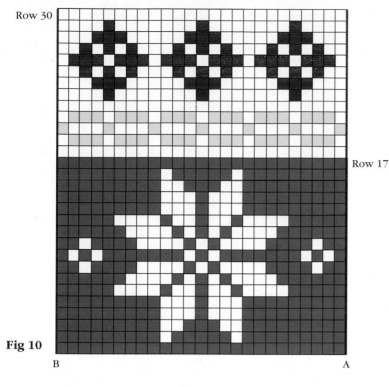

Row 30

Row 17

Fig 10

B   A

HEEL

Hold stocking with right side facing you and heel sts on 2 dpns at top (outer edges of stocking will be in the center between dpns). Sl sts from left dpn onto right dpn, having all 26 sts on one dpn. Continuing with both dpns and lt green, work back and forth in rows as follows:

Row 1 (right side): Sl 1 as to purl, knit rem sts.

Row 2: Sl 1 as to purl, purl rem sts.

Rep last 2 rows until heel measures about 2" long, ending by working a knit row.

TURN HEEL

Note: Heel is turned by working short rows. When instructions say "turn," leave rem sts unworked.

Row 1 (wrong side): Sl 1 as to purl, P4, P2 tog; P1; turn.

Row 2: Sl 1 as to purl, K5, sl 1 as to knit, K1, PSSO; K1; turn.

Row 3: Sl 1 as to purl, P6, P2 tog; P1; turn.

Row 4: Sl 1 as to purl, K7, sl 1 as to knit, K1, PSSO; K1; turn.

Row 5: Sl 1 as to purl, P8, P2 tog; P1; turn.

Row 6: Sl 1 as to purl, K9, sl 1 as to knit, K1, PSSO; K1; turn.

Row 7: Sl 1 as to purl, P10, P2 tog; P1; turn.

Row 8: Sl 1 as to purl, K 11, sl 1 as to knit, K1, PSSO; K1, turn.

Row 9: Sl 1 as to purl, P12; P2 tog, P1, turn.

Row 10: Sl 1 as to purl, K13; sl 1 as to knit, K1, PSSO; K1: 16 sts. Cut yarn, leaving sts on needle.

GUSSET AND FOOT

With right side of heel just made facing you, join green and, with free dpn, pick up 8 sts along right edge of heel; K16 (heel sts), then pick up 8 sts along left edge of heel: 32 sts. Continue with both dpns and work back and forth in rows as follows:

Row 1 (wrong side): Purl.

Row 2: K1, sl 1 as to knit, K1, PSSO; knit to last 3 sts, K2 tog; K1: 30 sts.

Rows 3 through 6: Rep Rows 1 and 2, twice: 26 sts.

Rows 7 through 10: Beg with a purl row and work 4 rows even in stock st.

Row 11 (wrong side): P2 tog, purl rem sts: 25 sts. Rows 12 through 25: Following chart in **Fig 10**, work last 14 rows only (beg with Row 17 and work through Row 30). When last 14 rows of chart have been completed, cut white; join green.

TOE

Rnd 1 (joining rnd): First needle: knit across 25 sts of foot just worked; 2nd needle: knit 13 sts from straight needle (instep sts); 3rd needle: knit rem 12 sts from straight needle: 50 sts.

Join and continue shaping in rnds as follows:

Rnd 2: First needle: K1, sl 1, K1, PSSO; knit to last 3 sts, K2 tog; K1; 2nd needle: K1, sl 1, K1, PSSO; knit rem sts; 3rd needle: knit to last 3 sts, K2 tog; K1: 46 sts.

Rnd 3: Knit. Rep Rnds 2 and 3 until 14 sts rem. Cut yarn, leaving about a 12" end. Thread into tapestry or yarn needle and weave through rem sts twice (removing knitting needles). Draw up tightly and fasten securely.

LOOP

With straight needles and red, cast on 3 sts. Knit each row until piece measures about 4" long. Bind off, leaving about a 6" end for sewing.

Finishing

Weave in all yarn ends. Lightly steam press design on wrong side. Weave seams tog. Fold down hem to inside and slip stitch loosely in place. Fold loop in half and sew ends to top of stocking at seam.

185

Jingle Bell Tube Socks

designed by Mary Thomas

Keep a child's feet warm and cozy on even the most frigid winter's night. Add bells and ribbon to the cuffs to put a festive jingle in their steps.

SIZE:
One size fits all

MATERIALS:
Sport weight yarn, 4 oz (280 yds) red
Sizes 1 and 3, 7" double pointed needles (dpn),
  or size required for gauge
1 yd 5/8"-wide green satin ribbon
1/2 yd 1/16"-wide green satin ribbon
eight 1/2" diameter gold jingle bells

GAUGE:
With larger size needles in stock st, 13 sts = 2"
9 rows = 1"

Instructions

SOCK (make 2)
With larger size dpn, CO 56 sts loosely on one needle; change to smaller size dpn and divide sts on 3 needles: 16-20-20 sts. Join, being careful not to twist sts. Work in K1, P1 ribbing for 1 1/2". Change to larger size dpn and work in patt as follows:

Rnd 1: * P2, K2; rep from * around.

Rnd 2: * P2, make a RT (right twist) as follows: K2 tog but do not remove from left-hand needle (**Fig 1**); insert tip of right-hand needle into first st (**Fig 2**) and knit it again, then sl both sts off left-hand needle (RT made); rep from * around.

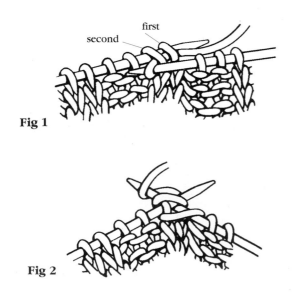

Fig 1

Fig 2

Rnds 3 through 5: Rep Rnd 1 three times.

Rnd 6: Rep Rnd 2.

Rnd 7: Rep Rnd 1.

Rnd 8: * K2, P2; rep from * around.

Rnd 9: * RT over next 2 sts, P2; rep from * around.

Rnds 10 through 12: Rep Rnd 8 three times.

Rnd 13: Rep Rnd 9.

Rnd 14: Rep Rnd 8.

Rep Rnds 1 through 14 until sock measures about 20" or 2" less than desired length.

SHAPE TOE:
Rnd 1: * K6, K2 tog; rep from * around: 49 sts.

Rnds 2 and 3: Knit.

Rnd 4: * K5, K2 tog; rep from * around: 42 sts.

Rnds 5 and 6: Knit.

Rnd 7: * K4, K2 tog; rep from * around: 35 sts.

Rnds 8 and 9: Knit.

Rnd 10: * K3, K2 tog; rep from * around: 28 sts.

Rnds 11 and 12: Knit.

Rnd 13: * K2, K2 tog; rep from * around: 21 sts.

Rnds 14 and 15: Knit.

Rnd 16: * K1, K2 tog; rep from * around: 14 sts.

Rnd 17: Knit.

Cut yarn, leaving a 12" end for sewing.

Divide sts on 2 needles—one behind the other (**Fig 3**). Thread yarn into tapestry needle; with wrong sides together, work from right to left as follows:

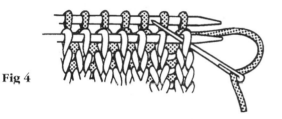

Fig 3

Step 1: Insert tapestry needle into the first st on the front needle as to purl (**Fig 4**). Draw yarn through st, leaving st on knitting needle.

Fig 4

Step 2: Insert tapestry needle into the first st on back needle (from back to front) as to purl (**Fig 5**). Draw yarn through st and slip st off knitting needle.

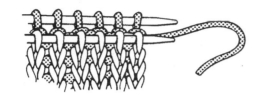

Fig 5

Step 3: Insert tapestry needle into the next st on same (back) needle (from front to back) as to knit (**Fig 6**), leaving st on needle.

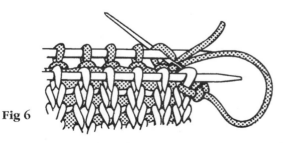

Fig 6

Step 4: Insert tapestry needle into the first st on front needle as to knit (**Fig 7**). Draw yarn through st and slip st off knitting needle.

Fig 7

Step 5: Insert tapestry needle into next st on same (front) needle as to purl. Draw yarn through st, leaving st on knitting needle.

Rep Steps 2 through 5 until one st is left on each needle. Then rep Steps 2 and 4.

Bind off.

Finishing

Cut 1/16"-wide ribbon into four pieces; tie a jingle bell to each end of each piece, knotting securely. Fold ribbons with bells in half allowing ends to hang unevenly (see photo); stitch folds to cuff.

Cut 5/8"-wide ribbon in half; tie each piece into a bow. Sew bow at top of jingle bells and ribbon.

Little Merry Janes

designed by Mary Thomas

Even babies need new fashion accessories to complete their holiday look. These festive Mary Jane style booties feature little satin bows with Christmas-red ribbon roses.

SIZE:
About 4" measured from heel to toe

MATERIALS:
Worsted weight yarn, 1/4 oz (18 yds)
  each black and white
Size 6, 10" straight knitting needles,
  or size required for gauge
two 5/16" heart-shaped buttons
10" piece 5/8"-wide green satin ribbon
1 yd 3/8"-wide red satin ribbon
sewing needle and matching thread

GAUGE:
In stock st, 5 sts = 1"
7 rows = 1"

Instructions (make 2)

Starting with sole and with black, cast on 28 sts.

Row 1 (right side): K1, inc in next st as follows: knit in front and in back of same st; K10, inc as before in each of next 4 sts, K10, inc as before in next st, K1: 34 sts.

Row 2: Knit.

Row 3: K1, inc in next st, K13, inc in each of next 4 sts, K13, inc in next st, K1: 40 sts.

Row 4: Knit.

Row 5: K1, inc in next st, K16, inc in each of next 4 sts, K16, inc in next st, K1: 46 sts.

Continuing in garter st (knit each row), work even until piece measures 1 1/2", ending by working a wrong side row.

INSTEP

Row 1 (right side): K17, K2 tog, K8, K2 tog, turn, leaving rem 17 sts unworked.

Row 2: Yarn to back of work, sl 1 as to purl, K8, K2 tog, turn, leaving rem 16 sts unworked.

Rows 3 through 5: Rep Row 2 three times, having one less unworked st at end of each row.

At end of Row 5: 15 sts remain unworked at each end.

Cut black.

Row 6: With white, sl 1 as to purl, P8, P2 tog, turn, leaving rem 14 sts unworked.

Row 7: Yarn to back of work, sl 1 as to purl, K8, K2 tog, turn, leaving rem 14 sts unworked.

Rows 8 through 15: Rep Rows 6 and 7 four times, having one less unworked st at end of each row.

At end of Row 15, do not turn; knit across rem 10 unworked sts: 30 sts.

Row 16: P19, P2 tog, P9: 29 sts.

TOP

Starting with a knit row, work 2 rows in stock st. Now work in lace patt as follows:

Lace Pattern (multiple of 4 sts + 1)

Row 1 (right side): K1, * YO, K3, YO, K1; rep from * across.

Row 2: Purl.

Row 3: K2, * sl 1 as to knit, K2 tog, PSSO, K3; rep from * across to last 5 sts, sl 1 as to knit, K2 tog, PSSO, K2.

Row 4: Purl.

Rep last 4 rows until top of bootie measures 2" from instep, ending by working Row 4.

Purl 3 rows.

Bind off loosely in purl. Cut white, leaving an 18" end for sewing. Sew bottom and back seam. Weave in ends.

ANKLE STRAP (make 2)

With black, cast on 44 sts.

Bind off in knit.

Finishing

Place one strap around ankle of each bootie, having ends overlapped at outer side. Tack in place. Sew buttons through both thicknesses of overlapped ends of each strap.

Cut green ribbon in half; form each piece into two loops with ends overlapping at center and stitch centers to tops of shoes.

Make two ribbon roses with red satin ribbon (instructions below). Stitch roses to centers of green loops.

FOLDED RIBBON ROSE

Step 1: Using 1/2 yd of red satin ribbon, fold left end up at center forming an "L" (**Fig 1**); mark left end so you can identify it while following these instructions.

Step 2: Fold right end of ribbon to front and across to left side (**Fig 2**).

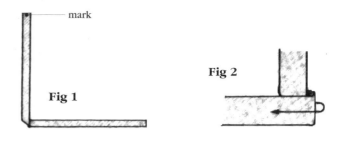

Fig 1   Fig 2

Step 3: Fold right end to back and across to right side (**Fig 3**).

Step 4: Fold left end to the back and down (**Fig 4**).

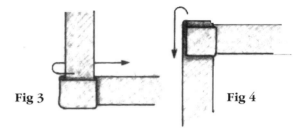

Fig 3   Fig 4

Step 5: Fold right end back and across to left side (**Fig 5**).

Step 6: Fold left end up and to the back (**Fig 6**).

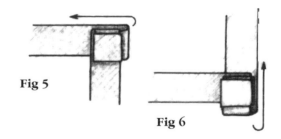

Fig 5   Fig 6

Step 7: Rep Steps 3 through 6 three more times (12 more folds).

Step 8: Hold ends of ribbon together and let go of the folds; ribbon will form a woven chain. Gently pull on the left end until ribbon gathers up into a rose florette (**Fig 7**). Take a few hand stitches through center of flower to secure. Trim ribbon ends close to stitching.

Fig 7

Sewing

Sewing Notes

1. All yardage amounts are based on 44"-wide fabrics.

2. Pattern pieces include seam allowances unless otherwise noted. The broken line is the sewing line and the outside line is the cutting line.

3. Trace pattern pieces onto tracing paper; include all markings.

4. Use a 1/4" seam allowance for all machine stitching unless otherwise noted.

Fabric Hints

1. Use quality 100% cotton fabrics for all projects unless otherwise noted.

2. For projects that are going to be washed, pre-test all your fabrics for colorfastness and shrinkage. Cut a strip of each of the fabrics that you plan to use for your project. To determine if the fabric is colorfast, put each strip separately into a clean bowl of extremely hot water or hold the strip under hot running water. If fabric bleeds a great deal, wash the fabric until all excess dye has washed out. Fabrics that continue to bleed after they have been washed several times should be eliminated.

To test for shrinkage, take each saturated strip and iron it dry with a hot iron. When strip is completely dry, measure and compare it to original measurements. The fabric industry allows about 2% shrinkage in cotton fabrics. If all of your fabric strips shrink the same amount, then you really have no problem. If only one of your fabrics is shrinking more than the others, it should be discarded.

Foundation Method

The Foundation Method is a wonderful method for piecing small patchwork. We have used it in five of our sewing projects. It may take a little more time than traditional patchwork piecing because the block patterns are traced onto a muslin or paper foundation. However, the accuracy it provides makes the Foundation Method worth the effort and it saves time in the long run.

Another advantage of using the Foundation Method for piecing is that you don't have to cut your pieces to the exact shape until you have sewn them to the foundation piece. Therefore, as long as your fabric covers the numbered area, overlapping it at least 1/8" on all sides, you don't have to cut it until after it is sewn to the block. (This will be illustrated later.)

The block patterns for the Foundation Method have pieces that are numbered in the numerical sequence that they must be sewn. Therefore, always start with #1, then #2 and so on.

TRANSFERRING THE BLOCK
There are two ways to transfer a block pattern onto the muslin or paper that is referred to as the foundation:

1. Trace block, centered on a muslin or paper square using a permanent marking pen. If you are unable to see the design through the muslin or paper, use a light source such as a light box, sunny window or glass-top table with a light under it.

2. Trace block onto tracing paper using a transfer pen or pencil. Transfer block onto muslin or paper foundation using an iron and following manufacturer's instructions.

Whatever method you use to transfer block pattern, be as accurate as possible.

CUTTING FABRIC PIECES

Cut fabric pieces for the block using one of the three following methods:

1. Use strips the width of the spaces on the block, plus 1/4" seam allowance on both sides, **Fig 1**.

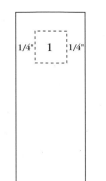

Fig 1

2. Use scraps that will overlap the numbered area to be covered, **Fig 2**; trim seam allowance after sewing.

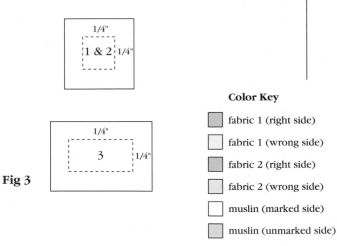

Fig 2

3. Cut pieces into the exact shapes in the design, being sure to add 1/4" seam allowance on all sides, **Fig 3**.

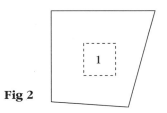

Fig 3

Color Key

▨	fabric 1 (right side)
☐	fabric 1 (wrong side)
▨	fabric 2 (right side)
☐	fabric 2 (wrong side)
☐	muslin (marked side)
▨	muslin (unmarked side)

PIECING THE BLOCK

Once you have transferred the block design onto your foundation (muslin or paper), you can begin to piece. You will always be placing pieces on the unmarked (right) side and stitching them to the foundation from the marked (wrong) side.

1. Position piece #1 over space marked #1 on unmarked (right) side of foundation, making sure that piece overlaps all marked sides, **Fig 4**; use glue stick or pin to hold in place.

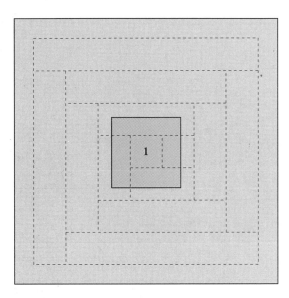

Fig 4

2. Place piece #2 over first piece right sides together, **Fig 5**.

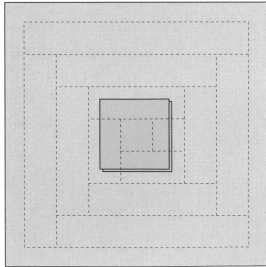

Fig 5

3. Carefully turn over foundation to marked side; stitch on marked line between #1 and #2, beginning and ending two stitches beyond line, **Fig 6**. Turn foundation to right side.

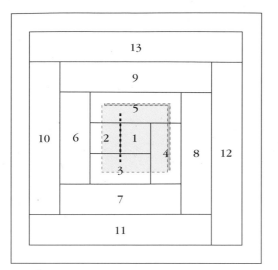

Fig 6

4. Fold foundation back along seam just sewn and trim seam allowance to 1/8", **Fig 7**.

Fig 7

5. Fold open piece #2 and finger press; pin or glue in place, **Fig 8**.

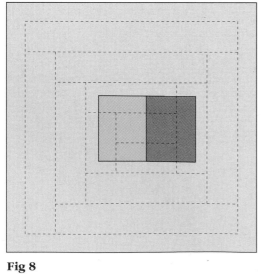

Fig 8

6. Place piece #3 right sides together with pieces #1/#2, **Fig 9**.

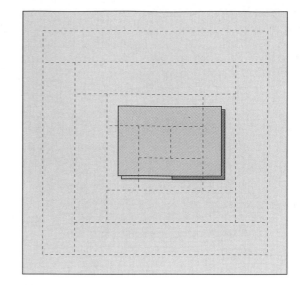

Fig 9

7. Turn foundation over; stitch, **Fig 10**.

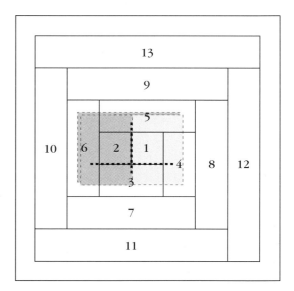

Fig 10

8. Trim seam allowance to 1/8", fold piece #3 open and pin or glue in place, **Fig 11**.

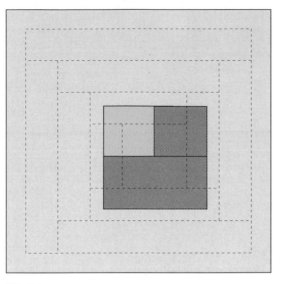

Fig 11

9. Repeat with remaining pieces following numerical sequence in block until entire block is completed.

Color Key

 fabric 1 (right side)

☐ fabric 1 (wrong side)

 fabric 2 (right side)

☐ fabric 2 (wrong side)

☐ muslin (marked side)

☐ muslin (unmarked side)

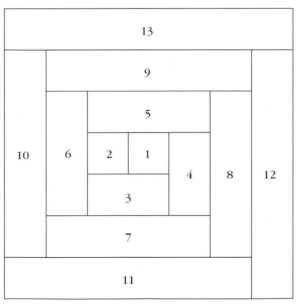

Block Pattern

Celestial Cherub Wall Hanging

designed by Linda Causee

The simple Log Cabin Block is the basis for this angelic beauty. You'll be amazed at how you can transform a little pile of pretty fabrics into an eye-catching wall hanging. Use shiny lamé and star-printed satin as we've shown here or choose bright holiday cottons for a more countrified look.

APPROXIMATE SIZE:
20" square
***Note:** Quilt is made to hang diagonally.*
MATERIALS:
1/4 yd gold lamé (A)
1/8 yd silver lamé (B)
1/8 yd cream satin (C)
1/8 yd white satin with gold stars (D)
1 1/4 yd lt blue print (E)
1/4 yd white and lt blue print (F)
1/8 yd white and silver print (G)
scraps rust print for hair (H)
1/2 yd muslin (foundation) (I)
1/2 yd lightweight fusible interfacing*
batting
rust embroidery floss
rose embroidery floss
embroidery needle
cosmetic blush
mini gold star wire garland
* Following manufacturer's directions, carefully fuse interfacing to wrong side of silver and gold lamé.

Instructions:

1. Cut fabric into 1" crosswise strips:
   four gold lamé (A)
   four silver lamé (B)
   three cream satin (C)
   four white/gold satin (D)
   seven lt blue print (E)
   five white/lt blue print (F)
   two white/silver print (G)
   one rust (H)
   one muslin (I)

2. Cut thirty-six 4" squares of muslin for foundation pieces.

3. Refer to Foundation Method, pages 194 to 197, and transfer Log Cabin Block pattern onto the thirty-six squares of muslin.

4. Using 1" strips and referring to Layout and Color Key, make thirty-six Log Cabin Blocks in the following quantities and fabric combinations:
   one block, muslin (I)/rust (H)
   nine blocks, cream satin (C)/white satin (D)
   two blocks, gold lamé (A)/gold lamé (A)
   four blocks, gold lamé (A)/silver lamé (B)
   six blocks, silver lamé (B)/lt blue print (E)
   nine blocks, lt blue print (E)/white and lt blue print (F)
   three blocks, white and lt blue print (F)/white and silver print (G)
   two blocks, lt blue print (E)/lt blue print (E)

5. Place blocks in rows referring to photograph and layout for placement. Sew blocks together in rows, then sew rows together. Check placement of blocks as you sew.

6. Trace face placement, **Fig 1**, onto muslin/rust block. You may need to use a light box for this step.

7. Using an Outline Stitch, **Fig 2**, embroider eyes and nose with rust embroidery floss and mouth with rose. Apply cosmetic blush onto cheeks.

8. Cut 1 1/4" strips from lt blue print for borders. Attach to two opposite sides of quilt, then to the remaining sides.

9. Cut 22" square from lt blue print for backing. Place wrong side up, then batting and quilt top right side

Color Key

- lt blue
- gold lamé
- silver
- cream satin
- muslin
- rust
- white/lt. blue print
- white/silver print
- white satin with gold stars

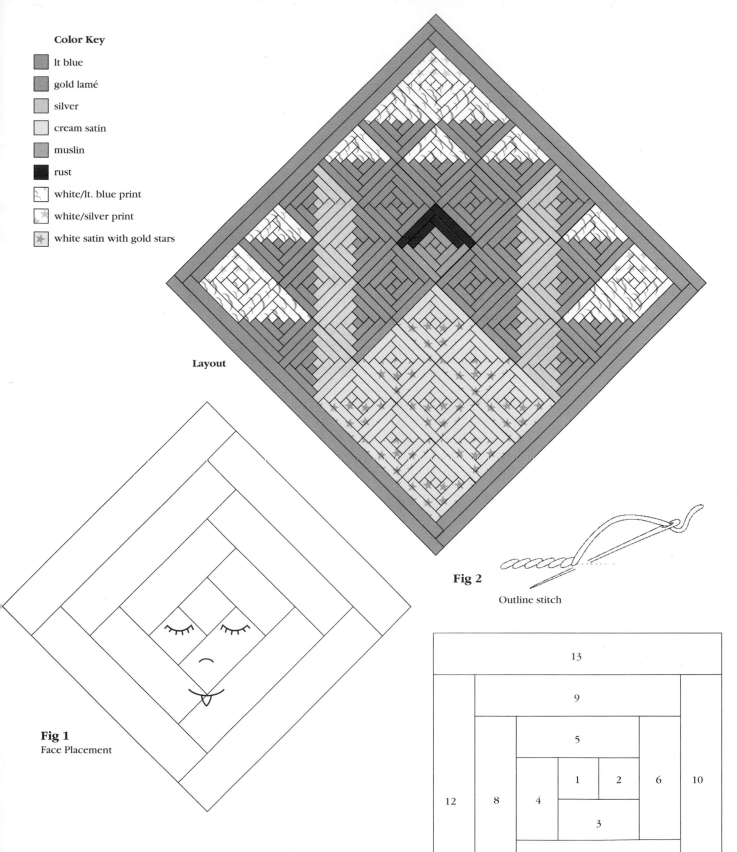

Layout

Fig 1
Face Placement

Fig 2
Outline stitch

Log Cabin Block Pattern

up. Baste, then quilt as desired. Photographed model was machine quilted in the ditch around cherub's head, gown and wings and next to border.

10. Trim batting to 1/4" beyond quilt top; trim backing 1/2" beyond batting. Fold backing edges toward top; blind stitch in place, folding raw edge under as you stitch.

199

"Pieced on Earth" Ornaments

designed by Linda Causee

These clever ornaments may look like they'd be hard to piece with perfectly matching points, but they are created using the Foundation Method, so the stitching is easy!

Holiday Basket

APPROXIMATE SIZE:
3 1/2" square
MATERIALS:
4" square muslin (foundation)
3 1/2" square backing
scraps white print (background)
scraps red/green print (basket, binding)
3 1/2" square batting
1/2 yd 1/8"-wide red satin ribbon
1 yd 1/8"-wide green satin ribbon
five red buttons, 3/8"-1/2" diameter
matching thread and sewing needle
optional: tacky craft glue

Instructions:

Note: *1/4" seam allowances are used throughout this project.*

1. Refer to Foundation Method, pages 194 to 197, and make one Basket Block on muslin square using Basket pattern. Trim block to 3 1/2".

2. Layer backing wrong side up, then batting and Basket Block right side up; baste layers together.

3. Cut two binding strips, 2" x 3 1/2", and two binding strips, 2" x 4".

4. Fold one 2" x 3 1/2" binding strip in half lengthwise with wrong sides together; sew to side of layered block. Bring strip toward backing and blind stitch in place using seam line as a guide. Repeat with remaining 3 1/2" strip on opposite side of block.

5. Fold one 2" x 4" strip in half lengthwise with wrong sides together; place along top edge of block, with each end extending 1/2". Stitch in place. Bring strip toward backing; blind stitch in place, folding in ends neatly as you sew. Repeat on bottom edge of block.

6. Referring to photograph, sew (or glue) four buttons randomly in basket.

7. Cut 10" length of green ribbon; tack one end at each top corner. Cut red ribbon in half; make two bows with 1" loops. Tack bow at each corner; trim ends if desired.

8. Cut a 6" length of green ribbon. With remaining ribbon, make bow with four 1 1/4" loops on each side; tie center with 6" length of ribbon. Tack bow at top of basket handle. Sew button in center of bow.

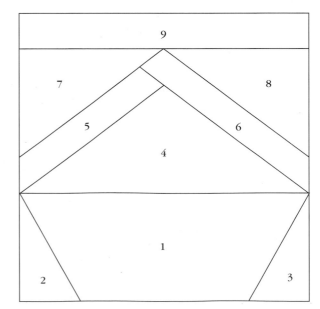

Holiday Basket Pattern

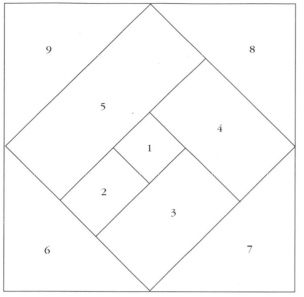

Holly Wreath Pattern

Holly Wreath

APPROXIMATE SIZE:
3 1/2" square
MATERIALS
4" square muslin (foundation)
3 1/2" square backing
scraps white print (background, binding)
scraps green print (wreath)
3 1/2" square batting
26 red seed beads
12" piece 1/4"-wide red satin ribbon
1/2 yd 1/8"-wide green satin ribbon
12" piece 1/8"-wide red satin ribbon

Instructions:

Note: 1/4" seam allowances are used throughout this project.

1. Refer to Foundation Method, pages 194 to 197, and make one Wreath Block on muslin square using Holly Wreath pattern. Trim block to 3 1/2".

2. Layer backing wrong side up, then batting and Wreath Block right side up; baste layers together.

3. Cut two binding strips, 2" x 3 1/2", and two binding strips, 2" x 4".

4. Fold one 2" x 3 1/2" binding strip in half lengthwise with wrong sides together; sew to side of layered block. Bring strip toward backing and blind stitch in place using seam line as a guide. Repeat with remaining 3 1/2" strip on opposite side of block.

5. Fold one 2" x 4" strip in half lengthwise with wrong sides together; place along top edge of block, with

each end extending 1/2". Stitch in place. Bring strip toward backing; blind stitch in place, folding in ends neatly as you sew. Repeat for bottom edge of block.

6. Sew seed beads randomly on wreath. Make bow with 1/4"-wide ribbon; tack at top of wreath.

7. Cut 10" length of red ribbon; tack one end at each top corner. Cut green ribbon in half; make two bows with 1" loops. Tack bow at each corner; trim ends if desired.

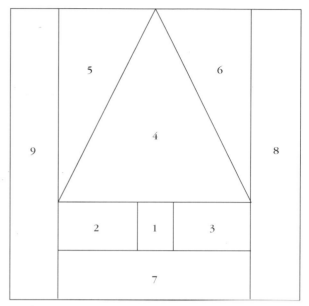

O' Christmas Tree Pattern

O' Christmas Tree

APPROXIMATE SIZE:
3 1/2" square
MATERIALS:
4" square muslin (foundation)
3 1/2" square backing
scraps lt print (background)
scraps green/red prints (tree, tree base, binding)
scrap green solid (tree trunk)
3 1/2" square batting
1 yd 1/8"-wide green satin ribbon
gold star jewel, 7/8" diameter
tacky craft glue

Instructions:

Note: 1/4" seam allowances are used throughout this project.

1. Refer to Foundation Method, pages 194 to 197, and make one Christmas Tree Block on muslin square using Christmas Tree pattern. Trim block to 3 1/2".

2. Layer backing wrong side up, then batting and Tree Block right side up; baste layers together.

6. Referring to Santa Star pattern for placement, glue or stitch ribbon in place for belt. For face, use puffy paint for nose, gold fabric paint for belt buckle, black pen for eyes and pink pencil or paint for cheeks.

7. From fleece or fur, cut out a beard and two small mustache pieces for each Star Santa; glue to Santa faces following Star Santa pattern for placement.

8. Pin batting to wrong side of skirt Sections 1 and 2. Machine baste 1/4" from outer edges. Trim batting close to stitching, **Fig 4**.

9. With right sides together, stitch skirt sections together in a 1/4" seam along one straight edge. Press seam open, **Fig 5**.

11. With right sides facing, pin backing to skirt matching seams. Stitch entire outer edge, straight edges and inner circle with a 1/4" seam allowance, leaving an opening along one straight edge for turning, **Fig 6**. Trim seam and corners; clip curves. Turn skirt right side out. Press edges carefully. Slipstitch opening closed. Topstitch 1/4" from all edges.

10. With right sides together, stitch backing sections together along one straight edge (see **Fig 5**) as for skirt section .

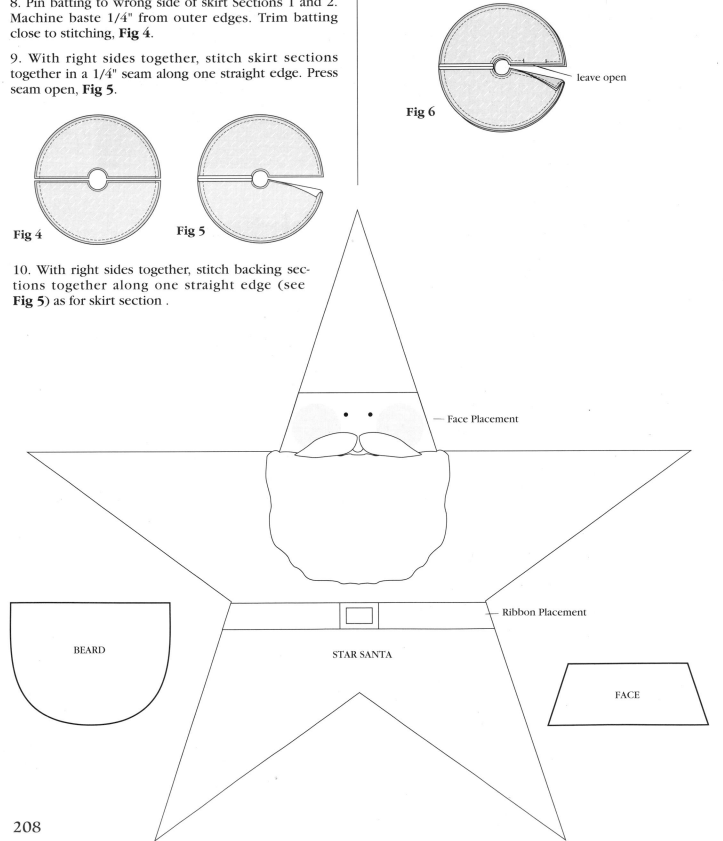

Fig 4

Fig 5

Fig 6

leave open

Face Placement

Ribbon Placement

BEARD

STAR SANTA

FACE

Frosted Fabric Trees

The Christmas season is a season of entertaining friends and family. Decorate a holiday buffet table with a forest of fabric pine trees or use them on the mantel with a ceramic village setting.

APPROXIMATE SIZE:
13" tall

MATERIALS:
1 1/2 yds assorted green fabrics
12" Styrofoam™ cone
white puff paint or Snow Accents™
glitter
ball ornament, about 1 1/2" diameter
pinking shears (or rotary cutter with pinking blade)
tacky craft glue
small phillips screwdriver or size 6 to 8 knitting needle (to push fabric into cone)
sponge brush

Instructions:

1. Using pinking sheers, cut fabric into 3" strips; cut into 3" squares. You can get approximately 238 to 252 squares per 1-1/2 yds of fabric, and you will need at least 200 squares to complete tree.

2. Place tip of screwdriver or knitting needle in center of fabric square; wrap fabric square around pointed end, **Fig 1**. Put dab of glue at tip of fabric.

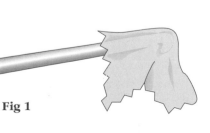

Fig 1

3. Starting at bottom of cone, push square into cone just enough for fabric to "bunch up," **Fig 2**.

4. Continue pushing squares into cone about every 1/2" to 3/4" around. For second row, place squares 1/2" to 3/4" above first row, staggering squares between first row. Work additional rows in same manner, working your way up to top. *Note: Be careful when pushing squares in at the top of the cone where it is very narrow. Push squares into cone at a downward angle instead of straight in and space a little farther apart. If the cone does break, use tacky glue to hold the piece back on. Put a toothpick or small dowel through top of cone to hold broken section in place.*

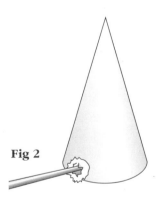

Fig 2

5. Fill in any empty spaces with squares for a full tree.

6. Brush white paint or Snow Accents™ on tips of fabric; sprinkle glitter on snow. Let dry; shake excess glitter from tree.

7. Glue ornament on top of tree.

FA-LA-LA-LA COW WITH WREATH

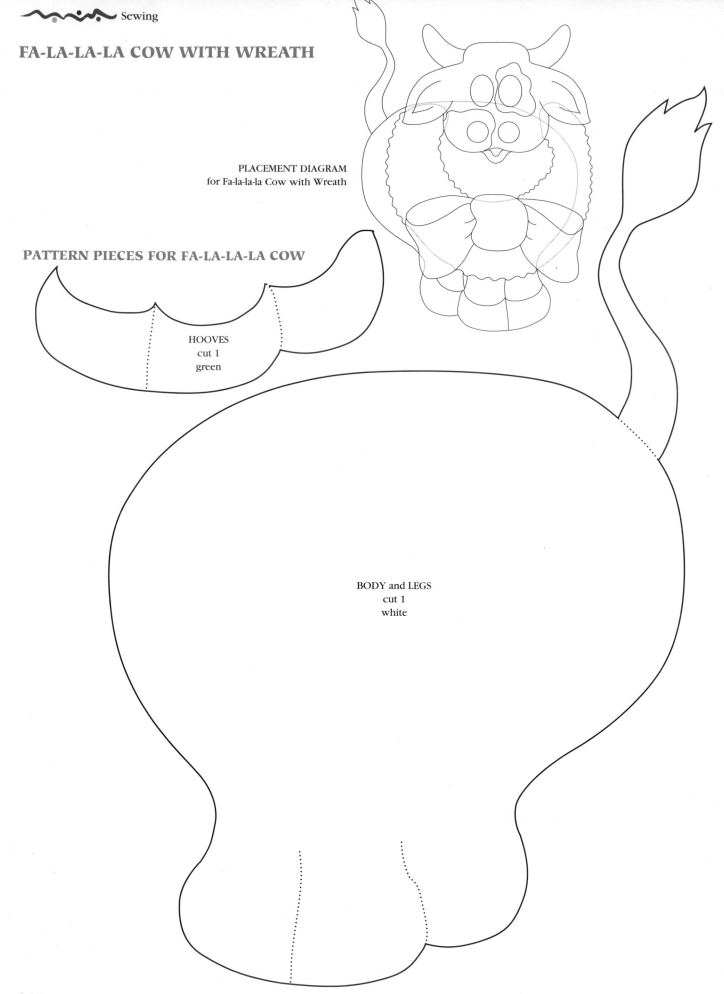

PLACEMENT DIAGRAM
for Fa-la-la-la Cow with Wreath

PATTERN PIECES FOR FA-LA-LA-LA COW

HOOVES
cut 1
green

BODY and LEGS
cut 1
white

PATTERN PIECES FOR FA-LA-LA-LA COW

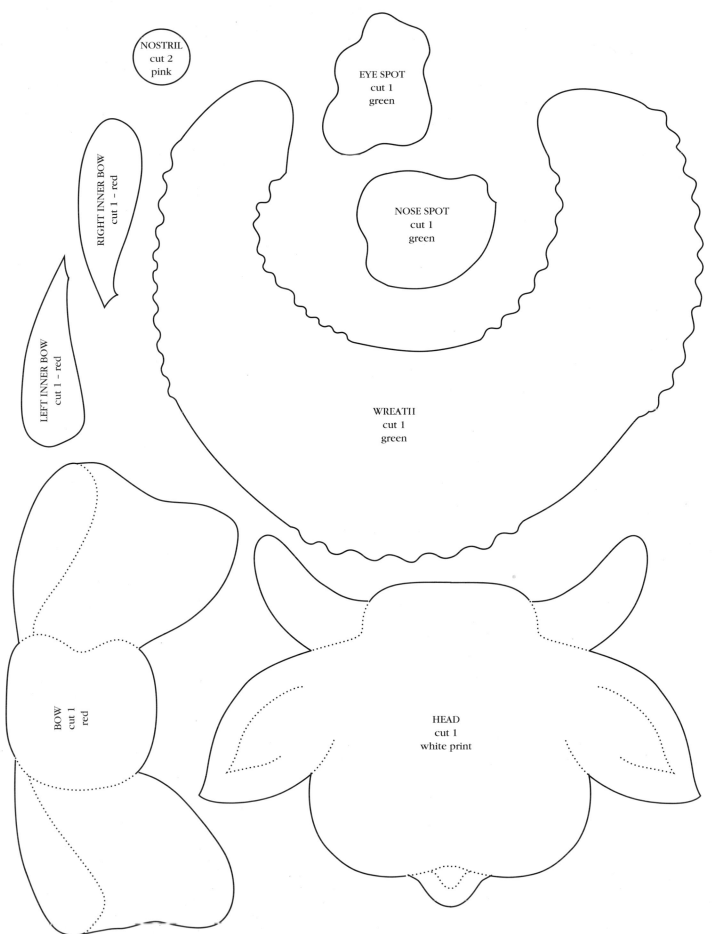

NOSTRIL
cut 2
pink

EYE SPOT
cut 1
green

RIGHT INNER BOW
cut 1 – red

NOSE SPOT
cut 1
green

LEFT INNER BOW
cut 1 – red

WREATH
cut 1
green

BOW
cut 1
red

HEAD
cut 1
white print

HOLLY COW WITH SANTA HAT

PLACEMENT DIAGRAM
for Holly Cow with Santa Hat

PATTERN PIECES FOR
HOLLY COW WITH SANTA HAT

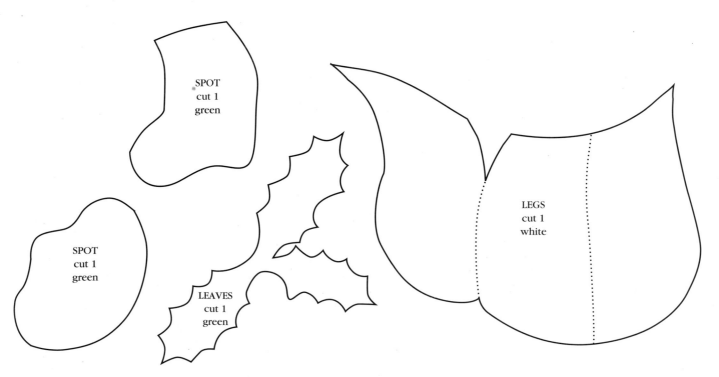

SPOT
cut 1
green

SPOT
cut 1
green

LEAVES
cut 1
green

LEGS
cut 1
white

PATTERN
FOR POI

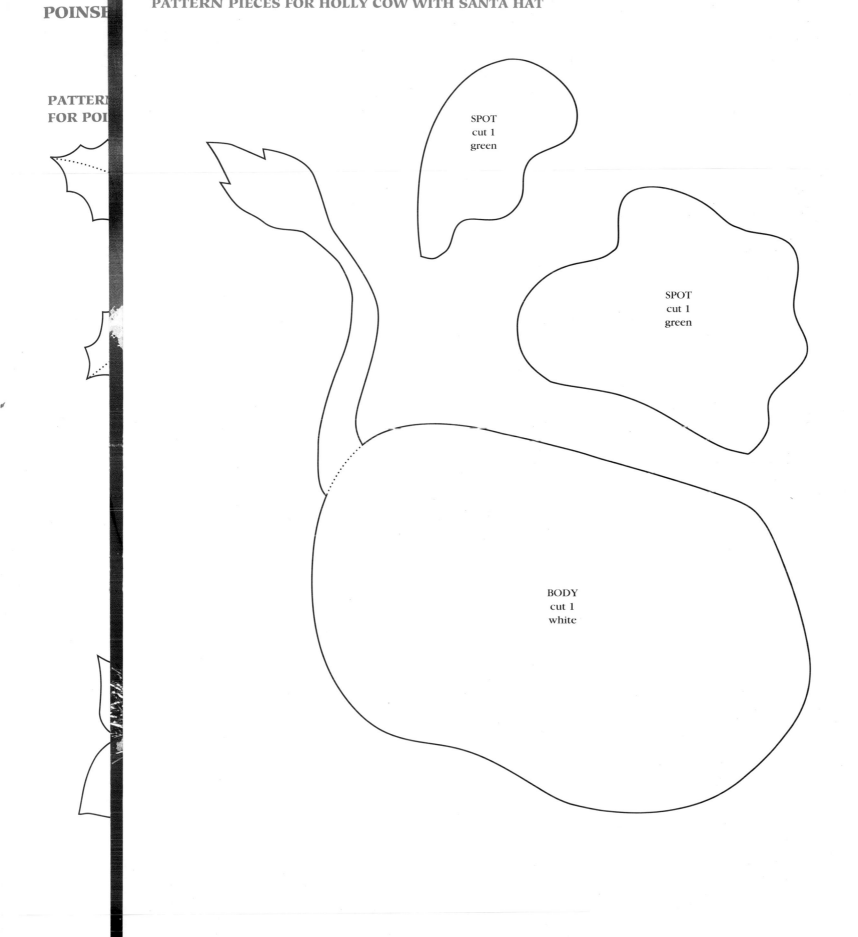

SPOT
cut 1
green

SPOT
cut 1
green

BODY
cut 1
white

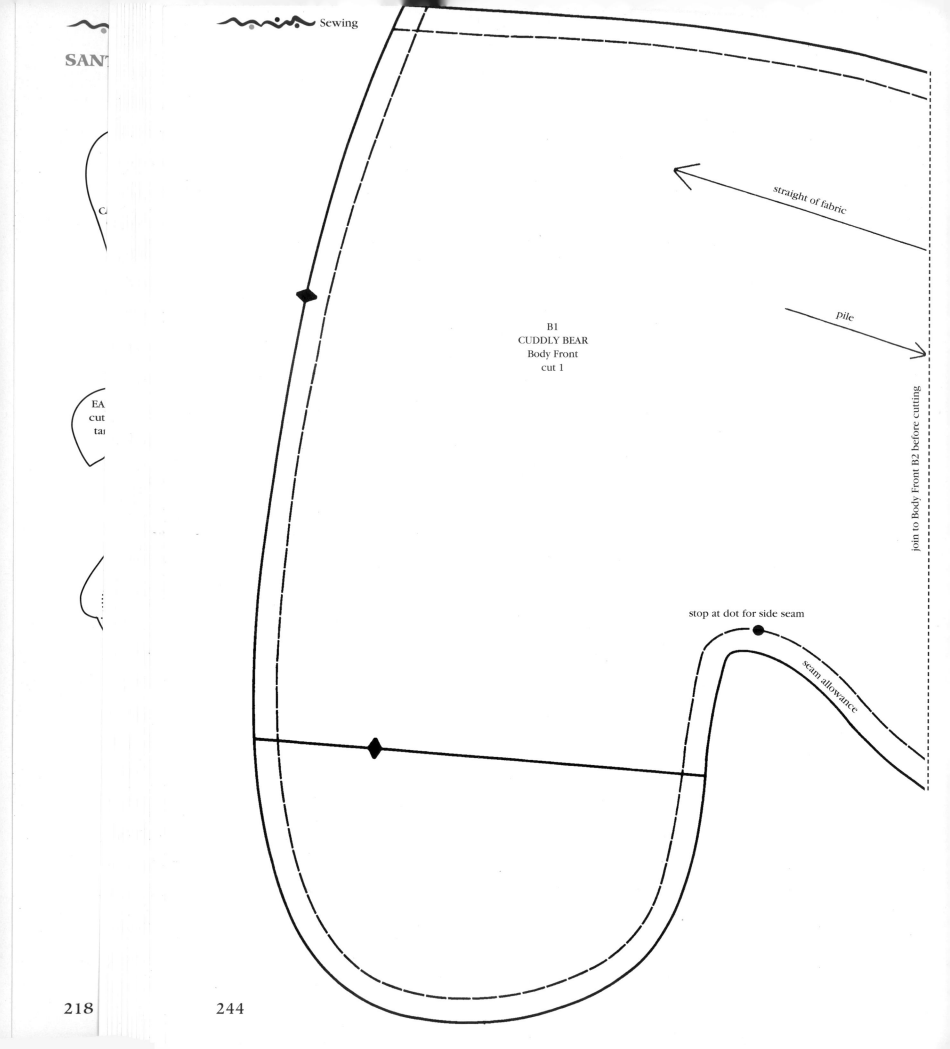

SANT

C

EA
cut
tar

B1
CUDDLY BEAR
Body Front
cut 1

straight of fabric

pile

join to Body Front B2 before cutting

stop at dot for side seam

seam allowance

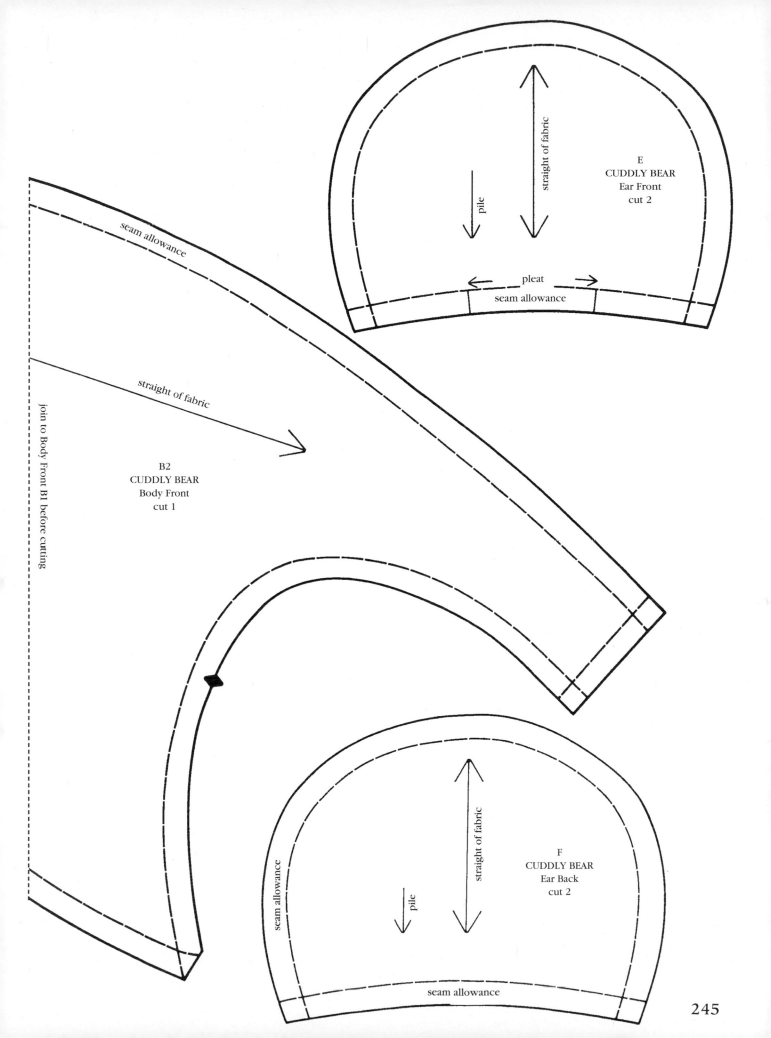

seam allowance

straight of fabric

pile

E
CUDDLY BEAR
Ear Front
cut 2

pleat

seam allowance

seam allowance

straight of fabric

join to Body Front B1 before cutting

B2
CUDDLY BEAR
Body Front
cut 1

seam allowance

straight of fabric

pile

F
CUDDLY BEAR
Ear Back
cut 2

seam allowance

245

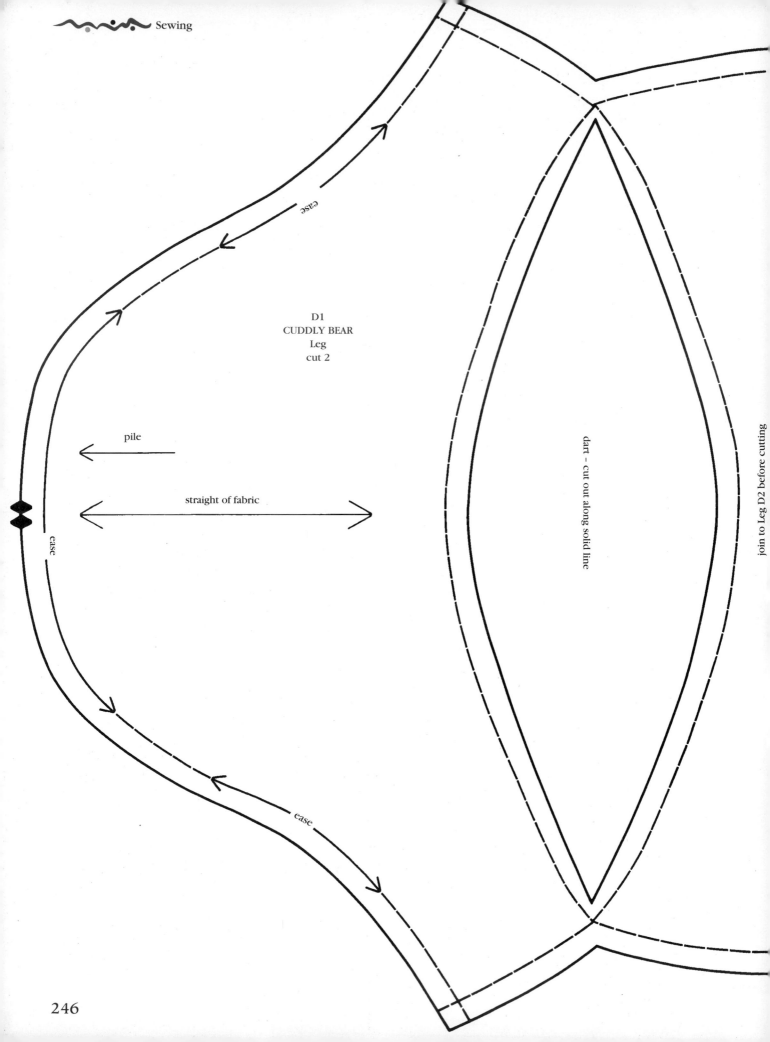

D1
CUDDLY BEAR
Leg
cut 2

pile

straight of fabric

ease

ease

ease

ease

dart – cut out along solid line

join to Leg D2 before cutting